DRIVING FORCES

By the same author

Fifty famous motor races
Derek Bell—my racing life
Ferrari—the Grand Prix cars
Brabham—the Grand Prix cars
March—the Grand Prix and Indy cars
Jackie Stewart's principles of performance driving
Williams—the business of Grand Prix racing

Patrick Stephens Limited, a member of the Haynes Publishing Group, has published authoritative, quality books for enthusiasts for more than twenty years. During that time the company has established a reputation as one of the world's leading publishers of books on aviation, maritime, military, model-making, motor cycling, motoring, motor racing, railway and railway modelling subjects. Readers or authors with suggestions for books they would like to see published are invited to write to: The Editorial Director, Patrick Stephens Limited, Sparkford, Nr Yeovil, Somerset, BA22 7JJ.

DRIVING FORCES

Fifty men who shaped the world of motor racing

ALAN HENRY

Patrick Stephens Limited

First published in 1992

British Library Cataloguing in Publication Data
Henry, Alan. 1947–
   Driving Forces: fifty men who have shaped motor racing.
   1. Racing cars. Racing—Biographies—Collections
   I. Title
   796.7210922

ISBN 1-85260-302-X

Patrick Stephens Limited is a member of the Haynes Publishing Group P.L.C., Sparkford, Nr Yeovil, Somerset, BA22 7JJ.

Typeset by MS Filmsetting Limited, Frome, Somerset
Printed in Great Britain by J. H. Haynes & Co. Ltd.

Contents

Introduction

THE 50 PERSONALITIES contained within these pages have all played pivotal roles in the development and evolution of motor racing over the years. They represent a broad cross-section of driver/constructors, team owners, patrons, manufacturers and administrators, without whom the many dazzling stars behind the wheel would have been bereft of cars, finance and technical support.

Their personalities range from the philanthropic and self-effacing through the gifted and dynamic to the arrogant and self-centred. All have been enormously motivated and determined, but I propose to let readers form their own conclusions from my text as to who falls into which category—and why.

Inevitably people will have favourites who have not been included within these pages—I tussled good-naturedly with publisher Patrick Stephens himself to exclude some of his nominees!—and the ultimate justification for the final list is purely subjective. Not only do I believe we have included a representative selection of the right people, but the bottom line is that they are personalities who I myself have found interesting to read about and absorbing to research.

I would like to thank the following for help, advice and assistance with various aspects of the narrative and photographic content: Michael Bowler, Mike Doodson, Danny Hindenoch, Denis Jenkinson, Fiona Miller, Doug Nye, David Phipps, and Nigel Roebuck.

Alan Henry,
Tillingham,
Essex.
February 1992.

1

J. C. Agajanian

J. C. AGAJANIAN was born Joshua James Agajanian and picked up his initials thanks to an elderly aunt nicknaming him 'Jacie' during his youth. But to everybody in the US racing scene he was popularly referred to as 'Aggie', the distinctive, immaculately dressed character in the cowboy hat who, as a car owner, became one of the archetypal Indianapolis heroes as well as a shrewd and successful circuit owner in California.

Possibly his greatest success was the 1963 Indy 500 when Parnelli Jones drove his Watson-Offy roadster 'Ol' Calhoun' to a controversial victory over Jim Clark's rear-engined Lotus 29. The circumstances of this success, and Aggie's role in achieving it, represented a triumph of the entrenched Indianapolis establishment over the precocious newcomers. Jones's roadster had been losing oil for many laps during this event, coating the track with a treacherous sheen of lubricant. But Aggie successfully prevailed upon officials not to black flag Parnelli, much to the disgust of Colin Chapman, and Clark had to settle for second place on his Indy début.

Aggie's close friends used to joke that his business was 'second-hand food' and his family's story of success epitomized the true nature of the Great American Dream. His father arrived in the US at around the turn of the century, reputedly fleeing from Armenia to avoid being drafted into the Tsar's army. Agajanian Senior apparently learned English by the obvious, if somewhat complicated, expedient of comparing English and Armenian bibles. He washed dishes in Los Angeles for some years, during which time he casually inquired what happened to the kitchen garbage.

The explanation was that it found a home as pig feed, a discovery which would change the immigrant's life. He saved his money and eventually bought himself some pigs of his own—then went into the garbage collection business. He was on the way to a huge fortune which J.C. would add to and expand in the half century that followed.

In 1932, at the age of 19, J.C. withdrew $1,500 from his father's savings account and—unbeknown to his parent—acquired an elderly racer called a Cragar. When Aggie's father saw it in the garage, he hit the roof. It was made plain to the young man that it was either him or the car—one of them had to go. Happily, Aggie placated his father and they reached a compromise. The car would stay, but 'Jacie' would not drive it. Instead, he would get another driver—at no cost to the family—to handle the machine.

Thus Agajanian took his first step down the road to becoming a highly successful Indy car entrant. In the wake of America's economic depression, he also expanded to assume the role of promoter, helping the sport back onto its commercial feet as he helped organize the Western Racing Association. Events sanctioned by the Automobile Club of America—the predecessor of USAC—had virtually died on the West Coast and it was not until 1947 that the WRA, by now virtually controlled by Aggie, was invited back into the fold. In 1948, J. C. Agajanian entered a car at Indianapolis for the first time.

Two years later Walt Faulkner became the first Rookie to start from pole position, driving one of Aggie's cars. In 1952 Troy Ruttman became the youngest winner, again at the wheel of a machine owned by the California-based entrepreneur. Thereafter, Aggie entered a rather bleak spell, but in 1957 fellow enthusiast Vel Miletich introduced him to a man who would play a major role in his racing life. It was Rufus Parnell Jones, universally known to friend and rival as 'Parnelli'.

By the end of the 1960s, Agajanian reckoned that he had spent something in the region of $500,000 at the speedway 'for a return of about $350,000. In pure business terms it made no sense, but then you have to be an enthusiast about this game.' And by then he was keeping a firm eye on Parnelli's progress, impressed at the way in which the quiet young man shook his head and declined the offer of an Indy drive in 1959, reckoning he was not yet ready for the big jump.

Finally, in 1961, Jones joined up with Agajanian's team, bringing with him his highly regarded mechanic Johnny Poulsen. Aggie, a thoroughly nice, popular extrovert, was also about to reap the benefits of a favour he had done for car builder A. J. Watson a few years earlier. Watson had wanted to purchase a road car and Aggie loaned him the necessary money. Now Watson's roadsters were required hardware for success at Indy and the chassis specialist bumped Agajanian up towards the front of the queue of those teams waiting to take delivery.

The combination of Parnelli, Aggie, Poulsen, and 'Ol' Calhoun' would notch up a total of two Indy pole positions and six championship race victories, one of which was that historic 1963 Indy 500 success. Jones started from pole in his regular machine, breaking record after record with the Agajanian roadster. He made his first routine fuel stop after 64 laps, dropping briefly back to eighth place and allowing Roger McCluskey's similar Watson–Offy roadster to take the lead.

Shortly afterwards, it started to become clear that the stock Ford-engined Lotus 29s, running more economically on pump fuel than the alcohol-drinking Offenhausers, would be able to run through to the finish on two fewer fuel stops than their establishment rivals. So it proved, and by lap 80 Jim Clark and Dan Gurney were running first and second, Jones charging hard to make up ground from third place.

Eventually Parnelli made it back into the lead, but there was just no way he could shake off the bottle green Lotus. Then 'Ol' Calhoun' began leaking oil, apparently from a horizontal split in its rear-mounted oil tank. On the startline, Clark of the Course Harlan Fengler was urged by Aggie not to black flag him until he'd studied the problem through field glasses.

Agajanian takes up the tale:

I had to stop him somehow. I said 'We were throwing oil, but we're not throwing any anymore. Harlan, you can't call us in now'.

And just then Colin Chapman comes rushing up with his English accent and says 'Pull that car off of there before he kills all the other drivers' and I yelled at him 'Get your butt back over that wall, Chapman ... Fengler and I are talking. It's not your car that's in trouble'. And Fengler turned to Chapman and said 'Get back please, Mr Chapman' ... and all the while I was saying 'You can't take the race away from us this late, you just can't do it'.

Fengler agonized, studied Parnelli's car through the glasses for two or three laps, and then nodded to J.C. 'OK, Aggie, we'll let him finish ...' The establishment had won, and Chapman took a long time to stop bristling about the way in which he had been treated. Clark finished second behind Parnelli.

Yet, somehow, Agajanian could be forgiven his enthusiasm and pressure. There was none of the bitter rancour surrounding his intervention, for this extrovert, wealthy team owner was a passionate enthusiast, a showman and a man who genuinely cared about the way in which the sport developed in the USA. He wasn't just any old car owner trying it on. Chapman would have done exactly the same had the position been reversed and Clark been the one dropping the oil.

Whilst gradually dropping out of Indy car participation in the late 1960s, Aggie stepped up his promotional activities at Ascot Park Speedway in Gardena, California. Backbone of his operation were the CRA Sprints, with the USAC Midgets running them a strong second.

He banged the drum and promoted this quarter-mile dirt oval with a flair and commercial pizzaz which would have done credit to any European Grand Prix organizer. Aggie knew, more than most, that motor racing was supposed to be entertainment and he did more than his share, hauling the paying public through the gates and sending them away satisfied customers. Saturday night at the Ascot sprints became as much a part of Long Beach Grand Prix weekend as the Formula 1 race itself, with many of the Grand Prix fraternity—drivers, mechanics, and journalists—cramming into the little dust bowl which oozed its own unique atmosphere.

His three sons—Carey, Chris, and J. C. Junior—were groomed to take over the running of J. C. Agajanian Enterprises, which to this day, continues to promote Ascot as the top Southern Californian sprint car venue. Sadly, in 1974, Aggie was diagnosed as suffering from cancer.

He fought the disease manfully for a decade, doggedly giving it a splendid run for its money. But it was one race he was destined to lose and, in May 1984, this larger-than-life showman succumbed at the relatively early age of 73. He had outlived his old rival Colin Chapman by just 18 months.

2

Jean-Marie Balestre

REASSERTING THE INFLUENCE and authority of motor racing's governing body, the Federation Internationale du Sport Automobile, became an all-consuming crusade for the highly political Jean-Marie Balestre throughout the 1980s. Energetic and dramatically confident, this volcano of a personality effectively re-wrote the rules of the game by transforming FISA from an almost mute, compliant organization into an assertive and authoritarian regime.

From the viewpoint of Grand Prix motor racing, Balestre's rise to power would become a matter of even more significance, leading to a head-on collision between FISA and the Formula One Constructors' Association, whose President Bernie Ecclestone had been largely responsible for transforming the Grand Prix business into a multi-media international sport.

Born in 1920, Balestre has had a colourful and action-packed career ever since his teenage years and recounts with enthusiasm how he served in the pro-Government international Brigade during the Spanish Civil War when he was only 15 or 16 years old. After that he took up law studies in Paris, followed by a spell as a journalist on a number of left-wing publications. Once the war had started, though, amidst the chaos of a disintegrating Europe, he tells of becoming involved in the organization of an anti-German 'action group' in Paris as early as 1940.

He subsequently served in the French Resistance, carrying out assassinations, bomb attacks and other covert activities against the Nazi German forces occupying France at the time. He has papers to prove this, although they were issued by the authorities some ten years later as it obviously took a great deal of time after the end of hostilities to establish who had been a collaborator and who had not.

When, in the late 1970s, photographs began to circulate of Balestre wearing a German uniform, he took unsuccessful legal action to suppress their publication. He explained that he was a double agent, having volunteered to infiltrate the enemy on the orders of the Resistance. This claim was confirmed in 1968 when he was invested with France's most valued civil award, the Légion d'Honneur.

In addition, Balestre insists that he was once arrested by the Gestapo, tortured for a month, and condemned to death. He escaped execution when the arrival of the Allied invasion forces forced the Nazis to deport him back to Germany. Returned to France in 1945, he was by then suffering from tubercolosis, typhus and diptheria which led—in 1966—to his being awarded a disability allowance and state pension.

The business fortunes of this returning war hero were established in 1949 when he helped to found an important Paris-based publishing group. Its first product was a motoring magazine that was usually candid and outspoken for its era, unafraid to criticize many new models, something which outraged several French manufacturers. Balestre spent a spell as production editor and chief editor of this magazine.

He is remembered by some of his rivals as an extremely intense competitor when it came to journalistic activities, qualities he subsequently put on regular display as president of FISA. When plans for the new Citroen DS19 went astray, the car maker sent the police into his office in search of them.

In the cautious 1950s, car makers were often unhappy with what they read in Balestre's magazine and legal actions frequently ensued. Whether his fondness for calling in the lawyers dates back to this period is unclear, but Balestre has felt it necessary to resort to legal actions himself—proving particularly sensitive to references about his wartime activities, as journalists in several countries have discovered over the past decade.

A motorsporting enthusiast from an early age, Balestre founded the Fédération Française du Sport Automobile (FFSA) in 1952 at a time when a handful of regional race-organizing clubs dominated the administration of French motorsport. It would be ten years before the FFSA became officially recognized as a national club, by which time Balestre had ensured his future with the organization.

Balestre had a hand in the introduction of kart racing to France; almost inevitably it proved a tremendous success and, with hundreds of appreciative kart racers supporting him, he could muster the votes necessary to impose himself on French motorsport. By 1973 he was President of the FFSA, by then officially recognized by the Ministry of Sport as the country's representative body, and, shrewdly, offered his candidature in elections for the Vice-Presidency of the CSI, the international commission nominally in charge of world motorsport. He then set about revitalizing its influence with considerable energy.

Changing the CSI's name to FISA, Balestre embarked on a crusade against Ecclestone and FOCA, which he felt had too much commercial control over motor racing. On the face of it the arguments raged between the two over such technical items as qualifying tyres and, notably, aerodynamic side skirts, the latter being used to splendid effect by the British-based non-turbo teams to counter the burgeoning power of a new breed of turbo engines developed initially by Ferrari and Renault. Widely, Balestre's stance was seen as siding with the major manufacturers against the FOCA-aligned majority.

Many historians now believe such arguments to have been a smoke-screen behind which the real battle—for the financial control of Grand Prix racing—was fought out between the two protagonists. The battle was finally resolved by the signing of the Concorde Agreement that has formed the comprehensive administrative framework by which Formula 1 has been policed ever since the start of 1981. However, although FISA swore to take over financial control of Grand Prix racing, many judge that Balestre scored a qualified success in this respect. FISA only gained a small percentage of the television coverage and circuit publicity rights, most of which continue to accrue to the Constructors' Association.

Balestre's power within motor racing stemmed from the votes he was able to muster during presidential elections at both FISA and, more recently, the FIA itself. Yet it was always a matter of some irritation amongst those in the motor racing business that no more than a handful of delegates to the meetings of these two Federations had anything more than a fleeting knowledge of motorsport. However, much of this criticism came from those who were merely disappointed that Balestre was not as easily bullied as they would have liked, and, despite the controversy he caused, there were several key manufacturers who regarded him as preferable to some other potential candidates whose names had been put forward.

Balestre's 13 year stint as the most powerful man in motorsport finally came to an end in the autumn of 1991. Having last faced a challenge to his FISA Presidency back in 1981, when Britain's RAC representative Basil Tye was roundly beaten off, Balestre had been re-elected unopposed on two occasions.

However, in October 1991, Balestre's regime was toppled when British lawyer Max Mosley, one of the co-founders of March Engineering and by then president of the FISA Manufacturers' Commission, toppled him by 43 votes to 29. Balestre took the defeat with commendable dignity, for while he was bowing out from the top job at FISA, he was still President of the FIA—which nominally controlled FISA—and the FFSA, France's national motorsporting authority.

Unquestionably, this pivotal personality is a consummate showman as well as a shrewd politician. He has the constitution of an ox, enjoying excellent health in the wake of a heart bypass operation in 1986, although it is known that, when attending the 1990 Brazilian Grand Prix, he needed a whiff of oxygen to overcome the lingering effect of bronchitis.

Balestre has been quoted as saying that he will never allow himself the luxury of dying in office. He may attribute his heart trouble largely to the stress of administering international motor racing, and the conflicts stemming therefrom, but the signs are that there is plenty of life in the old chien yet ...

13

3

John Barnard

WHEN JOHN BARNARD left the Benetton team before the midway point of the 1991 World Championship season, Formula 1 racing suddenly found itself deprived of one of the handful of designers who had been responsible for laying down the design guidelines for a whole generation of Grand Prix machines. One of the few truly original thinkers in a business where technical mimickry is frequently the norm, Barnard would gain a reputation as an uncompromising perfectionist who was found difficult to work with by those not sharing his single-mindedness.

Yet Barnard was no sudden design prodigy. Before forging his highly successful partnership with Ron Dennis in 1980 that formed the bedrock on which today's spectacularly successful Honda Marlboro McLaren team was built, Barnard's experience of motor racing design stretched back to 1969 when he first joined the Lola drawing office as a junior.

Born in 1946 in the north London suburb of Wembley, Barnard had initially studied engineering at Brunel Technical College and Watford Technical College, ending up in the GEC design department working on machinery for producing electric lightbulbs. For a lifelong car enthusiast, this was an understandably short-term project and, in accepting the position with Eric Broadley's company, Barnard could hardly have landed a better opportunity as a starting point for career in motor racing design.

At the turn of the 1970s, Lola was producing a wide range of proprietary racing cars for every imaginable international and national formula. Moreover, by curious coincidence, it was in the Lola design office at Huntingdon, near Cambridge, that John met up with a like-minded young engineer called Patrick Head. Over a decade later, Head's Williams F1 designs would shape up as the most consistent and competitive rivals to the Barnard-designed McLarens.

In 1972, Barnard received an invitation to join McLaren in a number two capacity to Gordon Coppuck, who was then in the final stages of producing his epochal M23 design that would take Emerson Fittipaldi and James Hunt to the World Championship in 1974 and 1976 respectively.

Barnard carried out much of the detail design work on the M23 monocoque, but found that his burgeoning perfectionist streak sat uncomfortably with the slightly free-wheeling atmosphere in the team—a throwback to the relaxed days of its late founder, Bruce McLaren. Input from the, admittedly highly-experienced, mechanics might have been all very well, but Barnard already took the view that the Chief Designer should be just that.

It was just a touch too informal for his taste, so when an invitation came his way to join the Vel's Parnelli Indy car team, he quickly accepted. Although the project was underfinanced, the Barnard-designed Parnelli VPJ 6B would go on to win its first race and the promise shown by his cars led to an invitation for him to join Jim Hall's Texas-based Chaparral team, where he designed the Chaparral 2K that won both the Indy 500 and the CART Championship in 1980.

By this time, however, Barnard had split with Hall. He felt that he had reached an agreement with the car owner that due credit for the design should be accorded to him and that, in the event, Hall neglected to make sufficient acknowledgement of his role. On his return to the UK Barnard was contacted by F2 team boss Ron Dennis with a proposal to design an F1 chassis.

The partnership started on an uncertain note. Their first task was to find a company willing to collaborate with them on the manufacture of a carbon-fibre composite chassis: Dennis also needed to raise finance. Their timing was superb. By then McLaren had fallen from the competitive high wire and their sponsors, Marlboro, engineered a merger with Dennis's existing Project 4 organization to found McLaren International.

In 1981, Barnard designed the first of the carbon-fibre MP4 (standing for Marlboro/Project 4) McLaren chassis with which John Watson won the British Grand Prix at Silverstone. For the next two seasons the team continued to use Cosworth V8 engines, but early on in the partnership Dennis had appreciated that they would have to follow the turbo trend.

Although their partnership would subsequently end in some acrimony, Barnard gives Ron Dennis credit for what he describes as 'the master stroke'. While most teams were making approaches to engine manufacturers to build a turbo engines, Dennis engineered outside sponsorship from Techniques d'Avant Garde (TAG), the Franco-Saudi high technology corporation, and with their financial backing approached Porsche on a customer basis with a request that they build a tailor-made turbocharged engine.

This was right up Barnard's street because it meant he could build a totally integrated Grand Prix design with virtually no compromise in terms of technical specification. Once the agreement with Porsche was finalized, it was Barnard who decided on the engine specification, Barnard who said where the exhaust pipes would go, and Barnard who meshed the whole concept in with his chassis concept.

'Too many engine makers give absolutely no thought as to how an engine is going to be installed in a chassis,' Barnard states firmly. 'They get it running on a test bed and then wonder why the chassis designer isn't interested. With the TAG-Porsche project, I had the final say and I think subsequent events proved that had been worthwhile.'

Barnard was understandably frustrated when his carefully prepared McLaren-TAG design was compromised at the last moment by FISA's decree that, from the start of 1983, a flat bottomed chassis would be mandatory in F1. The TAG engine had been designed for installation in the ultimate ground-effect car, so 'at a stroke, part of the whole concept's rationale had been wiped out'.

Nevertheless, Barnard's design would rule the World Championship scene through 1984, 1985, and 1986 with Niki Lauda and Alain Prost (twice) taking the Drivers' World Championships. By the end of 1986 he was finding it hard to sustain his motivation and inwardly knew that he needed a new challenge. He had sold his shares in McLaren International to TAG boss Mansour Ojjeh and, in the autumn of 1986, accepted an invitation from Ferrari to set up a new design studio in England at premises situated only a few miles from his home in Surrey.

Barnard's brief was to build a new car for the 3.5-litre naturally aspirated regulations that were due to be instigated at the start of 1989. John was to be answerable directly to the ailing Enzo Ferrari, who would in fact die in August 1988; yet there was no doubt that the English designer's direct and uncompromising approach resulted in his ruffling some feathers within the highly political Ferrari establishment.

His type 640 Ferrari turned out to be a radical departure from established tradition, featuring strikingly different aerodynamics and a novel electro-hydraulic gearchange. In the hands of Nigel Mansell, the new Ferrari won its first race in Brazil at the start of 1989 and although John left the team at the end of the year, after barely three years, its direct descendant, the type 641, would take Alain Prost to within sight of the 1990 World Championship before the Frenchman lost out to Ayrton Senna.

Barnard's perfectionist approach was clearly a costly luxury for any F1 team, both in terms of salary and the corresponding investment in equipment to get the job done to his demanding standards. After McLaren and Ferrari, it was in truth rather difficult to see who else would have the financial commitment to take Barnard on, but in 1990 he joined Benetton with a brief to establish a new Technical Centre and initiate a long-term development programme to produce a winning car round the Cosworth HB engine.

Yet again, Barnard came up trumps. Although the new Benetton B191 would only win the 1991 Canadian Grand Prix because of Nigel Mansell's last lap retirement, in doing so it sustained the Barnard reputation for producing F1 designs that win in their first season. Within days of that success, Barnard was ousted in what amounted to a palace coup and, in a matter of weeks, Jaguar racing boss Tom Walkinshaw took a major stake in the Benetton team. In retrospect, it seems that the Benetton management took the view that Barnard had became a little too autocratic for their comfort, although this is not the emphasis Barnard himself would put on the interpretation of events.

However, as the 1991 season moved towards its close, it became increasingly clear that Benetton was missing Barnard's technical contribution. Meanwhile, John was sitting quietly at home in rural Surrey, considering his future options at leisure, doubtless with a wry grin on his face. He was undecided whether or not he wanted to continue in the F1 maelstrom, although, as he admitted, 'I think I might have one more Grand Prix design in me for the right team!'

4

Sir Jack Brabham

SIR JACK BRABHAM was one of Grand Prix racing's great practical heroes, applying a down-to-earth straightforwardness to everything he tackled. Whether it was the challenge of winning three Drivers' World Championships or the business of manufacturing and running his own Grand Prix cars, Jack could be relied upon to take a direct, no-frills approach.

Jack's paternal grandfather, a Cockney, was born in Bow, East London, in 1869 and emigrated to Australia at the age of 16. John Arthur Braham, always known as Jack, was born in Hurstville, about ten miles to the south of Sydney, on 12 April 1926, the only son of a greengrocer. His education embraced a course at a local technical college once he had finished with his routine schooling, but he quickly decided to abandon his first job in favour of maintaining his father's trucks and cars at a local Hurstville garage. This imbued him with a mechanical aptitude and resourcefulness that were destined to produce repeated benefits in the years that followed.

At the age of 18, Brabham joined the Royal Australian Air Force. He dearly wanted to fly, but by now it was 1944 and at this stage of the Second World War there was more demand for flight mechanics than aircrew. Most of his time in the forces was spent working on Bristol Beaufighters until he was demobbed in 1947 and, rather uncertainly, looked around for something to do with his life.

Together with a close friend, Brabham decided to start up a small engineering business of his own, but it was not long before the lure of motor racing exerted its pull. His interest was sparked by the then-fashionable midget car racing category, a highly popular class for which the races were staged on rutted, makeshift oval tracks.

Jack's first season was pretty successful. He won the New South Wales championship after helping to develop a JAP-engined special for dirt track ace Johnny Schonberg, taking over behind the wheel of this machine after Schonberg retired from active racing due to pressure from his wife.

In this close-fought, uncompromising dirt track environment Jack developed his distinctive oversteering—and defensive—driving style, a technique that would stay with him throughout his racing career. However, there was a brief hitch; when a broken connecting rod cost

Jack the South Australian championship, he briefly opted out of the motor racing game and tried his hand at the truck business with his father. He didn't take long to change his mind ...

It was in 1951 that Brabham made a chance acquaintance that was to affect the long-term development of his racing career. Two brothers, Ron and Austin Tauranac, called in on Jack's machine shop to see whether he would be interested in selling them one of his single-cylinder Velocette engines. As it happened, Brabham wasn't interested in this particular deal but he kept in touch with Ron Tauranac, who was actually to beat him to the 1954 New South Wales hillclimb championship title.

Brabham aspired to a professional future in the sport and was well ahead of his time when he attracted Redex sponsorship for his Cooper-Bristol during the 1954 season, although the Australian motorsporting authorities were extremely sniffy about the whole business and he was obliged to remove the identification. In 1955 Jack made tracks to England where he became involved with Charles and John Cooper, forging a partnership that would result in the taciturn Australian winning the 1959 and 1960 World Championships for the famous team from Surbiton.

Having a pretty shrewd engineering mind of his own, Jack was always keen to check up on Cooper progress, more often than not by bouncing ideas off Ron Tauranac through continuous correspondence with his compatriot. Some of Ron's suggestions included interesting little sketches, showing Jack how to surmount some problem or other, and the wily Brabham would discreetly feed them into the Cooper design system if he thought they fitted the bill.

Jack had long-term plans to set up as a production racing car manufacturer in his own right, and with this in mind he asked Ron to come over to England late in 1959. By this time Jack was also exploiting his Grand Prix success by means of a thriving garage business, a speciality of which was the installation of Coventry Climax engines into otherwise innocuous Triumph Heralds.

Brabham and Tauranac also started Motor Racing Developments to build a range of production single-seaters, a project which understandably cut across Cooper's business activity. Moreover, with Jack also keen to build his own Grand Prix car, the parting of the ways with Cooper came at the end of 1961. Eight months later, at the 1962 German Grand Prix, Jack gave the new Brabham-Climax BT3 its Formula 1 debut after initially campaigning a private Lotus 24 while Tauranac worked on completing the new machine.

For the 1963 season, Jack signed the lanky American Dan Gurney as his second driver and the Climax-engined Brabhams quickly developed a reputation for setting a competitive pace, though they also fell victim to mechanical problems far too frequently. It was not until the 1964 French

Grand Prix at Rouen that Dan scored the Brabham marque's maiden World Championship success, following that up with victory in the Mexican Grand Prix.

There would be no more wins coming their way in 1965, but Brabham's shrewd sense of anticipation ensured that his team was well placed to achieve almost instant success when the 3-litre Formula 1 was instigated at the start of the following year.

Having originally received some assistance from Repco, the Australian manufacturer of replacement car components, in locating premises in Surbiton when he started his production racing car business (the cars were dubbed Repco Brabhams from the outset), Jack again beat a path to their door. Repco had developed a lightweight V8 engine, based on the General Motors Oldsmobile F85 block, to replace the ageing 2.7 Climax four-cylinders that were the mainstay of the Tasman series, the most prestigious racing category in Australia and New Zealand. Brabham not only became involved in racing that 2.5-litre Tasman engine from the outset, he also persuaded Repco that they should produce a 3-litre F1 version. They agreed and the rest, as they say, is history.

Brabham's victory in the 1966 French Grand Prix at Reims was the first ever to be scored by a driver in a car bearing his own name. He followed this up with wins in the British, Dutch, and German races, celebrating his 40th birthday at Zandvoort with a touch of wry humour, limping out to the grid with a false beard and walking stick. It was his way of getting back at those amongst the media who believed he was past it!

The following year, the Brabham-Repcos continued their reliable, winning ways, but this time it was Jack's second-in-command, Denny Hulme, who took the title. The rugged New Zealander remembers that Jack probably lost his chance of a fourth World Championship by too frequently opting to use new technical developments before they were sufficiently reliable.

Brabham never wasted words; monosyllabic responses were generally all that could be expected by even his closest friends. He was also shrewd to the point of sheer cunning. His former chief mechanic Ron Dennis, today boss of the World Championship winning McLaren International team, recalls Jack spending hours tyre testing in order to find the best covers for his own use. The ones he rejected were reserved for Hulme's cars.

He was also ready and willing to turn his hand to any chore. When the troublesome 1968 four-cam Repco V8 developed a penchant for dropping valves, he commandered his wife's kitchen oven to 'cook' the cylinder heads that had been re-drilled with new valve seats, Jack having flown them back to England for attention following practice problems in the 1968 French Grand Prix at Rouen. Once the job was done, he placed the reassembled engine on to the right-hand passenger seat of his Piper Twin Comanche and flew it back to France for the following day's race.

Jack was disappointed that the failure of the four-cam Repco engine resulted in his losing the highly-rated Jochen Rindt to Lotus for 1969, even though he finally dropped Repco engines in favour of the ubiquitous Cosworth DFV. Brabham admired Jochen enormously and moved heaven and earth to try and persuade the mercurial Austrian to rejoin his team for 1970. Jack would have retired at the end of 1969 had he managed to lure Jochen back into the fold, but Lotus boss Colin Chapman was prepared to pay whatever was necessary in order to outbid the Australian.

So Brabham raced through 1970, winning the South African Grand Prix and actually running a strong third on his final outing in Mexico before engine failure thwarted his bid to challenge the much more powerful Ferrari flat-12s. Once out of the game, he sold his shares in MRD to Ron Tauranac who, in turn, quickly sold out to Bernie Ecclestone.

Jack Brabham, knighted at the end of 1984, never had second thoughts once away from the cockpit and never looked back. His sons Geoff, Gary, and David continue the proud family tradition as professional racers in a wide variety of categories, with the Old Man occasionally turning out to watch them with impassive paternal approval.

5

Eric Broadley

WHILE COLIN CHAPMAN'S name was thrown into the motor racing spotlight with his Formula 1 achievements during the 1960s, there was another key specialist racing car builder making its own significant impact on the European motor racing scene. The company was Lola Cars, its founder Eric Broadley, an ambitious and imaginative enthusiast who emerged from the same 750 Motor Club beginnings as the likes of the late Lotus boss and racing engine specialist Brian Hart.

Yet although his company would be associated with Grand Prix racing from time to time throughout its history, Lola would make its mark and livelihood manufacturing commercially available cars for other national and international racing categories. In that respect, Lola would outlast such famous names as Cooper, Brabham, and Lotus when it came to marketing off-the-shelf proprietary racing machinery.

Back in 1956 Eric's cousin, Graham Broadley, was racing a Formula 750 car at a time when Eric was involved in building and site management. On a couple of occasions Eric helped out his relative and was rewarded with a race in the car, which duly fired his appetite for the sport. It wasn't long before Eric started to manufacture his own car for the equally popular 1172 category, which relied on Ford side-valve production engines.

From premises in Bromley, Kent, Broadley established his reputation as a practical and reliable engineer, and in 1959 the first of the Coventry-Climax, 1100-cc Lola Mk 1 sports cars were manufactured. These really helped put the company's name on the map, spawning a succession of sports cars and Formula Junior single seaters which attained much European success, Richard Attwood's triumph in the 1963 Monaco Grand Prix supporting Formula Junior event being one such typical example.

In 1962 he manufactured a Climax-engined Grand Prix car which John Surtees drove for the Reg Parnell-managed Bowmaker F1 team, and the following year built the Ford V8-engined Ford GT as the first step in the programme that would eventually produce the GT40. Ironically, once that consultancy contract had expired in 1965, Broadley's company went on to produce the delectable T70 sports racers and coupés, machines that are now even more highly esteemed in some collectors' circles than the GT40.

Broadley's work for Ford had been based at the Ford Advanced Vehicle Operations headquarters at Slough, managed by former Aston Martin General Manager John Wyer, and when he was back in harness with Lola he moved their base to the area. It was here that the T70 was designed and evolved, giving Denny Hulme and John Surtees a winning edge in Group 7 sports car races, and on the Can-Am scene before the all-conquering McLarens got into their stride.

In 1966 Lola went to Indianapolis after being commissioned by Texan oil millionaire John Mecom to build a trio of cars operated by ace mechanic George Bignotti. One of them, driven by Jackie Stewart, was deprived of a near-certain début victory by engine failure in the closing stages, as the rightly proud Scot never ceases telling anybody who will listen. JYS did, however, win the one-off Japanese Indy car race at the Mount Fuji circuit later that same year at the wheel of one of Broadley's cars.

Lola was one of the first constructors to announce that it would support the fledgling Formula 5000 when it got off the ground in 1969, initially with the T142 and T190, neither of which were particularly easy machines to handle.

Mike Hailwood and Frank Gardner did a lot of development work on the latter model, Broadley following along with a sensational rethink when he took the smaller F2 monocoque into which was installed the inevitable 5-litre Chevrolet V8. In the early 1970s the European 2-litre sports car championship also proved to be good business for the firm with Jackie Stewart's much-publicized efforts with the T240 Can-Am machine.

The company relocated to Huntingdon in 1970 and, four years later, Broadley was invited to have his second stab at a Grand Prix contender with a contract to build the Formula 1 chassis for Graham Hill's Embassy team. This was a purely commercial arrangement and Eric has steadfastly remained reluctant to take the plunge himself into Grand Prix waters. At the time of writing his company is manufacturing the Lamborghini-engined Grand Prix chassis used by the French Larrousse team on a purely commercial basis, and while the technology involved in this project is well on a par with that employed in Lola's Formula 3000 and Indy car racing, Broadley is content to remain a supplier and spend most time doing what he knows best.

In the 1980s, the Indy car scene really opened up as an attractive and lucrative market for customer cars, with Lola snatching a large share of what had previously been the March market from 1987 onwards. Ironically, while Lolas have swept the board over the past three or four seasons, Graham Hill's 1966 win and Al Unser's 1978 victory at Indianapolis stood as Lola's only prior successes at the Brickyard through those halcyon days of the 1980s, despite some tremendous performances from Mario and Michael Andretti on behalf of Lola's long-time US importer Carl Haas. The Huntingdon-based constructor only notched up its third Indy victory when Dutchman Arie Luyendyk emerged triumphant in 1990.

In 1985 Andretti came closer to victory than at any time since his, so far, sole success in 1969. His Beatrice Lola T800 finished only a couple of seconds adrift of Danny Sullivan's March after the Kentucky driver survived a hair-raising spin which Mario missed by the skin of his teeth.

As far as the future is concerned, Eric Broadley will continue in his low-key, unobtrusive manner—and Lola will almost certainly prosper consistently as it has done over the past three decades.

6

Sir David Brown

DAVID BROWN WAS a millionaire who bankrolled a decade of Aston Martin racing effort mainly as a hobby, a spin-off from his family's highly successful, wide-ranging industrial empire. He was an unusual personality, enjoying his money and surrounding himself with all the accoutrements of the super wealthy, such as ocean-going yachts and private aircraft, while at the same time adopting a far from frivolous approach both to his business and his motor racing.

A measure of his financial status can be gauged from his decision to purchase the bankrupt Aston Martin company on a personal whim for a mere £20,000 in 1946, having responded to an advertisement in *The Times*. That was a great deal of cash for any company to have at its disposal in those days of austerity, let alone a private individual. Shortly afterwards, David Brown acquired Lagonda for a further £55,000, merging the two concerns to produce one worthwhile whole.

Although Aston designer Claude Hill took umbrage when Brown sanctioned fitting the W.O. Bentley-designed 6-cylinder Lagonda engine to the first of the cars to be manufactured under the new regime—the DB1—the new proprietor generally had a sure touch with his employees. He made it his habit to hire good men and, having done so, listened to them attentively. He very rarely contradicted the judgement of his key employees when it came to engineering and strategic motor racing matters.

The Brown family fortune came from a Huddersfield-based engineering dynasty, specializing in gear-cutting for a wide range of industrial and marine applications, started by DB's grandfather—also David Brown—in 1860 when he was only 17. It started as a partnership, Brown and Broadbent, but by 1870 the name had been changed to David Brown and Company. His two sons, Frank (father of DB) and Percy, duly came into the family firm, which became titled David Brown and Sons in 1912.

Young David was bought a motorcycle by his father to ensure that he got to work on time in the mornings. Born in 1904, he developed a keen interest in motorsport, riding in hillclimbs and races at an amateur level, and had his first serious contact with car racing when Amherst Villiers approached the Brown company to sort out a problem with the gear-driven supercharger on a Vauxhall he was preparing for Raymond Mays.

By August 1932, the death of his father had left him the challenge of running the David Brown empire singlehanded, a challenge which he met with great enthusiasm and considerable success. For the next forty years this industrial conglomerate expanded to become leading manufacturers of products as diverse as farm tractors, machine tools, and steel and bronze castings, in addition to its specialist gear making.

Absolutely central to the success of the burgeoning racing effort proved to be the personal relationship between 'DB' and his team manager John Wyer, whom he later promoted to be General Manager of the whole Aston Martin Lagonda combine. Wyer was recruited from Monaco Engineering, the specialist race preparation company, whose director Dudley Folland had himself raced a private pre-DB Aston Martin in the immediate post-war years. From the outset, Wyer had an almost unfettered hand on the management and administration front, only occasionally feeling a subtle nudge from his employer.

Brown also developed a close affinity with Frank Feeley, Aston Martin's talented body designer. They spent long hours together, DB hovering close to Feeley's drawing board discussing body styles, making helpful and positive suggestions, letting his own preferences be known without ever becoming over-assertive. As with Wyer, he was prepared to defer to what he considered a well-reasoned argument.

With his workforce, the sartorially impeccable Brown seemed a trifle shy, but displayed an interest in their jobs which they all felt was far from superficial. Like Ettore Bugatti, he was not averse to diverting factory staff away from car production duties to refurbish the interior fittings of his ocean-going yacht.

The off-duty trappings of his considerable wealth included, in addition to a succession of yachts, a large country estate and a private de Havilland Dove aircraft that was frequently used in conjunction with the motor racing programme. He made a point of keeping himself extremely fit, was an accomplished tennis and polo player, and a capable private pilot.

It was once rumoured in the popular press that David Brown was spending in the region of £1 million per year keeping his Aston Martins racing throughout the 1950s. This seems a vastly inflated sum and DB would later tell racing historian Chris Nixon that, in his estimation, the total 'over fifteen years was between £1$\frac{1}{2}$ and £2 million'. That, of course, would barely pay the salaries for a single year in a contemporary Grand Prix or sports car racing equipe, but Brown was not a big spender on unnecessary items.

In the early 1950s Stirling Moss was outraged when he was offered a £50 retainer from Aston Martin shortly after Jaguar had awarded him a £1,000 bonus for winning the Tourist Trophy. But that was par for the course as far as DB and John Wyer were concerned. On the other hand, all the drivers testify to the fact that DB always booked them into first-class hotels, never stinting on their food and creature comforts when they were racing abroad. Brown certainly knew where to spend money best to extract maximum loyalty per pound, for none of the surviving team members have anything but delightful memories of their time spent racing for the Feltham-based team.

Brown budgeted for Aston Martin to run at a loss in the sense that such deficit was not intended to exceed the notional advertising benefits accruing to the main David Brown Group from its racing activities. It was an exceedingly pragmatic approach, something of a contrast to the way that, say, Enzo Ferrari operated his automotive dynasty. But then Maranello was the Commendatore's sole source of income; Aston Martin did not fulfil that role for David Brown.

The high-water mark of achievement for the David Brown Aston Martins came in 1959 when Roy Salvadori and Carroll Shelby won Le Mans in the elegant DBR1 and the team also clinched the World Sports Car Championship. Brown and Wyer had made this an overriding priority to the point where the team's ambitious F1 plans, based round the front-engined DBR4, were shelved until 1960, by which time they had been overtaken by the rear-engined revolution.

There would be works Aston Martins at Le Mans as late as 1964, after which financial prudence promoted DB to close down the racing side after a splendid 15-year run. The 1956 switch from Feltham to Newport Pagnell, occasioned by Aston's takeover of the Tickford coachbuilding concern and the need to integrate production between the two, started a steady financial decline which an unnecessarily conservative attitude towards pricing the much-acclaimed DB4, which began production in 1961, simply accelerated.

Knighted in 1968 for his services to racing and the motor industry, Sir David Brown sold Aston Martin to Company Developments in 1972 and moved, with his millions, to an active semi-retirement in Monaco. He would, of course, retain control of the David Brown Corporation until January 1990, when a management buy-out headed by directors Chris Cooks and Chris Brown finally brought 130 years of family ownership to an end.

Above all, Sir David Brown is recalled fondly by his team drivers as a man with remarkable equilibrium, never marked by great swings of temperament. He never seemed unduly elated by success, nor dejected in defeat. He underpinned their efforts with a quiet confidence, sticking resolutely behind any decisions he made and gaining a reputation as an outstandingly supportive employer. Without him, Aston Martin and Lagonda would almost certainly have dwindled into financial oblivion in those dank days of the post-war 1940s.

7

Ettore Bugatti

ETTORE BUGATTI WAS possibly the most remarkable of all the distinguished personalities who feature in this volume. He combined an unstinting enthusiasm for fine engineering with commercial aspirations that were always firmly subjugated to artistry and with a commitment to producing aesthetically beautiful cars. This rare mix enabled Bugatti to produce some magnificent road and racing cars—identified by the distinctive horseshoe-shaped radiator—between the wars; but it also ensured that the dynasty founded by the man known universally as 'Le Patron' was always operating on a precarious financial base.

Ettore Bugatti was born in Milan on 15 September 1881, although he would steadfastly regard himself as a Frenchman from the moment he moved to Alsace to take a design job with the de Dietrich company in the early years of the century. Subsequently working for Mathis, then Deutz, it was in 1911 that Bugatti established his own car factory in the outbuildings of a dye factory in the village of Molsheim, a picturesque Alsatian village nestling in the foothills of the Vosges mountains between Strasbourg and Saverne.

Bugatti was a dictator, the absolute ruler of all he surveyed. Yet such a label implies a ruthlessness which those who worked with him testify was pleasantly absent from his personality. He was a warm-hearted family man who generously indulged his wife, sons Jean and Roland and daughters Lydia and L'Ebe, and seemed never happier than when he was at home in Molsheim, in surroundings he loved passionately.

Bugatti's greatest and most famously successful cars were produced after the First World War. In 1924 the superb type 35 was unveiled, winning countless races in the hands of works drivers and privateers alike over the next few years, followed two seasons later by the Type 39A—effectively a supercharged version of the earlier car.

In 1929, Bugatti would gain great distinction when the enigmatic Englishman William Grover-Williams triumphed in the inaugural Monaco Grand Prix, the Molsheim firm notching up a hat trick when René Dreyfus and Louis Chiron repeated that victory in 1931 and 1932 respectively.

Of that trio of Monaco winners, only the urbane Dreyfus survives at the time of writing, now a spritely 85. Grover-Williams did heroic espionage work for Britain during the Second World War, only to be betrayed to the Gestapo and executed; Chiron survived to race in the post-war era, dying in 1979 at the age of 80. They were all debonair, dashing, and handsome young men at the turn of the 1930s, each adding another layer of veneer to the increasingly lustrous and romantic Bugatti legend.

Dreyfus had a keen eye for detail and was fascinated by what a patriarchal society existed not just in the Bugatti factory, but in Molsheim as a whole. In his splendid volume of memoirs, *My Two Lives*, he pointed out that almost everybody in that village worked for 'Le Patron' during the late 1920s, either directly or indirectly.

When René was invited to join the Bugatti works team at the start of 1933, the population of Molsheim was around 3,000—and the Bugatti workforce around 800. The prosperity of every shopkeeper in the area depended directly on the Bugatti company's personal success. Dreyfus also recalled that there were very few private cars; all the workers rode round on bicycles. René quickly acquired one in order to feel at home in this contented social backwater!

Bugatti designed everything. Whilst his engineers were briefed on the technical specification of the cars—and there is no evidence to suggest that 'Le Patron' interfered unduly on this front—he put his personal touch on the internal plant fittings. Even the choice of vases was down to the boss.

Bugatti also displayed an extraordinary tendency towards pulling his engineers off mainstream motoring projects in order to pursue his personal pet projects. For example, the men who worked in the trim department, preparing the cars' sumptuous leather interior appointments, would suddenly be switched to manufacturing exquisitely intricate saddles and reins designed by their employer. Dreyfus remembers these as singularly first-rate products—quite the equal of the top Paris brands—but Bugatti never showed any interest in marketing these leather goods on a commercial basis. Unbelievably, the works team missed the 1933 French Grand Prix simply because the cars were not ready. The engineers had been occupied on some personal project of the boss's—like manufacturing a bureau, containing a secret compartment, for his beloved wife.

In 1935 Bugatti decided to manufacture what he intended would be the most prestigious and elegant road car ever made. This, of course, was the massive 13-litre, straight-eight Royale. Only six of these gigantic motor cars were ever constructed, even the richest of international tycoons regarding Bugatti's latest dreams as prohibitively expensive.

Under such circumstances, one might have expected Bugatti to be personally gratified when King Zog of Albania expressed interest in purchasing one of these monsters. 'Le Patron' declined the invitation. Later he confided that he couldn't possibly sell one of his automotive works of art to a man with such deplorable table manners ...

His personal idiosyncrasies also extended to dealing with local trades-men. He might have been a late payer on occasion, but took the view that nobody had any cause for concern over this habit. A wealthy man on paper, he was always financially over-stretched. No matter. He was Bugatti; his word was his bond.

The local electricity company was not so philosophical when the bill for the factory's electricity supply fell overdue. The matter was raised with 'Le Patron', who promptly responded by installing his own generating plant. He also reputedly added insult to injury by inviting the chief of the electricity company to a formal opening of his alternative power source!

With the Royale clearly not destined to sell in the numbers originally anticipated, Bugatti now turned his attention to the tangential consider-ation of precisely what to do with over twenty 13-litre engines that were now surplus to requirements. He laid plans to manufacture a railcar *par excellence* with a planned performance well in excess of 120mph.

Powered by four Royale engines, the first such railcar was built at the Bugatti factory without anybody bothering to think how it would be removed on completion. Subsequent scrutiny revealed there was no way that it could be removed through the existing gate, so 'Le Patron' instructed his staff to knock an additional hole in the perimeter wall. By marshalling the entire workforce, the railcar was then pushed out to freedom, down the road to the local railway station!

Six were sold to three French railway companies and, indeed, after serious car production ceased in the late 1940s, Bugatti continued to build railcar engines of slightly less lavish performance than that provided by the Royale units.

Just prior to the Second World War, Ettore Bugatti was dealt a body blow from which many believe he never recovered. On 11 August 1939, his eldest son Jean was killed when he crashed the Le Mans-winning T57 whilst trying to avoid a cyclist on a local public road. Bugatti survived the war, although because he was still technically an Italian citizen he had to fight with all the resources at his disposal to prevent his factory being confiscated as war booty. Finally, in 1946, he was granted the French citizenship he had craved for so many years.

In the economic chaos of the immediate post-war years, Bugatti attempted to reactivate the road car manufacturing side of his business. But the moment had passed for this automotive master. After a short illness he died on 21 August 1947, ending a remarkable era in the history of car making.

His younger son Roland tried to revive the near-lifeless corpse of Bugatti as a car maker. As late as 1956 the company would even launch an abortive return to Formula 1 with the ill-starred, central-engined T251. But there was to be no Indian summer. The last vestiges of the famous company were snapped up by Hispano-Suiza in 1964.

8

Colin Chapman

HAD COLIN CHAPMAN been alive today, he might well have had his qualities of diplomacy and charm taxed to their utmost in explaining the DeLorean affair. For years, the motor racing community dutifully projected a deferential public face to the memory of this remarkable engineer, and there is no doubt that his contribution to motor racing history deserves in no way to be tarnished by what might or might not have happened in connection with certain of his business activities.

Nevertheless, what had hitherto been little more than lounge bar gossip about Chapman's true role in the collapse of the DeLorean company, was suddenly thrown into sharp public focus in 1989. His loyal right-hand man Fred Bushell, then Chairman of Team Lotus International, was arraigned on charges of conspiracy to defraud the DeLorean company 'together with the late Colin Chapman'.

Chapman's sudden death, from a heart attack in the small hours of 16 December 1982, was certainly hastened by worries over these and other business problems. The controversy over his business dealings in the years immediately prior to his death has yet to be resolved and, consequently, it may be many years before the full details of this complex matter surface for public scrutiny. It is an increasingly sad memorial to Chapman's life and times that, however inevitably, so much dirty washing now has to be aired in public. For, as the role played by this vibrantly energetic and imaginative engineer slips into an historical perspective, it is certain that he was the pivotal personality on the post-war international motor racing scene, and possibly the most significant of all time.

Born the son of a publican in Richmond, Surrey, on 19 May 1928, Anthony Colin Bruce Chapman was to gain legendary status as an original thinker, motivator, and leader of men. Graduating in engineering from London University, he spent his National Service in the Royal Air Force just as he was becoming embroiled with manufacturing Ford Ten-engined specials for the burgeoning 1172 formula, run by that power-house of enthusiasm and mechanical ingenuity, the 750 Motor Club.

Many potential geniuses fail because they are out of step with the period in which they live. By contrast, Colin Chapman was always well in harmony with his era, almost anticipating the mood of the times, both on and off the race track, with an endearing, breezy confidence. Lotus Engineering was born on 1 January 1952, followed by Team Lotus in 1954.

The origin of the company name is lost in the mists of time, perhaps known only to Colin's widow Hazel, who, as his fiancée, lent him a crucial £25 back in February 1953, enabling him to form the business into a limited company. It began as an essentially spare time activity, Colin attempting to dovetail its operation with carving out a career working for British Aluminium. Eventually, from 1 January 1955, he was able to focus his energies on Lotus full-time.

A host of lightweight, agile, and affordable sports racing cars flowed from the tiny Lotus factories throughout the 1950s, first in the North London suburb of Hornsey, later in the Hertfordshire dormitory town of Cheshunt. Like Enzo Ferrari, Chapman designed road cars to provide the bread and butter; his real joy was his racing team, the organization always staying in private hands and not included in the Group Lotus flotation on the London Stock Exchange in the summer of 1968.

On the racing front, Chapman shrugged aside many prevailing design conventions. His astute understanding of tubular chassis dynamics, suspension design, and the key role played by aerodynamics were far ahead of his time. Lotus's first Grand Prix car was two years away when Colin was invited to redesign the chassis of the Vanwall Formula 1 challenger. The autocratic Tony Vandervell was impressed with his frank and outspoken views on the original Cooper-designed frame, and gave him *carte blanche* to revamp it. Chapman also called in aerodynamicist Frank Costin, whose brother Mike was already one of Lotus's key men, and he evolved the distinctive wind-cheating profile that would race away to the 1958 Constructors' World Championship.

Team Lotus was at last in Formula 1 by 1958, precariously at first, but Chapman pressed ahead with audacious plans for the future, even though he ran the company hair-raisingly close to the financial bone in those early days. While Cooper certainly pioneered the central-engined revolution, winning the World Championship in 1959 and 1960, this was essentially the one brilliant shot in their F1 locker. Chapman and Lotus picked up the theme, crafting and refining it to a level far beyond anything Cooper could achieve. When wealthy privateer Rob Walker bought a Lotus 18 for Stirling Moss to drive in 1960, Chapman's reputation was poised on the verge of the big time. Moss duly won the marque its first Grand Prix at Monaco and, indeed, by repeating that achievement in the Principality and at the Nurburgring in 1961, the Walker team had three such victories under its belt before Team Lotus broke its Grand Prix duck.

The extrovert, roistering Innes Ireland won the 1961 United States Grand Prix at Watkins Glen and was duly rewarded for this achievement when Chapman dropped him from the team a couple of weeks later. Beneath Chapman's superficially suave, good-natured gloss there lurked the ruthless pragmatism that motivates so many truly outstanding businessmen. Colin could see that young Jim Clark was a better bet, so

Innes had to go. The trauma of that experience still dominates Ireland's life thirty years later.

The 1960s and 1970s passed amidst a kaleidoscopic blur of mounting achievement, World Championship victories, and a rise to commercial respectability for Lotus and its founder. Far from being burnt out by the pressure, Chapman seemed to thrive on it. His workforce, whether design staff, mechanics, or administrators, would grumble over the way in which Colin always wanted his pound and a half of flesh, but he would always cajole, romance, or bully them into a superhuman effort time and again.

Lotus old hands always talk affectionately about how 'The Old Man' could marshal those inspirational qualities. For them, it wasn't simply a question of being associated with Lotus's success. An essential element of the appeal was the proximity of Chapman himself, almost as if some of the greatness might rub off on them.

In 1968, Chapman suffered his first major derailment. Jim Clark, the quiet, affable Border farmer who drove to stardom and 25 World Championship Grand Prix victories for Lotus over the previous six seasons, died in a minor league Formula 2 race at Hockenheim. For Chapman, it was like losing a brother. Together, they had not only scaled the peaks of Formula 1 achievement, they had also destroyed the bastions of technical conservatism in the USA by winning the 1965 Indianapolis 500 to initiate a design revolution in this very specialized area of racing.

Fleetingly, Colin considered stopping racing, but returned with renewed vigour. Jochen Rindt, Emerson Fittipaldi, and Mario Andretti would win him more World Championships, but none of them ever quite rekindled the personal spark that existed between Chapman and Clark. There were fresh technical furrows to plough, however, the most significant of which was the harnessing of under-car aerodynamics to produce ground effect in the late 1970s.

In his later years, Chapman found his taste for F1 slightly muted when his unique 'twin chassis' Lotus 86 and 88 designs, intended to separate aerodynamic from suspension loadings within the chassis, were deemed illegal by the sport's increasingly pugnacious governing body. He was also getting into the realms of very big money when Lotus Cars were commissioned to re-engineer the controversial DeLorean gull-winged sports car that was to be manufactured in commercially over-ambitious quantities in Ulster.

Colin Chapman's sudden death robbed his family of a father and husband who motivated and inspired them in much the same way as he did his employees. His son Clive and daughters Jane and Sarah recall that outings with their father were exciting, challenging, and enormously competitive, whether they were water-skiing or hang gliding. He was a man who squared up to life at a thousand miles an hour, whose personality left a profound impression on all who were touched by him. In motor racing terms, he was a giant.

9

Luigi Chinetti

PUTTING IT BLUNTLY, there was always something distant, almost tense, about the relationship between Enzo Ferrari and his US distributor; yet over the years Luigi Chinetti probably sold more of those delectable Italian supercars than any other man on earth. Post-war America was ripe for the picking when it came to marketing exclusive European high performance cars. Ferrari's products fitted the bill perfectly and Chinetti proved that he knew how to shift them out into the market.

For all that, the sense of mutual ambivalence between Chinetti and the Commendatore surfaces time and again if one trawls the history books. Ferrari makes only the most cursory mention of him in his memoirs, a strange state of affairs, one might conclude, bearing in mind that Chinetti was at the wheel of the winning Ferrari at Le Mans in 1949, the first occasion on which the Prancing Horse emerged triumphant at the Sarthe. Perhaps the key to this strange relationship stems from the fact that the two men came from broadly similar backgrounds, and that Chinetti had first known Ferrari way back in the 1930s when he was, arguably, the bigger celebrity. Born in Milan in 1905, the young Luigi qualified as an engineer and briefly worked for his father to get a feel for the business before joining Alfa Romeo. He was ambitious, confident, and pushy, transferring to the competitions department and getting a chance behind the wheel.

In 1932 he won Le Mans, sharing a 2.3-litre Alfa with Raymond Sommer. The history books record that Chinetti felt unwell after a few hours and that the Frenchman did the lion's share of the driving. In later life, Luigi would emphatically reject such a contention. Two years later he repeated the success, his car shared now with Philippe Etancelin under the Scuderia Ferrari banner, and went on to compete in every one of the 24-hour classics through to 1949, although the years separating his second and third victory would prove momentous for the confident young Chinetti.

During the 1930s he wandered about Europe, finally settling in Paris where he eventually started a small garage business. Just after the outbreak of war he was hired by the charismatic Lucy O'Reilly Schell to look after the two Maserati specials she was entering in the 1940 Indianapolis 500 driven by René Dreyfus and René le Begue. It was an enormously exciting opportunity for Chinetti, who grasped it with both hands. He sailed for New York on an Italian liner in a group that also included Lucy's son, the 19-year-old Harry Schell who would later become an accomplished F1 driver in his own right. As with Dreyfus, who was Jewish, it proved to be a one-way trip for Chinetti. After the Indy outing, he stayed on in the USA throughout the war, eventually making it his home. Although vehemently anti-fascist, Chinetti was still an alien and regarded with a certain degree of suspicion by the ultra-conservative Americans. Happily, he wasn't interned and was permitted to work in New York, although his movements were closely monitored through until the end of the war. It was not until 1946 that he was finally granted US citizenship.

After five years in America, Chinetti had got used to the way of life and had no real ambition to return to a Europe devastated by conflict. Yet, according to his recollections, it was on a trip back to Europe to tie up the loose ends of his old Paris garage business that he met up with Enzo Ferrari once again for the first time since the 1930s. The way Luigi tells it, he suggested that Ferrari consider manufacturing road cars using the engineering know-how garnered from his motor racing.

Whether such a tale stands up to detailed scrutiny is a matter of debate—Ferrari had already produced a couple of eight-cylinder sports cars for the 1940 Mille Miglia shortly after splitting with Alfa Romeo; but, either way, it was agreed that Chinetti should sell them in the US. His first sale was a 166 Spyder, delivered to Briggs Cunningham in 1948, the year Luigi opened his operations from a rented garage on New York's 49th Street.

That victory at Le Mans the following year helped boost the image of Ferrari and Chinetti together, and from that moment onwards the American distributorship advanced forward steadily: by the mid-1960s it was reportedly consuming between 35 and 40 per cent of the entire Maranello road car output. Hand in hand with this success, Luigi began to assume some of the Commendatore's individualistic truculence.

Just as Enzo Ferrari could keep international celebrities waiting on his pleasure at his Maranello fortress for hours at a time, for no better reason than a deliberate policy of wrapping the business in a uniquely mystical aura, so Chinetti could prove equally temperamental with his US customers. Once you'd bought a car from him, it seemed as though the normal dealer/customer relationship had gone through some bizarre role reversal.

Rather than it being a question of Chinetti catering to every whim and request of the rich and famous who patronized his business, he was often cool and aloof with his customers, giving the impression that he was rather doing them a favour attending to the expensive cars he had sold them. It might have been frustrating, but it was absolutely the correct approach from the standpoint of sustaining the exclusive, idiosyncratic image.

Ferraris supplied by Chinetti helped a whole host of American racing drivers to make the big time. Wealthy enthusiasts such as Temple Buell, Tony Parravano, John Edgar, and Allan Guiberson provided the steeds in which the likes of Phil Hill, Masten Gregory, Richie Ginther, Dan Gurney, and Carroll Shelby all cut their serious racing teeth. Chinetti also claims the credit of prompting Briggs Cunningham to think in terms of a Le Mans challenge after buying that first Ferrari in 1948.

On the international racing scene, of course, Chinetti's North American Racing Team (NART) campaigned with consistent zeal and enthusiasm. Luigi was delighted when his cars upstaged the works entries, something they did quite often. In 1960, he brought the dazzling duo of Pedro and Ricardo Rodriguez to Le Mans in NART's 250 Testa Rossa. Smashing lap record after lap record, at one point the teenage duo looked as though they would humble the factory cars in a straight fight.

With a Cheshire cat grin, Chinetti politely declined an 'invitation' from the works Ferrari pit to rein in these tempestuous young talents lest they embarrass the established hot shoes. As it turned out, the Rodriguez car eventually wilted under the strain, but Pedro would go on to win twice at Daytona for NART, and it was Chinetti who was responsible for fixing up Ricardo with a works Ferrari F1 drive at the end of 1961 at the start of the Mexican's tragically brief Grand Prix career.

In 1964, when Enzo Ferrari rampaged into a fury over the CSI's refusal to homologate the 250LM as a production GT car, NART would enter the works F1 Ferraris in the last two races of the season after the Commendatore surrendered the factory team's entrant's licence in a huff. Surtees and Bandini sported the distinctive blue and white US racing colours for these two races, much to Chinetti's delight and pleasure.

Chinetti also had the satisfaction of scoring Ferrari's last victory at Le Mans, in 1965, when Masten Gregory and Jochen Rindt barnstormed his 275LM to victory after the faster works 330Ps and the rival 7-litre Fords failed to last the distance. Thereafter, Chinetti would continue to support Le Mans with a variety of Ferraris, long after the works team withdrew to concentrate exclusively on Formula 1.

Throughout his time as a Le Mans entrant—and indeed fielding cars in the other endurance racing classics over three decades—Chinetti would almost shamelessly charge wealthy privateers for the privilege of driving his cars. It didn't matter, he said emphatically, whether they were the most highly talented drivers of all time.

If they were promising but had no money, then there was always the possibility of Chinetti giving them a chance anyway. But if they were rich they paid, no matter what. Perhaps even more so than Enzo Ferrari himself, Luigi Chinetti made certain that nobody short changed the Maranello dream ...

10

Charles and John Cooper

IN LIFE, THEY say, timing is everything, and the success of the Cooper Car Company bears out that old adage superbly. As a commercial manufacturer of racing cars they lasted barely two decades, as a Grand Prix contender only eleven years. For a variety of reasons, both human and technical, they proved unable to keep pace with accelerating F1 developments in the late 1960s, yet the contribution to motor racing history made by the company founded by Charles Cooper and his son John was monumental.

They complemented each other like Beaujolais and Filet Mignon. Had either operated alone, he would almost certainly have failed. Charlie was grumpy, conservative, and tight-fisted; John somewhat over-ambitious and impulsive. Yet together they somehow struck precisely the right blend of engineering audacity and business cunning in the immediate post-war years, riding a wave of success that only began to run short of momentum in the mid-1960s.

Charles Newton Cooper was born in Paris on 14 October 1893. His parents were in show business. His father was English, his mother, who died when he was very young, Franco-Spanish. From as early an age as he could recall, Charles was a mad keen motorcyclist. At the age of 15, he took up an apprenticeship with the Napier car makers and remembered with enormous satisfaction working on some of the record breaking machines driven by S. F. Edge.

Cooper Senior saw service in the First World War, was fortunate to survive being gassed on the battlefield, and returned to civilian life determined to make his mark in the motoring world. He subsequently built up a small garage business in Surbiton, Surrey, and married in 1922. On 17 July 1923 his son John was born.

An industrious, hard-working man, Charlie Cooper could be irascible and short-tempered. But he had an instinctive nose for business and managed successfully to combine this with a growing interest in motor racing. He was active at Brooklands and was actually employed by the famous record breaker and racing ace Kaye Don to travel to Molsheim and build up a Bugatti T34 for him at the factory. In retrospect, the contrast between the rough-and-ready Cooper and the artistic Ettore Bugatti epitomized opposite poles in terms of motor racing technology.

A practical man, his interests were diverse and he encouraged his son's interest in cars and matters mechanical. He built John a couple of small petrol-driven miniature cars during his youth. He also tried his hand at flying with one of the popular do-it-yourself 'Flying Fleas' which briefly proved such a fad in the 1930s.

John in turn took up an apprenticeship with one of his father's companies on leaving school, and then went to work for a toolmaker who specialized in Admiralty work shortly after the Second World War broke out. John Cooper really wanted to serve in the RAF, but by the time he was recruited the war was almost over and he worked out the closing stages of hostilities as an aircraft instrument maker.

In 1946 the Coopers built a 500-cc hillclimb special that would lay the foundations for the establishment of a business manufacturing racing cars on a commercial basis. By 1948 they were in serious production making 500-cc Formula 3 cars and, in those heady immediate post-war years, almost everybody who was anybody would learn their single-seater trade behind the wheel of one of the spindly little cars made in Surbiton.

Stirling Moss, Peter Collins, Harry Schell, Stuart Lewis-Evans—even Bernie Ecclestone—were all customers at one time or another, and there was not a circuit in England at which Cooper 500s didn't do battle at some time or another during the late 1940s and early 1950s.

Cooper Cars went steadily from strength to strength. Mike Hawthorn would cut his international racing teeth behind the wheel of a Formula 2 Cooper-Bristol in 1952, performing well enough to attract an offer from the Ferrari F1 team the following year. Subsequently, a succession of highly effective central-seater sports cars would give rise to the first rear-engined Cooper, purpose built for the 1957 1.5-litre F1 regulations, which directly led to Stirling Moss's sensational victory in the 1958 Argentine Grand Prix. Using a 2-litre Climax 6-cylinder engine in his Rob Walker-owned F2 Cooper, Moss scored an historic success that started a new chapter in Grand Prix racing history.

Yet Cooper's way of going motor racing was in stark and primitive contrast to the lavish life in the Formula 1 fast lane of the 1980s. Charlie Cooper's *modus operandi* avoided expenditure on all but the absolutely necessary. His works were dark, dank, and dingy; the staff were underpaid and often grumbled. Yet somehow he managed to imbue tremendous loyalty in the people who worked for him. He may have been a miserable old so-and-so, but he inspired a peculiar brand of affection in a workforce who frequently reckoned they were getting the rough end of a not very generous deal.

By contrast, the genial, pipe-smoking John Cooper was always straining in the harness of his father's penny pinching ways. He was imaginative and saw the scope for business expansion, but was prone to letting his enthusiasm for new and expensive projects get slightly out of control. Rows between father and son were predictable and numerous. Yet by 1959 they had recruited the rugged Australian Jack Brabham to lead their own Grand Prix team and stormed to two consecutive World Championship titles. Moreover, if anybody wanted an off-the-peg customer car, Coopers was the place to go and find it.

The timing of these Championship victories was superb. Cooper produced solid, unspectacularly reliable rear-engined Grand Prix machines at a time when their rivals were in disarray. Vanwall had just effectively quit the scene after taking the 1958 Constructors' title; Ferrari was too slow in abandoning the front-engined concept; and Lotus, from which Cooper had the most to fear, fielded cars that were too frail and unreliable. Charlie Cooper regarded Colin Chapman as a 'Flash Harry', but John quickly realized that Lotus had the obvious potential to seize the F1 initiative. And he was right.

By 1961 Cooper's F1 effort was going off the boil, hidebound by design conservatism, as the new $1\frac{1}{2}$-litre Formula 1 got underway. Jack Brabham could read the writing on the wall, figured that he could do better on his own, and set up his own team. By 1966, when he would win a third Championship at the wheel of a car bearing his own name, Cooper would be locked into a gentle decline.

His departure from the fold left amiable New Zealander Bruce McLaren as number one driver, but Charlie Cooper by now regarded him with a degree of suspicion, mindful of how Brabham had jumped ship to start his own operation. When Bruce couldn't persuade the Old Man that purpose-built Tasman chassis, rather than existing F1 machines, would be necessary to guarantee success 'down under' in the winter of 1963/64, he set up his own team and ran the cars he wanted in his own right. It was effectively the start of McLaren Racing and Bruce would be lost to Cooper at the end of 1965.

By then, however, Charlie Cooper would not be around to see the fruits of Bruce's labours. Having suffered with a heart condition for several years, he died at his home on Box Hill, Surrey, on 2 October 1964. In the summer of 1963, John Cooper had been involved in a terrible road accident when the prototype twin-engined Mini-Cooper saloon—one of his personal pet projects—somersaulted to destruction on the Kingston bypass. He took many months to recover and Ken Tyrrell obligingly took over as Cooper team manager while he recuperated.

That road accident caused John Cooper to sit back and take stock. With the team's competitive performance dwindling, and the new 3-litre Formula 1 scheduled to get underway in 1966, he felt extremely uncertain about the future. He was therefore particularly receptive to an offer from the Chipstead Garages Group—controlled by entrepreneur Mario Tozzi-Condivi and Marks and Spencer's heir Jonathan Sieff—to buy out the company. Before the end of 1965 he had concluded a deal worth in the region of £200,000 and signed a service contract to continue in charge of the F1 operation.

Tozzi-Condivi massaged a deal to access supplies of a 3-litre Maserati V12, progeny of the 2.5-litre unit used in the Maserati 250F almost a decade before. It proved a successful stop-gap measure at the start of the new formula. John Surtees used a Cooper-Maserati to win the 1966 Mexican Grand Prix, and Pedro Rodriguez to score a lucky success in South Africa the following year. But Cosworth's sensational DFV was on the horizon, and approaching fast. The F1 stakes were to be dramatically raised.

Although now out of John Cooper's immediate control, the team took a crucial wrong turn in 1968 by opting to use the new BRM V12 engine rather than the Cosworth V8. At the time it was reasoned that using the Ford-backed engine would compromise their relationship with British Leyland, which was still paying Cooper royalties on the high performance version of the Mini saloon that had been developed at the start of the decade.

By the end of that year, with no sponsorship in sight, and fuel and tyre contracts terminated, Cooper's F1 effort was dead in the water. Vic Elford would drive a privately owned Cooper-Maserati in the 1969 Monaco Grand Prix to rule off a distinctive and productive era in British Formula 1 history.

John Cooper continued fielding the works Mini-Coopers in the British saloon car championship until the end of 1969. After that, he retired to Ferring, on the Sussex coast, where he bought a small garage business which he runs to this day.

11

Briggs Cunningham

BRIGGS CUNNINGHAM PROBABLY did more for the image and development of American road racing in the post-war era than any other individual, his pioneering attempts to win Le Mans being financed purely from his own resources in the early 1950s. Over a decade later, it would cost the Ford Motor Company many millions of dollars to succeed where Cunningham had only just failed.

The scion of a Cincinnati family whose fortune came from meat packing, Briggs Cunningham was born in 1907 into circumstances that might best be described as 'seriously wealthy'. He was a tremendously accomplished youngster, turning his hand to boxing, sailing, and tennis with a natural deftness that must have been extremely frustrating for his rivals and opponents.

He was in his early twenties when he dropped out of Yale to marry Lucie Bedford, the daughter of a New York industrialist. A measure of their financial status can be gained from the fact that they returned from their European honeymoon having acquired from the Earls Court Motor Show a 1500-cc Alfa Romeo that had recently won the Double Twelve at Brooklands. In addition, whilst staying at St Moritz, Briggs found himself inveigled into taking part in an impromptu bobsleigh competition.

It was typical of his athletic, energetic approach to life that he embraced this unexpected challenge with all-pervading enthusiasm and commitment. Universally popular, even-tempered and genial, he would meet success and tribulation with the same wry smile and sheepish shrug of the shoulders. A much-loved man with many friends, his enthusiasm for sport in general—and for motor racing in particular—was built on a bedrock of fair play and consideration for others.

During the 1930s Briggs and his wife would race a variety of 6-metre yachts with distinction, in both American and Mediterranean waters, and developed an interest in aviation that saw him qualify for his private pilot's licence just before the outbreak of war. As a family man in his mid-thirties, Briggs was turned down for active service, but he put his aviation knowledge to good use patrolling Atlantic coastal waters as a member of the Civil Air Patrol, flying a single-engined Sikorsky amphibian.

In the immediate post-war years he branched out into motor racing, driving an MG TC in East Coast SCCA club events, but it was a chance meeting with Sam and Miles Collier that really sparked his enthusiasm in the direction of Le Mans. Back in 1939, in collaboration with Buick chief engineer Charles Chayne, Briggs had developed a racer dubbed the 'Bu-Merc'—a novel hybrid using both Buick and Mercedes components. Miles Collier drove it in a special race held at New York's World Fair during 1940, thereby establishing what proved to be a crucial link.

Cunningham and the Colliers enthusiastically discussed the prospect of building an all-American sports car that would be capable of taking on the best of the Europeans on their home ground—Le Mans. In preparation for building their own car, they agreed that they should enter the 1950 race using a pair of 5.4-litre Cadillac Series 50–61s.

Both these machines had their engines modified by Frick-Tappet, and whilst the Colliers shared a regular sedan, Cunningham and Phil Walters drove a bizarre special, the Cadillac strikingly rebodied under an aerodynamic skin to take the form of an open coupé. Dubbed 'Le Monstre' by the disbelieving French fans, it finished 11th, one place behind its more conventional stablemate. Sadly, Sam Collier was killed the following September driving Cunningham's Ferrari on the old Watkins Glen road course, while Miles succumbed, tragically and suddenly, to a respiratory illness just over four years later.

Enormously encouraged by that first Le Mans, Briggs Cunningham returned to his team base in Palm Beach, Florida, where his team began to lay plans for an all-new sports car with which to compete more seriously the following year. The result was a somewhat ordinary looking two-seater roadster, the C2-R, powered by an uprated version of Chrysler's 5.4-litre V8 engine mated to de Dion rear suspension.

The outcome of the 1951 foray to Europe proved quite satisfactory, for one of these C2-Rs, shared by Phil Walters and John Fitch, held second place behind the winning Jaguar on Sunday morning before a minor, irritating mechanical problem dropped it from contention to finish a distant 18th. The sister cars of Cunningham/Huntoon and Rand/Wacker failed to last the distance.

Convinced that his team was progressing in the right direction, Cunningham developed his most successful sports car for the 1952 Le Mans outing—the chunky, purposeful C-4R, also propelled by an uprated Chrysler V8 engine. It used a four-speed ZF gearbox and carried Briggs to his own personal best placing at the Sarthe; sharing with Bill Spear, he finished fourth behind two Mercedes-Benz and a Nash-Healey.

En route, the C-4R broke the distance record for its class (5 to 8 litres) that had been established by the Sydney Allard/Tom Cole Allard two years previously. Two others C-4Rs, driven by Fitch/Rice and Walters/Carter, both dropped out with valve trouble.

By this stage, Cunningham realized that Jaguar's progress with disc braking technology would ensure that the cars from Coventry exerted a major performance advantage in years to come. He reasoned that an even faster car would be required to challenge the British machines in 1953, the end product, being the striking, ultra-sleek C-5R which became nicknamed 'The Shark' because of its low-slung, fierce frontal appearance. Continuing to use the trusty 5.4-litre Chrysler V8, it broke fresh ground by employing torsion bar suspension.

During practice for the 1953 Le Mans epic, the Cunningham C-5R proved a tremendously quick contender. However, although the sleek Alfa Romeo Disco Volante coupés were slightly quicker than the C-type Jaguars, Briggs' worst fears were realized. The English car's disc brakes settled the matter when it came to the race.

Nevertheless, the C-5R proved a serious interloper and broke up a hoped-for Jaguar 1-2-3 finish by taking third place in the hands of Walters and Fitch. Cunningham and Spear finished seventh, Moran/Benett tenth.

In 1954, the C-4Rs were destined to produce the Cunningham team's most rewarding Le Mans result of all, Spear/Johnson finishing third with Cunningham/Benett fifth. The team also entered a 4.5-litre Ferrari 340 for Walters and Fitch that suffered rear axle failure just before half distance. Cunningham's great dream of building his own Le Mans winner finished in 1955 when his prototype C-6R, powered by a 2.9-litre Offenhauser 4-cylinder engine, lasted eighteen hours but never climbed higher than thirteenth.

Later Briggs would install a 3.8-litre Jaguar engine into this machine for US domestic competition, but the Cunningham roadsters were gone from America for good. Everybody was depressed following the Levegh tragedy in 1955, the Frenchman's Mercedes killing more than 80 outlookers when it vaulted catastrophically into the spectator enclosure opposite the pits following a collision with Lance Macklin's Austin-Healey, and Briggs suddenly found his hands full when Sir William Lyons suggested he took on the Jaguar distributorship for the North-East United States. Over the next few years he would race D-type, Formula Junior single seaters and Oscas, as well as selling Maseratis.

During this period he became immersed in the world of yachting once again, successfully defending the Americas Cup in 1958, the first occasion on which it was contested for 12-metre yachts instead of the larger J-boats. Briggs, at the helm of *Columbia*, won four straight victories over the British challenger *Sceptre*.

Five years would elapse before Briggs Cunningham's distinctive blue and white team livery was seen once again at Le Mans. In 1960 he fielded four Chevrolet Corvettes (which benefited from quite considerable 'back door' assistance from General Motors), John Fitch and Bob Grossman surviving to take eighth place. From then on, Briggs Cunningham ran the occasional Jaguar and Maserati at Le Mans up until 1963, but by then he had moved to California where the business pressures of building up and operating his highly successful motor museum at Costa Mesa, on the Pacific coast south of Los Angeles, were occupying an increasing amount of his time.

Over the years, this precious collection of automotive gems sky-rocketed in value to the point where Cunningham decided they should be found a safe home while he still had the faculties to do so. At the end of 1986, with Briggs approaching his 80th birthday—and by now the oldest sailing member of the New York Yacht Club—the 71 road and racing cars were sold for an undisclosed price believed to be in the region of $20 million.

Appropriately, the purchaser was Miles Collier, whose father of the same name had played such a key role in getting the Cunningham racing legend off the starting grid almost forty years before.

12

Ron Dennis

NOBODY HAS BEEN more responsible for enhancing Grand Prix racing's competitive image during the 1980s than McLaren International's Managing Director Ron Dennis. A brilliant organizer, yet so frequently a poor communicator, with a self-confessed ambivalence towards the press, Ron's single-minded personality initially harboured no great enthusiasm for racing cars as such. Born in Surrey on 1 June 1947, he was attracted to the sport simply because of its image of engineering excellence, starting out as a junior mechanic on Jochen Rindt's Cooper-Maserati back in 1967 at the age of 19.

When Rindt moved to Brabham the following season, Dennis made the switch with him and gradually earned promotion within the team to the point where Jack entrusted him with the overall operational management for the 1970 United States and Mexican Grands Prix. At this stage he decided to go it alone, correctly reasoning that it made no sense doing for somebody else what he could do just as well, if not better, for himself.

In partnership with Neil Trundle, then chief mechanic on the Brabham Indy car team, he set up Rondel Racing to field a couple of F2 Brabhams hired from Ron Tauranac. They had £2,000 between them plus a great deal of assistance from many willing helpers. They bought their first transporter on hire purchase and managed to cajole Graham Hill into driving for them. At only their second race, the prestigious Easter Monday Thruxton F2 International, Hill scored a splendid win to put Rondel firmly on the map.

Shipbroker Tony Vlassopulos and property developer Ken Grob later became involved and, after Tim Schenken had rounded off Rondel's first season with fourth place in the European F2 Championship, the team raised its sights for 1972. With sponsorship from the French Motul oil company Rondel fielded four Brabham BT38s for Schenken, Carlos Reutemann, Henri Pescarolo, and Bob Wollek.

Even at this early stage, you could see at work the Dennis approach which makes today's McLaren International equipe so special. The cars were spotless, always immaculately turned out and festooned with sponsorship decals. They proved to be front runners and, suitably encouraged, Rondel built its own cars, the Motul M1s. The plan was to use this as a springboard to F1 the following season, but the economic brakes were firmly applied in England as a result of the Arab-Israeli war, forcing Rondel to cease trading.

While Tony Vlassopulo took over the F1 project for a fleeting handful of races, Dennis fell back in an attempt to retrench in F2. After a hopeless 1974 season running a couple of Surtees TS15As for two slow-coaches from Ecuador, Ron forged a deal with March and began the long slog back to competitiveness the following year. In 1976, operating out of a new factory in Woking, he established Project Four Racing, the company that would eventually become amalgamated with McLaren Racing and perpetuated in the MP4 designation the cars have carried ever since the merger.

In 1976, Project Four ran Eddie Cheever in a Ferrari V6-engined March, swapping to the Ralt-BMW combination for 1977 when the 19-year-old American finished second in the European F2 championship. For 1979, Project Four amalgamated with Creighton Brown's ICI-backed F2 operation, fielding Stephen South and Derek Daly, and the company got involved in a profitable deal preparing the BMW M1 coupés for the 'Pro-Car' promotional races that were staged as support-ing events at many European Grands Prix. More significantly even, Project Four fielded its own Marlboro-backed M1 driven by Niki Lauda and won the Championship. The Austrian twice World Champion would crop again much later as a key player in the Ron Dennis story.

By 1979, Dennis also felt he was ready for a renewed assault on the F1 establishment. He teamed up with John Barnard, a young designer who had been responsible for the Chaparral 2K that had led the Indy 500 that year before its retirement. Barnard had earlier worked under Gordon Coppuck at McLaren and, like Dennis, was to prove a highly motivated perfectionist. He had audacious plans for a Formula 1 chassis manu-factured from carbon fibre, a very stiff and light material used mainly in the aerospace industry up to that point, so the two men forged a partnership, with Dennis confident that he could raise the necessary capital.

Meanwhile, the Marlboro cigarette people were becoming increas-ingly nervous about McLaren's dwindling competitiveness. Dennis suggested a merger in 1979, but senior McLaren director Teddy Mayer rebuffed his advance. Twelve months later Marlboro told Mayer that he'd better get on and amalgamate with Project Four if the team was to have any realistic future. Thus a new company, McLaren International, was born out of the old.

Although Mayer held the majority shareholding in the new company, McLaren International quickly became perceived as a Dennis/Barnard operation. Ron stamped his rather clinical trademark on the team's *modus operandi*, while Barnard would tolerate no compromise on the technical front. The first result of their joint labours was the splendidly elegant carbon fibre McLaren MP4 which won the 1981 British Grand Prix at Silverstone in the hands of John Watson. McLaren was back in the winners' circle for the first time in four years.

At the end of 1982 Dennis became the majority shareholder when he bought out Mayer's stake in the company. By this time it was clear just how firmly he intended McLaren to become F1's pacemakers. Not only had he lured Niki Lauda out of a two-year retirement to win again behind the wheel of an MP4, he had also laid ambitious plans for a state-of-the-art Porsche-built turbo engine and raised the finance to pay for it from the Franco-Saudi high technology company Techniques d'Avant Garde. By the end of 1983 the new engine was race ready and, in 1984, the McLaren-TAGs took the Grand Prix world by storm.

Later, when John Barnard left, his shareholding would be acquired by Mansour, son of TAG's founder, the late Akram Ojjeh, who is now the majority shareholder in the TAG/McLaren organization.

In 1984 the Championship fell to Lauda, the following two years to Alain Prost. The team relinquished the Championship to Nelson Piquet in 1987, but bounced back commandingly in 1988, now with Ayrton Senna as Champion and Honda engines supplanting the German V6. It was a testimony to the team's strength in depth that Barnard's acrimonious departure to Ferrari, at the end of 1986, had virtually no effect on the McLaren organization's on-track performance.

Into the new era of naturally aspirated engines that began in 1989, the McLaren-Hondas continued winning with Prost regaining the Championship for the third time.

By this point Ron Dennis was just 42 years old and determined to expand the McLaren reputation into fresh fields of endeavour. Now operating from a striking high-tech factory, still in Woking, the company announced plans to manufacture an exclusive high performance road car aimed directly at the prestige markets hitherto so jealously guarded by the likes of Porsche and Ferrari.

Some people dismissed this project as symptomatic of Dennis's obsession for empire building, others just watched with a disbelieving fascination. If his team could produce a road car to the exacting standards already imposed on the racing team, it was clearly going to be something worth waiting for.

These days Ron commutes by executive jet and has homes in both Britain and France. He winces when people occasionally produce a faded photograph of an oil-stained youngster in Cooper mechanics' overalls. But deep down, most of his friends believe, he is privately very proud of what he has achieved from those modest beginnings.

13

Keith Duckworth

WHEN KEITH DUCKWORTH designed the Cosworth DFV 3-litre Grand Prix engine for Ford in 1967 it helped to rewrite the parameters of Formula 1 performance at a stroke. It propelled Jim Clark's epochal Lotus 49 to a début victory in the Dutch Grand Prix at Zandvoort, outclassing all the opposition in devastating fashion.

More significantly, from a long-term viewpoint, Duckworth's engineering genius changed the way people went F1 racing for the next two decades. The Cosworth DFV became widely available as a thoroughly dependable off-the-shelf racing engine, with the same rugged, straightforward, no-nonsense qualities as the man whose creation it was.

David Keith Duckworth was born in August 1933 at Blackburn, Lancashire. His father, Frank, owned a weaving shed and also sold cotton at the Manchester Cotton Exchange. His maternal grandfather was a blacksmith. Keith's family were comfortably off, but their relative affluence was the result of much hard endeavour and application.

Keith Duckworth was educated from 1942 to 1950 at Giggleswick, a highly respected public school near Settle in the Yorkshire Dales. He later did his national service with the RAF, although his aspirations to become a service pilot received a severe dent within hours of his being awarded his wings. Keith actually dozed off in the cockpit and was ejected from the course for 'dangerous and incompetent night flying'.

In 1952 he moved on to study at London's Imperial College, where an increasing inclination towards messing around with cars and motor racing people meant that he spent insufficient time concentrating on his degree course. In the end, he scraped through the BSc in 1957 and began to cast around for a proper job.

What he was really seeking was a post-graduate apprenticeship, but although offered opportunities with both Rolls-Royce and Napier—as well as the chance to stay on to do research at Imperial College—none of these possible choices seemed quite right. Intriguingly, Rolls-Royce had their doubts about young Duckworth's suitability as a member of a team, something Keith later recalled as an extremely astute observation. At 24 years old, he already had a deep-seated streak of independence, a quality which almost certainly contributed to his success as an engineer.

Finally, in the autumn of 1957, he joined Lotus at their Hornsey headquarters with a brief from Colin Chapman to sort out the troublesome new five-speed gearbox that was an integral design feature of the new Lotus 12 Formula 2 single seater. This complicated transmission, which inevitably earned the soubriquet 'The Queerbox', never worked successfully and there were robust disagreements between Chapman, ever the dynamic theorist, and Duckworth, the practical engineer, over whether it could ever be made to hold together.

After something less than a year, Duckworth felt he could no longer work with Chapman. He decided to start up his own, race engine development company in partnership with Mike Costin, who had been Technical Director for Lotus Cars since 1956. Unfortunately, whilst the acronym 'Cosworth' sprang up as the logical name for the new organization, getting Costin aboard proved rather more complicated.

Shortly before Duckworth told Chapman he was leaving, the Lotus boss shrewdly signed another three-year contract with Costin that specifically forbade any collaboration with Keith's fledgling company. As a result, Costin did not formally join Cosworth until 1961.

Cosworth started in business doing various engine preparation jobs on Coventry-Climax engines for Lotus Elites, as well as racing car preparation for a variety of private owners. Cash flow was always a problem in those early years, but Duckworth's pragmatic qualities extended to understanding the financial realities of being in business.

Whilst his family's comfortable background allowed Keith to take the moral high ground unavailable to many when it came to pronouncing on the questionable virtues of borrowing money, he was shrewd and efficient when it came to operating Cosworth Engineering. The company's fortunes really took off at the start of the 1960s when they began building Ford Anglia 105E-based engines for the new 1,100-cc Formula Junior, from which point the name Cosworth increasingly became synonymous with light, efficient, and reliable racing engines.

Cosworth had started with its headquarters in distinctly down-at-heel premises in Friern Barnet, moved to ex-Progress Chassis Co. premises at Edmonton in 1961, and finally to premises in St James Mill Road, Northampton, at the end of 1964. By now the company was also building the SCA engine for the 1-litre F2 category, but the big break came the following year when Colin Chapman persuaded Ford to finance the design and manufacture of a new Grand Prix engine for the 3-litre F1 that was due to start in 1966.

Thanks to the shrewd and perceptive influence of Walter Hayes, who was in charge of Ford's Public Affairs at that time, Lotus, Ford, and Cosworth were all brought together. Hayes successfully sold the idea to Ford of Britain Chairman Patrick Henessey and final approval came from Detroit to proceed with the project. Cosworth was commissioned to build the F1 engine and a four valves per cylinder, four-cylinder F2 engine, all for a budget of £100,000. By any standards, this deal would come to be regarded as the bargain of the age for Ford.

Duckworth set up his drawing board in the quiet of his home, away from the factory's frantic activity, and settled down to produce the historic Cosworth DFV. The project took just under two years from Keith putting pen to paper to the first Cosworth DFV being handed over to Team Lotus in April 1967. Duckworth sometimes worked for up to 16 hours a day during the height of the initial 9-month design process, during which he lost 40 pounds in weight. Keith himself was modest about the amount of effort required, although undeniably proud of the end result.

Giving himself a personal reward for Cosworth's endeavour in producing what would become the most successful Grand Prix engine of all time, Duckworth purchased a Brantley helicopter, but he would lose his licence when he suffered a heart attack in 1973. Despite making an apparently complete recovery, he declined to give up smoking and the problem came back to haunt him 14 years later.

During that intervening period Cosworth had deveoped into an outstandingly successful company, not only expanding and consolidating its collaboration with Ford—the Sierra Cosworth would become the first road car to carry the company's identification—but also carrying out prestigious freelance design work on the Mercedes-Benz 190 engine.

Nevertheless, Duckworth's heart attack had made a profound impact on his thoughts about the future. He held 85 per cent of the shares in Cosworth Engineering, so the prospect of what would follow in the event of his sudden demise might spell major problems with death duties for the family. They would almost certainly have been obliged to sell up.

As a result, and after careful consideration, in 1980 Cosworth was taken over by United Engineering Industries, a Manchester-based engineering firm. The deal comprised £4.5 million in UEI shares, £2.4 million in loan bonds, and an additional £425,000 in loan bonds at the conclusion of a satisfactory year's trading. It was a fair deal, but probably not the best Keith might have achieved had he been motivated by money alone.

This takeover in no way changed the manner in which Cosworth operated and Duckworth continued in his own personal fast lane, much to the detriment of his health. In 1987, during a period of some stress due to the break-up of his first marriage and the design problems associated with the 1.5-litre Ford F1 turbo engine, it became clear that open heart surgery was required. Even then, he was pragmatic about the whole thing, feeling that his body had let him down badly. But he gave up smoking immediately and, soon afterwards, relinquished his position as Chairman to Mike Costin. In 1989 Carlton Communications made a successful £492 million offer for UEI, so control of Cosworth passed into fresh hands for the second time in a decade, and the company subsequently passed into the control of Vickers PLC in April 1990.

Now retired from the executive management of Cosworth, the company he founded over 30 years ago, Keith Duckworth takes life at a somewhat more gentle pace than he did during his heyday as possibly the most accomplished race engine designer in post-war Grand Prix history.

Yet the image of Duckworth in a rocking chair on some distant porch could not be further from the truth. His acerbic wit has endured and his appetite for lengthy arguments, on all matters of engineering and motor racing, remains undiminished. Straight-talking to the point of bluntness, he has a wicked sense of fun and can be enormously congenial company. Above all, his inquiring mind is ever active, pondering any and every technical conundrum imaginable.

14

Bernie Ecclestone

MANY USED CAR traders are dapper, smooth talking and quick witted, but it takes a very special kind of business brain to dominate the financial side of a sport as intricate as Grand Prix racing. Yet that's precisely what Bernie Ecclestone has managed in his supposed sixty years.

I say 'supposed', for this pristine, compact wheeler dealer is reluctant to admit to his true age. The fact that he was grass track motorcycle racing at Brands Hatch as long ago as 1947 suggests that he must surely be approaching retirement age. However, unlike most of us, Bernie has maintained himself in pretty good nick and would still pass for a man in his late forties.

Bernie is an old motor racing hand. Motorcycle and Formula 1 World Champion John Surtees tells a fascinating story of being taken by his father Jack to buy motorcycle parts from an enterprising young Ecclestone who'd set up stall in his mother's kitchen. Apparently, Bernie originally planned to qualify as an industrial chemist, a sort of motor racing Guy Fawkes, as some of his motor racing colleagues have put it. In the event, the nearest he got to realizing that ambition was working in a local gas works where, legend has it, he was so busy with his freelance, spare-time dealing that he failed to perform a routine check on a filter, causing a dramatic loss in supply pressure over a wide area of South London.

His interest in motorcycles led him to compete in the 500-cc Formula 3 with a Cooper-Norton, later with a Cooper-Bristol single seater and a Cooper-Jaguar sports car. He established a very smart motorcycle dealership, Compton and Ecclestone Ltd, in Broadway, Bexleyheath, an emporium that was in stark contrast to the dingy, oily, and chaotic popular image of a British motorcycle dealer in the 1950s.

Ecclestone's showrooms were spotless, light, and airy and this trait was continued when he moved into car dealing, his premises in Bexleyheath mirroring similarly high standards of presentation. You could eat your lunch off the floor of Bernie's showrooms, and doubtless a lot of customers did just that ...

On the Formula 3 front, Bernie struck up a close friendship with Stuart Lewis-Evans, the talented young Kentish driver who would go on to drive alongside Stirling Moss and Tony Brooks in the Vanwall team during 1958. After Connaught Engineering went out of business and auctioned off its assets in 1957, Ecclestone purchased a couple of cars and entered them in the 1957/58 Tasman Series for Lewis-Evans and Ivor Bueb. He had longer-term plans to field Stuart at the wheel of his own Cooper-Climax in 1959, but the young English star was badly burnt when he crashed in the 1958 Moroccan Grand Prix and died a few days later.

Thereafter Bernie dropped to the fringes of the motor racing business, concentrating on building up his extensive interests in commercial property. During the boom times of the 1960s, Bernie became extremely wealthy indeed; to this day, his holdings reputedly include industrial property on estates adjacent to London's Heathrow airport, pretty valuable land by any standards. Towards the end of the 1960s, he picked up his links with the motor racing business via fellow motor trader-cum-racer Roy Salvadori, and Jochen Rindt, for whom he became something of a business advisor.

On visits to England, Jochen would borrow Bernie's white Rolls-Royce Silver Cloud to use as his transport. The two men got on well together. Rindt's friends say they recognized each other as kindred spirits, particularly as far as business was concerned. Bernie handled a lot of Jochen's complex negotiations with Colin Chapman in preparation for Rindt joining Lotus in 1969. Had Rindt survived to retire from the cockpit, many people reckon he and Ecclestone would have now been organizing F1 together, but the Austrian driver's death during practice for the 1970 Italian Grand Prix at Monza put paid to such ideas.

Bernie had taken a hand in running Rindt's F2 Lotus cars under the Jochen Rindt Racing banner and was beginning to get a taste for a racing team involvement. On the motorcycle racing front, in 1971 he acquired Colin Seeley's business and then received an approach from Ron Tauranac with the suggestion that he might like to purchase a share in the Brabham team. Bernie, being a loner, wasn't interested. What he did propose, though, was a purchase of the entire Motor Racing Developments organization, lock, stock, and barrel.

He took control at the end of 1971—and Formula 1 was never the same since. Hardly had the diminutive Ecclestone assumed his new role as an F1 team principal than he began marshalling his fellow constructors into what became his own personal motor racing power base, the Formula One Constructors' Association (FOCA). In the years that followed, he presided over commercial negotiations with race organizers, established television coverage contracts, and generally polished up the image of Grand Prix racing.

Due almost entirely to the efforts of this workaholic perfectionist, FOCA became the most powerful single lobby on the international motor racing scene. Eventually, the sport's administrators woke up to what was happening. And they did not like what they saw.

Into this commercial maelstrom plunged newly-elected FISA President Jean-Marie Balestre at the start of the 1979 season, determined to retrieve for FISA the notional concept of 'sporting power'. Bernie now led his FOCA teams into a battle over the fundamental matter of precisely who controlled motor racing. It was a turbulent period with races being boycotted, others taking place outside the official World Championship, legal action threatened.

Yet Bernie remained the most influential and powerful man in the Grand Prix business. He is the man who created, exploited, and still retains control of the golden purse strings of television coverage, the 'open sesame' to making his peers and rivals more well known and wealthy than they could ever have imagined twenty years ago.

In the Grand Prix paddock and pit lane, Ecclestone's word is law. FISA may sanction the races, but Bernie is the man on the spot. He can flick his fingers to make most FOCA team principals come running. His position as FOCA President is so deeply entrenched that there was no real question of anybody challenging for his position even when he sold Motor Racing Developments to Alfa Romeo at the end of 1987, thereby ceasing to be a team owner.

During his years as a team owner, Ecclestone's perfectionism used to drive his employees to distraction. He would fuss over a sticker on a rear wing end plate which didn't seem to be quite straight, get extremely angry if the factory working areas were not kept tidy and free of rubbish. Yet, on the other side of the coin, he has gained a reputation as a good employer. There have been several unmentioned examples of his assistance to employees who have encountered illness or other hardships over the years.

Overwhelmingly, though, Bernie Ecclestone is the man who made Grand Prix racing a multi-million dollar international televised sport. A succession of discreet fawn-liveried private jets and a penthouse apartment in the same block as Jeffery Archer's, on the Thames opposite the Houses of Parliament, testify to his shrewd judgement and remarkable business acumen.

15

Enzo Ferrari

WHEN ENZO FERRARI died on 14 August 1988, the last surviving link to the pioneering days of motorsport was finally severed. One of the last of the giants who shaped, steered, and moulded the very character of international motor racing, his influence was wide ranging and considerable across seven decades of motor racing. A self-made man, in many ways Enzo Ferrari was a rag-bag of contradictions. Unpredictable, volatile, and autocratic, he ruled his racing team on a day-to-day basis almost to the day he died.

He came from the humblest and most modest of beginnings. Born near Modena on 18 February 1898, Enzo Ferrari had ambitions to become an opera singer, a sports journalist, and a racing driver during his youth. He eventually achieved the third of those ambitions. Barely out of his teens, he got a job with the CMN company before joining Alfa Romeo. He was second in the 1920 Targa Florio and made quite a respectable reputation for himself in the years that followed.

Amongst the young Ferrari's personal victories were the 1924 Circuito del Savio at Ravenna and Circuito de Polesine at Rovigo, while his triumph in the Coppa Acerbo at Pescara was distinguished by his beating the Mercedes team, which had itself just won the Targa Florio. By this time his cars were sporting the distinctive prancing horse emblem which all Ferraris, whether road machines or racers, carry to this day. At the 1923 Circuito de Savio, which he also won, Ferrari was introduced to the father of the late Francesco Baracca, an Italian First World War fighter ace. Baracca had carried the prancing horse symbol on his aeroplanes and Count Enrico Baracca suggested the young Enzo now carried it on his cars.

Throughout that decade, despite problems with ill health, Ferrari increasingly involved himself on the technical side of the Alfa Romeo team's programmes, and helped lure the respected engineer Vittorio Jano from Fiat to enhance the famous Milan team's engineering capability.

In 1929, he effectively left Alfa Romeo and set up as the company's distributor for the Emilia Romagna area, based in Modena. On the back of this newly-established business, he set up the Scuderia Ferrari, an independent racing team that was to field privately-owned Alfa Romeos for wealthy local textile merchant Alfredo Caniato and clothing manufacturer Mario Tadini. The fledgling Scuderia would grow into what was effectively a works-blessed independent Alfa Romeo team after the factory team's withdrawal from motor racing early in 1933.

By this stage, the birth of Enzo Ferrari's first son Dino in 1932 had prompted his retirement from active driving. In any event, the management demands of his embryonic business empire were diverting his total attention and until 1938 Ferrari and Alfa Romeo became synonymous as Italy's leading international racing team.

Perhaps jealous of the Scuderia Ferrari's success, Alfa Romeo director Ugo Gobatto wanted the team's racing efforts to be returned from Modena to the parent company's Portello headquarters in Milan. Obviously impressed with the success of the new Alfa 158s designed by Giaochino Colombo, his plan was to absorb the Scuderia Ferrari within the Alfa Corse organization.

Enzo Ferrari, by now well accustomed to getting his own way, dug in his heels and steadfastly refused. The problem was further aggravated by his taking an immediate and overwhelming dislike to Gobatto's protégé, Spanish engineer Wilfredo Ricart. A rift was inevitable and final. In 1939 came the formal split, Ferrari going his own way bound by a clause in their severance agreement that precluded him from becoming involved in any motor racing activities, save with an Alfa Romeo product, over the next four years.

It is quite clear that Enzo Ferrari treated these terms with some leeway. By 1940, he had manufactured a couple of 8-cylinder sports cars, designed by former Fiat engineer Alberto Massimino, for local drivers Alberto Ascari and the Marchese Lotario Rangoni Machiavelli di Modena, a wealthy local aristocrat. They used these to compete in the 1940 Mille Miglia and, although these cars carried no name or designation beyond '815', they must go down in history as the first real Ferraris.

During the Second World War, Ferrari kept his company in business by carrying out specialist machine tool work, actually moving out of Modena in 1943 to establish a new factory on land he already owned in the village of Maranello. This was to become the home of the most famous and romantic Grand Prix team of all, not to mention maker of the world's most exotic road cars.

The first V12-engined sports car to carry the Ferrari name raced in June 1947, and in the years that followed the company would build up and expand its racing activities. Some finance for the increasingly expensive Grand Prix programme would come from motor racing's traditional paymasters, the tyre and oil companies, but Enzo Ferrari did not stint on his motor racing and it was only by the sale of sports racing cars to well-heeled amateurs, and mouth-watering production road cars to wealthy members of the café society, that the mathematics of the whole affair made any sense.

In fact, by the late 1960s, the economics of the Ferrari operation had become a complete nonsense and it was only through the discreet intervention of Fiat supremo Gianni Agnelli, tactfully and graciously proposed to the old autocrat, that the Ferrari company was rescued from impending bankruptcy in 1969.

None of these commercial considerations altered the devastation he felt when Dino died, from a kidney ailment, in the summer of 1955. Thereafter he increasingly withdrew to his Maranello fortress, which he seldom left during the last thirty years of his life. Thus insulated from the motor racing world, he relied heavily on a succession of not altogether impartial lieutenants for his information as to what was going on in the pit lane. It was not always a system that got the best out of his team.

During the 1950s and 1960s he seemed to gain a perverse sense of satisfaction from fostering a destructive sense of internal rivalry amongst his drivers, seldom nominating a specific number one and allowing them to race amongst each other in order to establish a pecking order.

In retrospect, too many Ferrari drivers spent too much time racing each other rather than the opposition. Yet to Enzo, who was still regularly addressed as 'Commendatore', despite the fact that the post-war government had annulled this honour bestowed by the Facists, this was simply part of the motor racing game. He could be remarkably warm and sympathetic to those drivers he liked, notably Peter Collins, Chris Amon, and Gilles Villeneuve, cool and unsympathetic to others, such as Eugenio Castellotti and Phil Hill.

When Jean Behra was killed, weeks after thumping Ferrari's team manager, there was not so much as a wreath from Maranello. Yet when Chris Amon reached forty, over a decade after last driving a Ferrari, he received a congratulatory message, as always penned in the Old Man's distinctive purple ink.

Like so many highly energetic autocrats, Enzo Ferrari was a libertine. He fathered an illegitimate son, Piero Lardi, only formally acknowledged as such after the death of his long-suffering wife Laura in the late 1970s. A girlfriend of Chris Amon's recalled the Old Man sliding his hand up her leg beneath the luncheon table on one occasion! He certainly was a game old boy.

Within his domain, Ferrari's word was law. While Agnelli and Fiat took the road car operation under their umbrella in 1969, the racing team remained Ferrari's personal property right up until the last year of his life. Through its corridors he would bellow at his employees, upbraiding and berating them for any deviation from his prescribed instructions.

Key personnel came and went, yet all would benefit and learn from their time working for this irascible, driven, inspired and charismatic Italian motor racing titan.

16

Emerson Fittipaldi

WHEN EMERSON FITTIPALDI emerged triumphant from a spectacular battle with Al Unser junior to win the 1989 Indianapolis 500, many fans regarded it as marking rejuvenation for the man who had became the youngest ever World Champion some seventeen years earlier. At the age of 43, this self-effacing, twinkling character seemed to be driving with as much determination and commitment as he displayed in his halcyon days at the wheel of a black and gold Lotus 72.

In reality, Fittipaldi's success on the Indy car scene came after four years of hard slog culminating in the restoration of credibility for a man who had slipped from the role of F1 pacemaker by dint of one crucial decision. At the absolute zenith of his achievement, Emerson had quit the McLaren team at the end of 1975 to throw in his lot with brother Wilson's fledgling Formula 1 team.

Sadly, the venture was not to be a success. While teams like Williams, Tyrrell, and McLaren would do credit to the reputation of their founder, Fittipaldi Automotive gradually became locked into a depressing downward spiral. It finally departed from the scene at the end of 1982, unnoticed and unmourned.

For those engineers and mechanics involved it was an obvious disappointment. For the Fittipaldi brothers, particularly Emerson, it was a tragedy. He was not 30 years old when he turned his back on the McLaren team, with two World Championships and fifteen Grand Prix victories to his credit. Had he not taken that crucial wrong turn Alain Prost might have been shooting at Fittipaldi's record tally of victories, rather than at Jackie Stewart's, in the late 1980s.

Emerson and Wilson were born into a motor racing family. Their father, Wilson Snr, was one of Brazil's most respected motor racing journalists and commentators, having followed Fangio's first foray to Europe in the late 1940s. Wilson Fittipaldi gave both his lads every encouragement, and while Wilson Junior became an undeniably accomplished performer, it was Emerson who displayed the star quality from an early age.

At the age of fifteen he won his first motorcycle race. By 1966 he was dominating the Brazilian national Formula Vee series and, three years later, he left his native shores to tackle British national Formula Ford. He could hardly have guessed at the time, but he was blazing a trail that would later be followed by Nelson Piquet and Ayrton Senna. At the time of writing, these three Brazilian drivers have scored eight World Championship titles between them.

Emerson mastered Formula Ford in a matter of weeks, graduating into Formula 3 mid-season and breezing away to win the important Lombank British Championship. At the start of 1970 he graduated into Formula 2 with a Lotus 69, but Colin Chapman had him marked out as a man to watch. After Piers Courage was killed in the Frank Williams de Tomaso at Zandvoort, Frank tried to lure Fittipaldi into his broke Formula 1 team. But Chapman headed him off. By July 1970, Emerson was finishing seventh in the British Grand Prix at Brands Hatch at the wheel of a Lotus 49D. Barely a year had elapsed since he stepped off the plane from Sao Paulo ...

Events now moved quickly. Chapman's superb Lotus 72 had at last provided the mercurial Jochen Rindt with equipment worthy of his talent. But tragedy intervened abruptly at Monza when Jochen died in a violent practice accident. Existing Lotus number two John Miles got cold feet and withdrew, so Emerson found himself propelled into the team leadership after only three races. He went on to win the United States Grand Prix at Watkins Glen, only his fourth Formula 1 race, thereby guaranteeing Rindt's posthumous title.

After that dramatic start, it was perhaps only to be expected that 1971 was something of an anti-climax. Emerson spent most of the year learning the F1 ropes, gaining several satisfactory top three placings. But his Grand Prix career did not yield another win until 1972 when he exerted an impressive level of dominance to snatch the Championship from Jackie Stewart's grasp.

Chapman was delighted with his Brazilian protégé, although less so with his number two, Australian Dave Walker. At the end of the year Walker was pitched out in favour of the dazzling Ronnie Peterson and the shrewd Fittipaldi could see the possibility of his position becoming undermined. Although he won three Grands Prix, Ronnie was clearly the faster driver, hijacking both Fittipaldi's team and Chapman's confidence. It was time for a move and Emerson accepted a big money offer to lead the Marlboro McLaren line-up for 1974.

Consolidating his reputation as a clever tactician, Fittipaldi may not have been the fastest contender for the 1974 title, but he displayed more guile and racecraft than his less experienced rivals. Niki Lauda might have made it to the title with a few more miles under his belt; but as it was, Fittipaldi bagged three victories and emerged with the crown for the second time in three years.

In 1975 Lauda really got a handle on the Formula 1 business, winning five races in the splendidly powerful Ferrari 312T to put the destiny of the Championship crown beyond doubt. But Emerson finished runner-up with two victories in a year that had seen him launch a one-man boycott of the troubled Spanish Grand Prix at Barcelona. Circuit safety facilities were just not up to scratch, but Fittipaldi alone chose to take a stand on the issue. When tragedy befell Rolf Stommelen's car during the race, resulting in the death of four onlookers, Emerson could allow himself a rueful shrug.

What followed next was a major misjudgement. Brother Wilson's suckling Formula 1 programme did not show much technical prowess throughout 1975, but at least it was well sponsored with financial backing from Copersucar, the Brazilian sugar marketing cartel. With Emerson now lending the team additional credibility, things would surely improve. They did, but only slightly. And briefly.

What followed was a gradual erosion of Emerson's competitive edge. Struggling with an uncompetitive car was not a role that fell comfortably onto his shoulders. He was determined enough, but the frustration gradually wore him down. There was to be one glorious moment when he finished second behind Carlos Reutemann's Ferrari in the 1978 Brazilian Grand Prix at Rio, but the vocal adulation from his fans could not blind him to the Copersucar's erratic development progress.

In mid-1979, Fittipaldi Automotive took over the assets of Walter Wolf Racing, and along with them inherited the neat ground effect Wolf WR9 and its designer Harvey Postlethwaite. In 1980 things were sufficiently promising to give Emerson and new team-mate Keke Rosberg a couple of podium finishes early in the year, but that initial optimism gradually evaporated amidst shortage of sponsorship and flagging morale amongst the workforce.

Emerson retired from the cockpit at the end of 1980, opting to concentrate his efforts on managing his youthful compatriot Chico Serra, who had been recruited to run alongside Rosberg through 1981. But the team's financial situation pushed it progressively further down the grid as the season dragged on. Postlethwaite left to take a design post with Ferrari and Rosberg quit because he was getting nowhere fast.

Backs to the wall, the Fittipaldi team soldiered through 1982 with a single car entry for Serra, although the young Brazilian was now struggling to get on the back of the grids. The money and motivation finally ran out, so the team closed its doors at the end of the year.

Wilson Fittipaldi turned his hand to managing the family businesses back in Brazil, including a prestigious Mercedes-Benz dealership, but Emerson headed for America, where he would rebuild his reputation as a driver to dramatic effect.

17

Mauro Forghieri

ANY DESIGNER WORKING for Ferrari necessarily lived in the shadow of the Commendatore's dynamic, forceful and idiosyncratic personality. Yet while some observers have found it fashionable to deride Ferrari engineering technology over the years, due credit must be given to Mauro Forghieri, a man whose versatility and design genius made a momentous contribution to the success achieved by the Prancing Horse for an incredible 25 years.

No designer before or since survived the political rigours at Maranello in the manner achieved by Forghieri. Sometimes in favour, sometimes not, his contribution to the marque's racing successes must be assessed as being more significant than any other engineer in the company's history. Giaocchino Colombo, Aurelio Lampredi, and Carlo Chiti all played their part, but the real core of the team's long-term success was down to Forghieri.

A key to Forghieri's special relationship with Enzo Ferrari may be found in the fact that his father, Reclus Forghieri, had been a pre-war pattern maker in the pioneering days of the Scuderia, working on the cylinder heads of the original Alfa Romeo 158s. Mauro's grandfather had been something of a poet and social commentator who spent much of his time prior to the early 1930s living on the Côte d'Azur and was only allowed back into Italy during Mussolini's Fascist regime on the strict understanding that he would not take part in any political activities.

Clearly, there was an excitable, imaginative, and theatrical streak coursing through the Forghieri family's bloodlines and Mauro inherited his fair share of these qualities. Despite the fact that his father had worked in such hallowed motor racing surroundings, Mauro's ambitions extended way beyond racing cars when he was studying at the University of Bologna.

'My great passion was aviation engineering,' he admits. 'I really wanted to go to the USA to work with Lockheed or Northrop, but just as I left university with a diploma in mechanical engineering at the end of 1958 I was called up to do my national service.'

His plans to go to America were side-tracked, never to be revived. Reclus Forghieri got on very well with Mr Ferrari on a personal level and the Commendatore made the suggestion that Mauro should join the company. He knew what he was in for. In 1957 he had briefly been to the famous Maranello factory to gather information for a university project he was completing, and he eventually started on a full-time basis at the end of 1959, working on calculations for the 120-degree $1\frac{1}{2}$-litre V6 engine.

'Engines have always been my principal interest,' he insists, 'and when I went to Ferrari I didn't know anything at all about chassis design. I suppose in the following 20 years you could say I became equally interested in chassis, suspension, and gearbox work, but engines were always my first love. I regarded my work on the $1\frac{1}{2}$-litre Ferrari 156 as my schooling period in the art of chassis development.'

Carlo Chiti had taken overall responsibility for the development of this car, which won the 1961 World Championship; but when he decided to join the disastrously unsuccessful ATS organization, formed by a group of Ferrari renegades at the start of the following year, Forghieri found himself propelled into a position of increasing responsibility. He admits he had nothing in common with Chiti, on either a personal or professional level, and faced an enormous challenge attempting to massage the 156 into some semblance of competitive order.

The scholarly, bespectacled engineer really began to make his name during the mid-1960s, developing the chassis which John Surtees eventually used to return the World Championship to Ferrari in 1964. After Surtees's departure in 1966, Forghieri then became responsible for the succession of fine-handling, if underpowered, 3-litre V12s that showed such promising form in the hands of Lorenzo Bandini, Jacky Ickx, and Chris Amon between 1967 and 1969.

It was an enormous disappointment to Mauro when Amon finally decided to leave Ferrari at the end of 1969, the straw that finally broke the camel's back coming in the form of a succession of engine failures with the new 3-litre flat-12 which would be at the core of Maranello's F1 efforts in 1970. Forghieri got on enormously well with Amon, both on a personal and professional basis. The Italian engineer puts the amiable New Zealander alone on a pedestal as far as all the drivers he had worked with were concerned. He judged Amon to have been a fine test and development driver, capable of describing a car's behaviour concisely and without superfluous waffle. And as a racing driver, Forghieri thought he was simply first rate. 'Jacky Ickx may have won more races on paper, so I suppose he must be regarded as more successful,' says Mauro to this day. 'But in my personal opinion Chris was as good as Jimmy Clark.'

During the summer of 1969 Ferrari F1 fortunes sank to a depressing level with Forghieri designing the new 312B1 flat-12 away from the mainstream action. This would propel Maranello back into the forefront of competitiveness in 1970 and Forghieri's personal star remained in the ascendant until 1973 when the whole programme fell apart at the seams again.

In 1972 the Ferrari 312B2 failed to deliver whilst Mauro was back at base developing his latest design concept—the squat, blunt-looking device nicknamed 'the snowplough', which reflected his efforts to concentrate as much weight as possible within the car's wheelbase. Ickx, by now approaching the twilight of his competitive F1 career, gave it the thumbs-down after initial testing and the Ferrari effort slipped further at the start of 1973.

Mauro was banished to a new special projects department, leaving former Innocenti engineer Sandro Colombo in charge of F1 design. By mid-season 1973, Maranello's Grand Prix challenge was almost dead in the water. Forghieri was summoned back from special projects and given the green light to revamp the new B3 chassis in time for the Austrian Grand Prix.

That car was developed into the 312B3 in which Niki Lauda made his name the following year. Then Forghieri came up with possibly the best design of his entire career: the neutral-handling 1975 312T, the most novel technical aspect of which was its transverse gearbox. Derivatives of this car kept Ferrari on, or close to, the top for the next five years, helping Lauda to World Championships in 1975 and 1977 and, as the 312T4, taking Jody Scheckter to the title in 1979.

Despite acknowledging Mauro's unquestionable talents, Lauda often found him impossible to deal with. 'They tell me Forghieri is a genius,' said Lauda acidly, 'so I suppose my problem is that I am unable to work with a genius!' The pragmatic and calm Austrian did not really know how to deal with a designer who could lay on the vociferous, extrovert pit-lane melodrama which Forghieri increasingly made his speciality!

Into the 1980s, with the advent of turbo technology, Forghieri gradually found his efforts supplemented when the Commendatore engaged English designer Harvey Postlethwaite to bring Maranello's chassis technology up to contemporary levels, particularly as far as the development of carbon-fibre manufacturing techniques was concerned. Yet Forghieri's contribution to Ferrari engine development programmes continued apace and he deserves a great deal of credit for helping the team win the Constructors' World Championship in both 1982 and 1983. Then, in 1984, Ferrari misjudged the tempo of the opposition and was totally floored by the brand-new McLaren-TAGs driven by Alain Prost and Niki Lauda.

Unquestionably, Forghieri was made the fall guy for the relatively unimpressive performance of the 126C4, which won only a single Grand Prix during the 1984 season; but a more accurate historic assessment must conclude that Maranello was beaten by the superior Porsche and Bosch technology that went into the TAG V6 engine powering the all-conquering McLarens. The Michelin radial tyres used by Prost and Lauda also had a very significant performance edge over the Goodyears used by Ferrari.

The first signs of Mauro's fall from grace came at the 1984 Italian Grand Prix. He was nowhere to be seen. Harvey Postlethwaite tactfully stayed away as well, ostensibly taking a timely holiday in England. He had more feeling than to embarrass his fellow engineer by turning up at Monza to feed the pressure cooker of gossip that inevitably erupted in the Italian press at that time in the season.

Despite outward assertions of continued confidence in his man, Ferrari transferred Forghieri sideways for the second time in his career, putting him in charge of a new department dealing with advanced engineering projects for the Ferrari company as a whole. But this time he was being moved closer to the door.

In reality Mauro's fall from grace was accelerated when he championed the cause of a four-cylinder turbo engine in the wake of Nelson Piquet's 1983 World Championship success using a BMW engine of this configuration in his Brabham BT52. Further encouraged by hints that FISA might reduce the maximum engine capacity to 1.2-litres in 1988, Forghieri embarked on this project with enormous enthusiasm during 1984. But the Ferrari four-cylinder turbo proved to be an unmitigated disaster, never running sufficiently long enough on the test bed even to produce a single power curve. The Commendatore, who was historically devoted to engine development above all else, never forgave Forghieri for this technical aberration.

In 1986, Forghieri finally left Ferrari to join the rival Modenese manufacturer Lamborghini with a brief to design a V12 engine for the new 3.5-litre naturally-aspirated F1 that came into being at the start of 1988. This duly made its race début with the Larrousse Lola team, was supplied to Lotus in 1990, and was then used by Ligier and the newly-formed Modena team from the start of 1991.

Early in 1990 Forghieri was requested to take over responsibility as Technical Director for the Modena Lambo team, but only a couple of months after taking up this appointment he returned to Lamborghini in order to develop a revised version of the V12, with five valves per cylinder, in preparation for the Italian Grand Prix.

Over thirty years after walking through the doors of the Ferrari factory for the first time, Forghieri was still in F1, still designing engines, still close to the centre of that grand drama which is motor racing, Italian style.

18

Bill France

CERTAINLY THE MOST successful form of motor racing in America—and, its supporters say, the world—is the highly specialized NASCAR stock car circus. It has grown up over the past forty years as a phenomenon almost entirely confined to the deep South, the high spot of its season being the Daytona 500 spectacular on that magnificent banked oval in Florida. The first Daytona 500 was staged in 1959, giving a well-deserved fillip to a category that had already been thriving for the best part of a decade. And the architect of its success was a genial giant by the name of Bill France.

France was born in 1911 and had started racing on Daytona Beach in a Ford Model-T special as long ago as 1936, squeezing his 6 ft 5 in frame into its tiny cockpit. He admits to enjoying his racing, but it didn't take long for what was later proved to be a successful entrepreneurial spirit to come to the surface. Sure, he reckoned, race driving was great fun; but promoting races made even more sense.

Daytona Beach, of course, is a name famed in motor sporting history. In the 1920s and 1930s the likes of Sir Malcolm Campbell, Henry Segrave, Ray Keech, and Kaye Don tore up miles of the golden foreshore into whirlwinds of sand as they pursued their spectacular record attempts. At the same time, the locals began holding their own impromptu speed trials, laying the foundations for one of the most fascinating of motor racing sub-cultures, which flourishes to this day.

The beach races survived through to the mid-1950s, steadily gaining in respectability and acceptance. Many of their participants honed their skills behind the wheel running moonshine—smuggling illicit booze across into those southern states still haunted by the spectre of prohibition—and France expanded his race promotional operations to a succession of country dirt tracks where the 'Good Old Boys' could take time off from their main line of business and earn a few dollars from racing.

However, despite the sustained success of the beach racing enterprises, France was astute enough to realize that stock car racing had to move with the times. Florida in general, and Daytona in particular, was becoming progressively more affluent and sophisticated with the onset of the 1950s.

The huge oceanfront building developments had pushed the sand racing further away from the centre of the city and although, with co-promoter Bill Tuthill, France had been staging between eight and ten races by 1947 under the title of 'National Championship Stock Car

Circuit', they needed something more upmarket.

Not only was there a pressing need for a permanent speed bowl, but also for the stock car racing business to be codified under some sort of national governing body. Prior to the formation of NASCAR, France had approached the American Automobile Association Contest Board to see if they would be interested in sanctioning the stock car racing circus. The board, effectively USAC's forerunner, proved extremely huffy and aloof about the idea and rejected it. Clearly, their only serious interest was focused on the Indy car fraternity. This rebuff led France to pay an increasing amount of attention and energy to the administration of NASCAR's interests. There were all manner of potential problems to be surmounted, not least the need to forge a set of workable technical regulations with which the racers could be expected to abide.

There was also the problem of offering a worthwhile number of races to the insurance companies—an absolutely crucial consideration in a country with a knee-jerk inclination towards initiating third party insurance claims. The insurance companies were not really interested in issuing cover for just a handful of events. So for 1948, France and Tuthill increased their promotional commitment from 85 to 394 races.

By the end of the following year NASCAR's highly professional approach paid off to splendid effect with a total of $64,000 in the points fund kitty. Even at this early stage it was clear that France and Tuthill were operating NASCAR as something of a dictatorship—they had reached the conclusion that trying to run the show on a wholly democratic basis, with a board of management being invited to vote on every contentious issue, was simply inoperable. But almost everybody agreed that theirs was a benevolent regime, committed to the furtherance of the NASCAR cause rather than pure commercial self-interest.

By the mid-1950s stock car racing at Daytona Beach had become well organized, promoted, and categorized, but it still nagged in Bill France's mind that NASCAR had no prestigious home circuit that would act as a show piece for the formula. He wanted to build a tri-oval super speedway, a permanent facility on which the hottest and fastest that Detroit could produce would do battle in front of a capacity crowd.

Thanks to his drive, determination and powers of persuasion, that's precisely what happened. The 2.5-mile tri-oval, with its turns banked at a lurid 31-degrees, presented a breathtaking challenge to NASCAR competitors, making the old beach course look like child's play by contrast. The track was ready to stage its first Daytona 500 in 1959 when pole position fell to the Pontiac of Cotton Owens at an average speed of just over 143 mph—more than enough to make the crowds rock on their heels in disbelief.

For France the showman, that first 500 was a classic for which he would have been hard pressed to write a more exciting script. The capacity crowd was spellbound by the intensity of the racing. In the end it came down to a two-car battle for victory between Lee Petty's Plymouth and Johnny Beauchamp's Ford Thunderbird. They crossed the line side by side, but the timekeepers' view was partially blocked by the third car of Joe Weatherly, which was being lapped at that precise moment, making it three abreast as they passed the flag. It would take four days of photographic examination and debate before Lee Petty was decreed the winner.

Over the years that followed, NASCAR would go from strength to strength, applying and policing its own firm regulations with just the correct blend of strength and sympathy. France's business empire expanded, usually smoothly, occasionally with the odd hiccup. One event that met with his overwhelming indignation was when the drivers boycotted the inaugural Talladega 500 at Alabama International Speedway in 1969, their verdict being that the track was too fast and no available tyre could stand up to the strain.

France was furious, feeling that the competitors were biting the hand that had fed them and, in the end, he managed to muster a sufficient number of competitors who were not members of the PDA (Professional Drivers' Association). The race went ahead, the field fleshed out with slower GT machinery. As France pointed out at the time, perhaps five out of the thirty-six cars that eventually took the start could run at the sort of speeds that were causing such concern to the aces. The dissenting drivers were eventually allowed back into the fold, while the introduction of a carburettor restrictor plate the following year helped allay their concerns in time for the second running of the Talladega 500.

Yet such confrontations were the exception rather than the rule. NASCAR thrives to this day as a living memorial to the man who built its strong foundations, while Daytona was soon expanded to become a regular stop on the World Sports Car Championship trail, the banking complemented by a twisty infield section to accommodate the European road racers.

In 1971, Bill France stepped down from the presidency of NASCAR, although he would retain his control of the corporation that ran Daytona and Talladega. His son, Bill France Junior, picked up the reins of control and has wielded them ever since, to equally productive effect.

Having reached the age of 60 'Big Bill' now turned his attentions to the furtherance of Alabama Governor George Wallace's presidential aspirations, a campaign that was prematurely ended when a would-be assassins's bullet crippled the right-wing politician. Wallace had been a staunch supporter of NASCAR and it was his influence that ensured a six-lane state highway was routed right up to Talladega's gates, the better to facilitate entry for the fans. Bill France was a loyal friend who appreciated such gestures and his support for the Governor's presidential challenge was his way of repaying a favour.

19

Amédée Gordini

AMÉDÉE GORDINI WAS a determined, dogged fighter whose attempts to put France on the map as a Grand Prix force in the 1950s were frustrated by a combination of optimistic over-commitment and dire under-funding. His cars were often frail and unreliable, but he could not be faulted for the sheer enthusiasm with which he tackled an obviously hopeless cause, fighting against Ferrari, Maserati, and Mercedes-Benz with a zeal that seemed almost irrational.

Born at Bazzano, near Bologna, on 23 June 1899, the young Gordini served an apprenticeship at a local Fiat distributorship, during which time he actually managed to build his first car out of unwanted spare parts. From there Gordini joined the Isotta-Fraschini concern, working briefly with Alfieri Maserati, before travelling to France where he decided to settle in 1922 for the straightforward reason that he had spent all his available money and had to get a job simply to make ends meet.

Gordini married a French girl and began a garage business on the Rue de la République, in Suresnes, which started out dealing in Fiats. He raced Bugattis for a while, including a Brescia and a T37, eventually taking out French citizenship. Simca, who were Fiat's French licencees, were impressed by Gordini's magic touch when it came to tuning Fiats and, in the immediate pre-Second World War years, Gordini began contesting the Monte Carlo rally in the French marque's products.

In 1939, sharing with José Scaron, Gordini won the 1,100-cc class on the Monte, but it was not until after the war that he established a joint racing programme with Simca's support. Operating from new Paris workshops, he began to develop some primitive 1,100-cc single seaters based on Simca components with a view to contesting the new international Formula 2 introduced in 1947. It was at the wheel of one such machine that the popular, debonair Jean-Pierre Wimille met his death whilst practising at Palermo Park, Buenos Aires, in January 1949.

Encouraged by his cars' agility, Gordini laid plans for graduation to F1, gradually expanding the 4-cylinder engines with their three-bearing crankshafts to encompass a $1\frac{1}{2}$-litre version that Gordini believed, over-optimistically, could be successfully supercharged to provide a worthwhile Championship contender in 1950. Using a Wade type RL compressor, a single-stage supercharged F1 Gordini duly made its Grand Prix début in that first season of the official World Championship.

Robert Manzon gave the car its only decent finish in a Championship event, taking fourth place behind the Alfa Romeos of Fangio and Fagioli in the French Grand Prix at Reims; but while the car was amongst the very lightest amongst its contemporaries, it was just not sufficiently durable. Moreover, the team was badly over-stretched. Competing in a full programme of Formula 2 events as well meant that the mechanics regularly had to remove the superchargers as the precarious Gordini budget certainly did not stretch to having separate engines for the junior category. The Simca-Gordinis would regularly frighten the drivers of more powerful machines, but were all too seldom in at the finish.

In 1951, undeterred by the fact that Simca's financial support was insufficient to expand as ambitiously as he would have liked, Gordini sanctioned the construction of a brand new engine that used none of the Simca production components his cars had previously employed. Now it had a five-bearing crankshaft, promising improved mechanical durability, but the chaotic situation continued. It seemed as though the whole equipe was wearing itself out with over-commitment and when, at the height of the season, Gordini absolutely insisted on contesting Le Mans, this sports car outing also degenerated into a fiasco. Theodore Pigozzi, the President of Simca, reached the conclusion that the partnership with Gordini was doing more harm than good to his company's interests and consequently terminated the collaboration at the end of the year. Even Maurice Trintignant's morale-boosting victory in the non-Championship race at Albi failed to change his views.

Gordini was now hanging by a slender thread over the financial abyss, to be saved from motor racing extinction when the sport's governing body decreed that the 1952 World Championship would be contested by F2 cars, in the absence of sufficient available machines to meet the $1\frac{1}{2}$ litre supercharged/$4\frac{1}{2}$ litre unsupercharged regulations. Not for nothing had veteran French journalist Charles Faroux dubbed Gordini 'The Sorcerer' back in the 1930s. His capacity for making bricks out of straw seemed unmatched.

Despite his lack of cash, Gordini designed and built brand new 6-cylinder 2-litre engines for 1952. They failed to win a single Championship race, but they were quick enough to keep the all-conquering Ferrari team on its toes, as Jean Behra's splendid third place in the Swiss Grand Prix would testify. Come the GP de la Marne at Reims, Behra would defeat the Ferraris of Farina and Ascari in a straight fight. Oh that it had been a World Championship qualifying event!

In 1953, Gordini, low on funds as usual, just had to keep plugging away with his existing machinery. Again he allowed an abortive Le Mans programme to be an unnecessary drain on the company's resources and, come the advent of the new $2\frac{1}{2}$ litre Formula 1 at the start of 1954, he replaced the crankshaft and cylinder liners in his existing 6-cylinder engine to magic up a power unit for the new regulations.

It was a forlorn hope. Behra drove like a tiger on every occasion, winning non-title races at Pau and Cadours, whilst his indomitable fighting spirit was never better demonstrated than the way in which he kept the Gordini tight in the slipstream of the infinitely more powerful Mercedes during the opening stages of the non-title Berlin Grand Prix at Avus. This attempt ended with engine failure and Behra could no longer afford the patriotic gesture implicit in driving for Gordini. Having forged his reputation driving for 'The Sorcerer' he signed for the works Maserati team in 1955.

How could Gordini continue? With Formula 1 hopes now pinned round the driving efforts of the capable, if unexceptional, Robert Manzon, the dauntless team boss prepared for his final throw of the Grand Prix dice—the 8-cylinder Gordini type 32. Late on the scene, it failed to make its Grand Prix début until Monza, where Jean Lucas, standing in for the absent Manzon, managed only eight laps.

Time was running out. Gordini struggled on, defiantly independent, through 1956 and into 1957, still fielding a sports car programme and manufacturing a limited run of high performance road cars. But it could not last. Even Amédée realized that, to survive, he would need to branch out into fresh fields.

To this end, in 1956 he concluded a contract with Renault boss Pierre Dreyfus for the development of a high performance version of the currently fashionable Renault Dauphine saloon. A total of 10,000 Dauphine-Gordinis were envisaged and, in 1957, after one final outing in the Naples Grand Prix, Gordini's F1 effort came to an end. This proud, gaunt-faced enthusiast finally capitulated to economic inevitability and wound up the racing team he had operated with such tenacity for almost a decade.

In the early 1960s, Gordini sold most of his surviving cars to the eccentric Schlumpf brothers, to grace the then-private collection of these acquisitive Alsatian textile millionaires. But the Gordini name would be perpetuated into the 1970s on a variety of high performance Renault road cars, as the Sorcerer settled into retirement, sustained by fond memories of what might have been.

By the time of his death, in 1979, Renault was poised to win its first Grand Prix with a turbocharged Grand Prix car, thereby succeeding on the post-war racing scene that had proved so frustrating for Bugatti, Talbot-Lago, and Gordini. It is all too easy to conclude that Amédée Gordini was a muddler who simply got out of his depth in Formula 1. In reality, he had considerable technical strength and optimism, but his hopes foundered on the rocks of financial reality.

20

Andy Granatelli

AFTER STP BOSS Andy Granatelli kissed Mario Andretti in the winners' circle at Indianapolis back in 1969, Mario jokingly muttered something about a clause in his contract debarring such extrovert outpourings of emotion in the future. Years later, Jackie Stewart suggested that the oil additive king should make a television advertisement in which he actually drank his product to make the point how pure it was!

These two stories capture the extrovert ways of the man who became one of US Indy car racing's larger than life characters throughout the 1960s and early 1970s. Granatelli's predilection for clowning around became an accepted part of the scene. He once stunned the Indianapolis pit lane by appearing in silk pyjamas decorated with hundreds of STP motifs. But it paid off in media coverage, and that's exactly why Granatelli became involved in motor racing as a sponsor.

Born amidst considerable poverty in Texas in 1923, he and his brothers Vince and Joe moved to California at an early age, then on to Chicago where they enjoyed their first taste of automotive competition in impromptu street drag races in the early 1940s which inevitably attracted the disapproving attention of the local police. Andy used a 1934 Ford convertible fitted with a 1939 Mercury V8 for these early adventures and his entrepreneurial ability also showed itself early on when he opened a successful petrol station/car wash business. Early setbacks included the business being robbed and a later venture being burnt out, but Andy really began to make his mark with a performance equipment company called Grancor and expanded into hot rod race promotion in 1947, a year after making his Indianapolis début with a modified flat-head Ford engine.

Danny Kladis drove Granatelli's car on its Brickyard début, but Andy himself tried driving the following year only to lose control and crash heavily on his qualifying run. He sustained fractures in his skull, ribs and arms and at one point was not expected to live. Whilst recuperating from this episode, he was later involved in a road accident that saw him thrown through the rear screen of a road car. He fractured his skull again and suffered a repeat arm fracture, effectively ending his serious racing career.

Jim Rathmann notched up the best finish for Grancor at Indy in 1952, then Fred Agabashian took fourth the following year, despite the fact that even the stewards privately admitted a lap scoring error which should rightfully have placed him second. In 1954 the stewards derailed Granatelli's efforts again, failing to see Rathmann's arm raised at the start of his qualifying run and his efforts were negated. Andy stormed out of the speedway, vowing never to return. Of course, this was an empty threat. In 1957, already a millionaire, he moved to Southern California, toyed with retirement, decided against it, and bought the financially beleagured Paxton Products gear concern, promptly turning it into a profitable company again. Paxton was then sold to the Studebaker division of General Motors, Granatelli being appointed President of the division that controlled his own company. Throughout this period Andy became embroiled in publicity-seeking record attempts, notably his own 1961 NASCAR-backed record run on Daytona Beach where he established a two-way average of 172.166 mph at the wheel of a supercharged Chrysler sedan.

It didn't take long for Andy to switch to Studebaker's STP division where he achieved his most spectacular marketing success. The oil additive business was an area regarded by many of the major oil companies with a degree of rather aloof disdain. They could be very huffy indeed about the likes of STP and Wynn's Friction Proofing, shrugging them aside as ineffective jollop. But Andy Granatelli swept STP to international prominence with an overwhelming promotional strategy, largely built round exposure at the Indianapolis Motor Speedway, the motor racing mecca to which he'd once vowed he would never return.

Andy came barnstorming his way back to Indy in 1961, buying the troubled Novi Indy project for what, at the time, seemed like an expensive $110,000. The precarious-handling machine, powered by a wailing 550-bhp supercharged V8, had resolutely defied the efforts of many drivers in the past. Andy, unable to sign a suitably qualified driver, withdrew from the 1961 500 and failed to make the cut the following year. But in 1963 Jim Hurtubise, Bobby Unser and Art Malone all made it onto the grid, but none finished.

In 1964, Granatelli brought four-wheel-drive technology back to the Brickyard after more than a decade's absence following a meeting with Stirling Moss. The English driver had enthusiastically recounted how well the Ferguson P99 four-wheel-drive Grand Prix car had performed to win the wet 1961 Oulton Park Gold Cup and Granatelli bore those remarks in mind. He subsequently asked Tony Rolt whether he would consider sending the P99 over for trials at the Brickyard. Rolt duly agreed, and Jack Fairman lapped the $2\frac{1}{2}$-litre Climax-engined car consistently at around the 140 mph mark. Granatelli was highly impressed and immediately commissioned Ferguson to design a new Indy car for him.

Conceived and manufactured in only five months at Ferguson's Coventry base, the car was again powered by a Novi V8, now developing about 740 bhp. Entered in the 1964 500, it was eventually qualified a splendid sixth by Bobby Unser who took over from originally nominated driver Jim McElreath who couldn't get used to four-wheel-drive characteristics and was unnerved when the car suffered some hub bearing troubles.

Unfortunately, Unser became involved in the tragic second lap accident that claimed the lives of Eddie Sachs and Dave MacDonald and the car was not repairable in time for the restart. In 1965 Unser qualified in the middle of the third row, but also failed to finish, and the Novi-Ferguson star gradually faded.

In 1967, after a year's absence from the Speedway, Granatelli returned with his most ambitious project yet. This was the striking STP Turbine car, variously nicknamed 'Silent Sam' and the 'Swooshmobile', possibly the most revolutionary and distinctive car ever to appear at the Brickyard. It was probably the most significant product of Granatelli's links with Paxton, who further modified the Ferguson 4WD system, mating it to a Pratt & Whitney turbine developing in excess of 500 bhp.

The monocoque backbone chassis had the engine slung along one side, the driver along the other, and, ironically, it was the Paxton-devised system of transfer gears from the turbine that proved to be the eventual problem which sidelined the dominant Parnelli Jones, a ball bearing in the transmission breaking up only seven miles short of the chequered flag.

Alarmed at the level of dominance displayed by the STP Turbocar, the traditionally conservative USAC rule makers rewrote the regulations to drastically curtail turbine engine performance in the future. Andy, with typical energy, hurled himself into a complex and expensive legal action against Indy's rule makers. He lost, but wasn't down for long.

Success at Indy may have eluded the flamboyant Granatelli yet again, but the publicity value to the STP corporation of all these racing activities had been valuable beyond their wildest expectations. Brushing aside the disappointment of the legal skirmish with USAC, Andy now threw his company's sponsorship behind Colin Chapman's exciting efforts with the Lotus turbine cars, machines which proved electrifyingly fast but worryingly fragile.

Jim Clark only briefly tried one before his tragic death at Hockenheim, early in 1968, but his replacement, Mike Spence, crashed heavily at the Brickyard soon afterwards and died from serious head injuries. Joe Leonard, Art Pollard, and Graham Hill drove the three entries in the 500; all proved extremely competitive, but none made it to the finish.

Finally, in 1969, Mario Andretti gave Granatelli his long-awaited Indy 500 victory, but the Italian-American's sole triumph at the Brickyard was achieved at the wheel of the STP team's old Hawk back-up car against a backdrop of bitterness and pending litigation. The STP Lotus partnership had planned to field mighty powerful 2.65-litre turbocharged Ford-engined, four-wheel-drive Lotus 64s, but Mario destroyed his machine after a suspension failure pitched him into a massive accident.

It had been the intention that Granatelli would purchase the cars for the rest of the USAC seson's races, but he and Chapman fell out amidst a flurry of writs and the deal fell through. Granatelli's great days at the Speedway were over.

21

Dan Gurney

AN AFFABLE, BEAMING giant of a man, Daniel Sexton Gurney approached his sixtieth year looking as taut and trim as many men half his age, a testament to the widely-held medical theory that stress is the key factor which ages the human being more than anything else. If Dan ever worried over-much, he certainly didn't let it show. Yet it is perhaps because of his laid back, easy going nature that he has been somewhat short-changed by the motor racing history books.

As an American, Dan Gurney did for Formula 1 what Carroll Shelby and Briggs Cunningham did for sports car racing. In his Grand Prix heyday he was acknowedged as the closest challenger Jim Clark ever had during his career and his efforts with his own Eagle-Weslake Grand Prix team were ambitious and extremely audacious. He stands shoulder to shoulder with Mario Andretti as the best American Grand Prix driver of the post-war era.

Born in Port Jefferson, New York, on 13 April 1931, Dan's family moved to Riverside, California, on his father's retirement as an opera singer. By 1950 Dan was knocking round the Bonneville Salt flats with the speed record crowd, but any motor racing aspirations had to be shelved in 1952 when he joined the army and was immediately packed off to Korea.

On his return, despite the added responsibility of a wife and young child, he took up the motor racing game with unstinting enthusiasm. First with a Triumph TR2, later with a Porsche 356, he eventually gained a sufficient reputation to be loaned other people's racing cars. In 1957 he had a ride in a Chevy Corvette at Riverside, beating a host of Mercedes 300SL gull-wings by almost half a minute. This led to his first outing in a really serious high performance machine, a 4.9-litre Ferrari belonging to vineyard owner Frank Arciero.

Suddenly it was all happening for the lanky Californian. Having shaped up successfully against the likes of Phil Hill, Masten Gregory, and Walt Hansgen on near-equal terms, he was suddenly a man to watch. Phil Hill dropped a word to Ferrari and, before Dan knew it, he was off to Le Mans in 1958 as a member of Luigi Chinetti's North American Racing Team challenge. Later that year Ferrari's works team beckoned; through Chinetti, he was invited to Modena for a test run.

That in turn led to a run at Sebring in 1959, in a 250 Testa Rossa. By

1960 he was in the factory Formula 1 team alongside Phil Hill and Tony Brooks, but found the draconian discipline and autocratic management style insufferable. He switched to BRM for 1961—an appalling mistake—before going on to drive the new Porsche flat-8 Grand Prix contender in 1962, winning the French Grand Prix at Rouen.

Between 1963 and 1965, he drove for Jack Brabham at the wheel of the fine-handling, spaceframe, $1\frac{1}{2}$-litre Climax-engined Formula 1 cars, consistently proving himself almost a match for Clark's dominant Lotus, though time and again let down by trifling mechanical failures. He would win the French Grand Prix again in 1964 and the Mexican Grand Prix the same year, but he never managed to sustain a consistent challenge for the Championship during his spell with Jack's team.

Although he and Clark were rivals in Formula 1, it was Dan who was inspired to suggest that Colin Chapman tackled Indianapolis. 'When I first saw the monocoque Lotus 25 in the pit lane at Zandvoort, I thought, "Wow, what would happen if we could take something like that to Speedway!"' he later recalled.

He drove Indy alongside Clark—a man he admired enormously—in 1963 and 1964, as part of the works Lotus-Ford set-up, before cutting out on his own. He remembers working alongside Chapman with considerable enthusiasm: 'He was a racer to the core. When you were part of his team you quickly came to realize that this was a guy working at redefining the cutting edge of racing technology. That was a real motivating factor, believe me ...'

With the change to the new 3-litre Formula 1 regulations at the start of 1966, Dan decided to go it alone and start his own F1 team—the first US Grand Prix effort since Lance Reventlow's abortive Scarab challenge at the turn of the decade. All American Racers Inc was established at Santa Ana, California, to field cars both in Indy and Formula 1 arenas. Starting the latter programme with an uncompetitive 2.7-litre Climax 4-cylinder engine, the sleek and elegant Eagles were soon to be fitted with Weslake V12 engines and, thus powered, Dan would storm to victories in the 1967 Race of Champions and Belgian Grand Prix.

It was a massively underfinanced project, as Gurney acknowledged to me some years later: 'We were a bit naughty even attempting it in the first place,' he allowed. 'We'd got the minimum of backing in every area. I think Weslake can be proud of their part in the organization, even though I think they would concede that their end of the operation was a little shy, even though they were working miracles.'

The first Weslake V12 cost $280,000, and each subsequent replica was hand fettled: 'We built about six and a half of the things!' It was a difficult time for Dan. Trying to deal with a failing marriage, an Indy schedule, and rattling back and forth like a transatlantic shuttlecock in an attempt to keep the F1 programme alive was too much to cope with. The striking, shark-nosed Eagle became an extinct Formula 1 species early in 1968, with Dan's enthusiasm for the Formula 1 game certainly further muted by Jim Clark's death at Hockenheim.

Dan would seek restoration on the F1 circuit as late as 1970, coming in to drive a few European Grands Prix for the McLaren team in the wake of Bruce McLaren's sad death. He wasn't in shape, and he knew it. He returned to the US, and to retirement from the cockpit.

However, all was by no means bleakness and despair. USAC racing in general, and Indianapolis in particular, would become a happy hunting ground for Dan the Man's Eagles, even though his own maiden outing at the Speedway in 1966 with one of his own cars was less than fulfilling. A multiple shunt on the startline wrecked Gurney's car, prompting his exasperated observation: 'Why thirty of the world's top racing drivers find it impossible to drive down a straight piece of track without running into each other sure beats the hell out of me ...'

Roger McCluskey would score the Eagle marque's first Indy car victory at Langhorne in August 1966, while a fruitful relationship with Bobby Unser paid off in 1968 when Dan's car won the Indy 500 for the first time. Eagles would also win the Memorial Day classic in 1973 (Gordon Johncock) and 1975 (Bobby Unser again). The last Eagle Indy car victory would be the late Mike Mosley's success in the 1981 Milwaukee 150.

By 1983 the Eagles had vanished from the Indy car scene, but Dan Gurney's All-American Racers were still in business. He concluded a deal to initiate Toyota's IMSA racing programme and this commitment has steadily expanded through to the present day, ensuring that Dan's genial countenance continues to be seen in pit lanes all over his home country.

22

Robin Herd

ROBIN HERD, MAX Mosley, Graham Coaker, and Alan Rees all invested £2,500 in establishing March Engineering at the end of 1969. Of the four, only Robin stayed in for the long haul, and when March Group plc was finally floated on the Unlisted Securities Market of the London Stock Exchange in 1987, that £2,500 translated into a healthy six-figure sum. Yet while Robin entered the 1990s as an extremely wealthy man, he would be the first to admit that he has still not achieved the Grand Prix design success that his meteoric early career had promised.

In 1970, when March first got off the ground, Robin was as highly qualified a race car designer as any of his contemporaries. Yet in the decade that followed he never quite rang the Formula 1 design bell, partly because he always had the company's commercial considerations in the back of his mind. Not for him the clean sheet that would later be handed to such talents as Patrick Head and John Barnard. Throughout Robin's Formula 1 career, the spectre of March Engineering's overdraft weighed heavily on his mind. Under the circumstances, he did remarkably well and proved extremely resilient.

As I write these words, Robin has just turned 52, yet looks about twenty years younger. He grew up near Ross-on-Wye and was educated at Monmouth School, where much of his time seems to have been frittered away sitting at the back of divinity classes reading *Motor Sport* magazine behind a half-opened desk lid in company with fellow pupil Alan Rees. No question about it, they were both mad keen on racing cars, so how Robin had time to graduate from St Peter's College, Oxford, with a double first in Physics and Engineering—scoring the second highest marks of all time—remains something of a mystery.

In fact, Robin was one of those natural academics to whom it all came easily. One of his contemporaries has described him as 'fundamentally lazy . . . Because he was so naturally talented, he just didn't have to try.' In reality, such an assessment short-changes Robin considerably. Yet, despite his early achievements, I think he would accept that he has become something of a hedonist in latter years. But at least he is a man who enjoys being wealthy and, in spending much of his money on his own club rallying programme, is merely doing what he would have loved to have done thirty years ago but couldn't afford.

In 1961 he joined the Royal Aircraft Establishment at Farnborough and progressed to the status of Senior Scientific Officer at the early age of 24, working at the National Gas Turbine Establishment. He had worked on some detail design aspects of the Concorde supersonic airliner before a career beckoned on the design staff of Bruce McLaren's fledgling company based at Feltham, Middlesex.

McLaren at this time was also involved as a member of the Ford endurance racing team that was seeking to storm Le Mans, that bastion of Ferrari domination, and Bruce had clearly become impressed with the aerodynamic qualities of the early GT40. With Herd able to draw on his aerodynamic experience, the team made considerable progress with aerofoil development.

Although Ferrari and Brabham are credited as the first teams to race with an aerofoil in 1968, the fact remains that McLaren's monocoque M2 test car, which ran during 1965 in preparation for the new 3-litre Formula 1, actually experimented with a large rear aerofoil that proved extremely effective. However, almost reluctant to believe the evidence of his own experiments, Robin shelved the concept with a view to employing it in 1966 when the team intended to use the Indy Ford V8 engine, reduced to 3 litres. When the moment arrived, this engine proved so spectacularly unreliable that the last thing anybody thought about was complicating the project with new-fangled aerodynamic developments.

Robin was a brave lad. In 1967 he not only rode round Goodwood with Bruce in the Can-Am McLaren M6A to monitor pressure readings on the inner and outer surfaces of the car, he also lay spreadeagled over the rear bodywork, watching the behaviour of the rear suspension through an aperture cut in the engine cover. Like something from a Marx Brothers comedy script, during the test one of his legs became tangled up with Bruce's left arm and the McLaren spun up the road in a cloud of tyre smoke, its precariously positioned passenger not really knowing whether to laugh or cry at his predicament.

McLaren and Herd got on well and Bruce had the feeling that they had the makings of a serious long-term relationship together. He was therefore understandably disappointed when Robin abruptly quit the team towards the end of 1967, accepting an invitation to join Cosworth Engineering to work on an ambitious project for a four-wheel-drive Formula 1 car. Robin now concedes that this was rather superficial thinking because the onset of the aerofoil era negated any theoretical advantage offered by four-wheel drive, and the Cosworth car never raced.

Robin was invited to stay on with the famous Northampton-based engine builders to concentrate on DFV development, but it wasn't a prospect that appealed. He wanted to design Grand Prix cars and began talking to Jochen Rindt about the possibility of designing a car specifically for the tempestuous Austrian driver, to be fielded by a team organized and set up by Jochen's manager, Bernie Ecclestone.

At the same time Mosley and Rees were attempting to get March off the ground, tempting Jochen with offers of a drive. For a short time Robin wasn't quite certain which way to jump, but he eventually threw in his lot with Max and Alan. March Engineering was on the road—and Herd was in the design hot seat.

Robin's first March Formula 1 design, the 701, was very much built down to a price rather than up to a specification. It wasn't a bad car, certainly not as bad as legend suggests, but it was not technically sophisticated by the standards of the radical Lotus 72, against which it was pitched throughout 1970. For 1971, still inhibited by budgetary constraints, Robin came up with the semi-streamlined 711, clothed in sleek Frank Costin-designed bodywork. It was much, much better, and perhaps if Ronnie Peterson had been more experienced it might have won a Grand Prix. As it was, the Swede finished second in the Championship behind Jackie Stewart.

The 1970s rolled past in a blur of successes in the junior formulae, March products reeling off a string of Championship victories in Formula 2, Formula 3, and Formula Atlantic. But Formula 1 success continued to elude them and, from 1973 onwards, financial necessity decreed that the March Grand Prix programmes should pay for themselves. March production car sales were not putting sufficient financial meat on the bone to sustain a programme of unrestricted Formula 1 development, and Robin's reputation suffered accordingly.

With March Formula 1 efforts petering out at the end of 1977, Robin concentrated his design work on other categories before making a disastrous return to the Formula 1 stage in 1981, producing a very poor copy of the Williams FW07 for use by John MacDonald's RAM racing organization. But at the same time as this débâcle, March received dramatically renewed impetus with a switch to Indy car racing in 1981, ironically using a modified, stiffened-up version of the RAM 811.

Once more, Robin's star was in the ascendancy as March introduced contemporary Formula 1 aerodynamic technology to the Indy car scene. Although by now he was far removed from day-to-day work at a drawing board, he would continue to be perceived as March's boss man, to whom both accolades and complaints would be directed as the firm's Indy cars took American oval racing by the throat in the mid-1980s.

On the one hand, his firm's successes produced a Duke of Edinburgh Design Award, plus a trophy from the Worshipful Company of Coachbuilders. On the other, he would be pilloried by customers dissatisfied over supply delays from Bicester, particularly when the company's Indy star began to fade in 1987 and the product was proving more fragile than ever. 'Mr Ninety Per Cent' and 'The Snake Oil Salesman' were but two of the sobriquets bestowed on him by frustrated March Indy car customers.

In 1987, the March name was back in Formula 1 thanks to a tie-up with Leyton House, the operating front for Japanese property tycoon Akira Akagi. It was a partnership that initially flourished, yet wilted towards the end of 1988 as the relationship between Akagi and Herd hit troubled times. It was dissolved at the start of 1989, both parties going their own ways.

Yet Robin seemed to remain untouched by the controversy and frustration. It would be too easy to say that financial security insulated him from too much stress; his relaxed and contented demeanour had never wavered over the twenty years of March's existence, even when bankruptcy stared them in the face.

At the end of 1989, at the age of 50, but looking little more than 30, he married for the second time. He and his new wife Diane enjoyed rallying together and life seemed pleasantly relaxed. He called me from his car 'phone shortly before March struck out into pastures new, acquiring a firm of stockbrokers in Southern England. 'We're expanding into the financial services business,' he said enthusiastically. I replied that I'd always been under the impression that March had been in the financial services business since day one.

I'm happy to say his sense of humour had not deserted him!

Right *J.C. Agajanian, debonair and extrovert, photographed at Indianapolis in 1971.*

Below *'Ol Calhoun' – the Agajanian Willard Battery Special – in the hands of Rufus Parnelli Jones, en route to victory in the 1963 Indy 500.*

Bottom *Former FISA President Jean-Marie Balestre (right) in eyeball-to-eyeball contact with his early 1980s sparring partner Bernie Ecclestone.*

Far left When this photograph of a youthful Alain Prost receiving his Volant Elf award from Ken Tyrrell was taken in 1975, Balestre (centre) had yet to become elected to the FISA Presidency. His most colourful years were still ahead . . .

Left John Barnard, possibly the most far-sighted F1 designer of the post-Chapman generation.

Right Eric Broadley's design experience stretches back to the mid-1950s when he built his own sports cars for the 750 Motor Club's 1172 formula.

Below left Jack Brabham shares a joke with his old confederate Ron Tauranac.

Below Broadley (centre) in company with John Wyer (left) and Ford's Roy Lunn and an early Ford GT40. Broadley played a key role in the development of this machine.

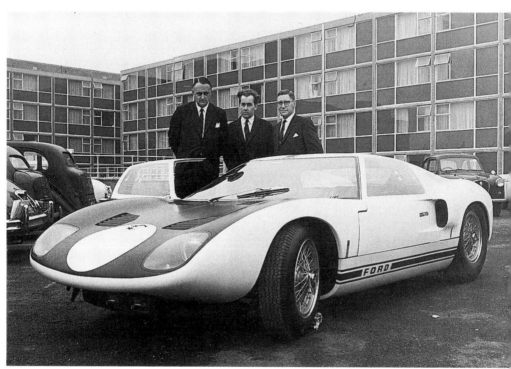

Top *Impeccably dressed as always, Aston Martin boss David Brown shares a winner's garland with Stirling Moss while Carroll Shelby (left) examines the silverware. Immediately behind Brown is Roy Salvadori.*

Above *The greatest moment in the David Brown Aston Martin era was the DBR1's victory at Le Mans, 1959, in the hands of Roy Salvadori (above) and Carroll Shelby.*

Left *Ettore Bugatti was a patriarchal figure for whom automotive engineering excellence represented an essentially artistic commitment.*

*__Right__ Dynamic, motivated, a leader of men
. . . all these soubriquets have been applied
to Lotus founder Colin Chapman, known to
his staff as the 'white tornado' in his latter
years.*

*__Right__ Ferraris supplied by Luigi Chinetti
helped a host of American racing drivers to
make the big time, yet relations were always
distant between Enzo Ferrari and his
brilliantly successful US distributor.*

*__Below__ Chapman employed many great
drivers in his time. He is seen here with the
late Ronnie Peterson who drove for Lotus
from 1973–76 and, tragically, in 1978 when
he died as a result of injuries sustained in a
startline accident during the Italian Grand
Prix.*

Left and below John Cooper (left) in reflective mood and (below) with a grimy Bruce McLaren in 1962.

Bottom Briggs Cunningham, then a spritely 69, at the wheel of the Le Mans Cunningham C4-R roadster gives the author a whirl round the huge car park of his motor museum in Costa Mesa, California, in October, 1975.

Right Mr McLaren – Ron Dennis.

Below Ron Dennis (holding lap chart board) at Mantorp Park, Sweden, during the summer of 1971, sitting alongside his Rondel Racing team driver Tim Schenken. Ron's then-partner Neil Trundle (yawning, far right) still works with him at McLaren International.

Bottom In the foyer at McLaren International's Woking headquarters.

Above *Bernie had few favourites amongst the drivers, but one of them was the late Carlos Pace, seen here heading one of the Ecclestone Brabham BT44Bs towards victory in the 1975 Brazilian Grand Prix at Interlagos.*

Left *Enzo Ferrari: the last of the old guard from motor racing's heroic pioneering era. Photographed holding forth at his Maranello fortress, September, 1986.*

Far left Bernie Ecclestone (right) in company with longtime Brabham chief designer Gordon Murray. The two men forged a partnership lasting almost seventeen years.

Left The smile of success: Cosworth DFV architect Keith Duckworth outside the Cosworth headquarters in Northampton.

Above right Emerson Fittipaldi, driver and constructor; World Champion 1972 and 1974, Indy 500 winner, 1989.

Right Emerson struggles round Monaco in 1980 at the wheel of the Fittipaldi F7. He would retire from the cockpit at the end of the season, but the team was locked into a downward performance spiral and went out of business just over two years later.

Below Ferrari designer Mauro Forghieri in conversation with team driver Patrick Tambay at the 1982 French Grand Prix.

Top left and right NASCAR's giant of a founder, Bill France Senior. And standing proudly by the start of the famous Measured Mile on Daytona Beach, scene of NASCAR's stock car events prior to the construction of the famous tri-oval banked permanent circuit.

Above Amédée Gordini (right) in conversation with Jean Behra, the gallant French driver who did so much for the French team's efforts in the early 1950s.

Left Andy Granatelli, still attending the Indy 500 in 1989.

Top left and right *Perpetually youthful, Dan Gurney's commitment and enthusiasm for motor racing has been unstinting for over thirty years.*

Above *Halcyon days: Dan's Brabham-Climax rounds La Source hairpin during the 1964 Belgian Grand Prix, a race he dominated until the legendary 'Gurney Luck' intervened and he ran out of fuel on the final lap.*

Right *Robin Herd (far left) sits on the right front wheel of the first March 701 shortly after the birth of the new racing car constructor in 1970. Alan Rees and Graham Coaker are towards the rear of the car while co-director Max Mosley (left front wheel) also features in this volume!*

Left Gift of the gab: Eddie Jordan made quite an impact with his F1 team during its maiden season in 1991.

Right Ligier with his early 1981 driving team, brothers-in-law Jacques Laffite (left) and Jean-Pierre Jabouille.

Below Gerard Larrousse (second from left) flanked with 1989 team drivers Philippe Alliot and Yannick Dalmas, plus former co-director Didier Calmels.

Left Still smiling at the world: Guy Ligier at the 1990 San Marino Grand Prix.

Right Brian Lister heads a family company renowned for its engineering ingenuity and versatility. He is seen here at the centenary celebrations, on 1 June 1990, flanked by the 1958 ex Briggs Cunningham car (present owner Andrew Barber) and one of the centenary edition Lister-Jaguars, identical to the 1958 version and built by the same craftsmen in the works.

Far right Sir William Lyons was one of the most formal and reserved of motor industry moguls. Yet that didn't prevent him from establishing Jaguar as one of the most thrusting British companies of the immediate pre- and post-war eras.

Above Alfieri Maserati (in car) was the driving force behind the Maserati brothers. His death in 1932, at the early age of 44, was a disaster for the company.

Left Raymond Mays (left) in company with Peter Berthon, fellow architect of the BRM project.

Below Mays photographed at Bourne in 1971 with the front-engined V16 (right) and the then-contemporary, Yardley-sponsored P160 V12 which would win the Austrian and Italian Grands Prix later that same season.

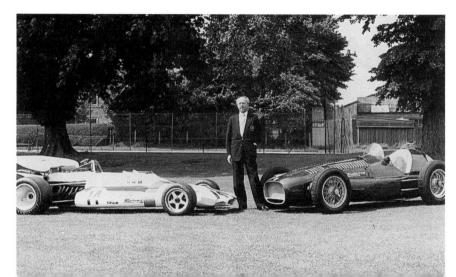

Right Bruce McLaren amidst his tranquil home surroundings.

Below Bruce heads his own Cosworth-engined M7A towards the McLaren marque's first Grand Prix victory at Spa Francorchamps in 1968.

Bottom Goodyear racing boss Leo Mehl (right) in conversation with McLaren team chief Ron Dennis.

Left *Max Mosley (left), new FISA President, in deep discussion with Donington Park owner Tom Wheatcroft.*

Right *BRM family snap: Centre, with spectacles, to the left of John Surtees, is Sir Alfred Owen, then his sister Jean Stanley, team manager Tim Parnell and Louis Stanley (in double breasted blazer).*

Below *Alfred Neubauer embraces Stirling Moss (right) and the bearded Denis Jenkinson after Mercedes-Benz's magnificent victory on the 1955 Mille Miglia.*

Left *Still trying to win a Grand Prix: Jack Oliver was unsuccessful behind the wheel, but is still aiming high as a boss of the Footwork team.*

Above right *BRM's zenith: Graham Hill at the wheel of the sleek BRM P261 during the 1964 Aintree 200 race.*

Right *A pensive Reg Parnell tries his hand at the wheel of the original BRM V16.*

Above A beaming Parnell shares the spoils of victory at Snetterton with Archie Scott-Brown (left).

Left Roger Penske issuing directions in the Indianapolis pit lane, 1989.

Below Penske with Bobby Allison and the American Motors Matador fielded for him by Roger's team in 1975.

Top *Ferry Porsche: carrying the torch lit by his father, he presided over the family company's fortunes over almost four decades of outstanding achievement.*

Above *Woolworth heir Lance Reventlow briefly tried his hand in this F2 Cooper-Climax after his Scarab Formula 1 project foundered mid-way through the 1960 Grand Prix season.*

Right *Carroll Shelby almost drifted into top line international motor racing by accident, but developed into an accomplished performer on the international sports car scene during the mid-1950s.*

Left John Surtees (right) shares a quiet moment with Mike Hailwood during the 1972 F1 season. Although men of widely differing temperaments, their motorcycle racing backgrounds forged a strong bond between them.

Right Six wheels: Ken stands with Tyrrell P34 designer Derek Gardner while Patrick Depailler tries the team's revolutionary 1976 contender for size.

Above Ron Tauranc (right) with fellow brylcreemed Brabham team co-director Phil Kerr (centre) and a sceptical looking Dan Gurney at the 1965 British Grand Prix.

Left Two wheels: Ken Tyrrell takes a break in the Monaco pit lane, 1974.

Above Tony Vandervell beams contentedly
after greeting a grimy Tony Brooks following
the latter's 1958 German Grand Prix victory
at the wheel of a Vanwall.

Right Rob Walker: gentleman racer.

Top *That great day for Walker as Jo Siffert wins the 1963 British Grand Prix at Brands Hatch.*

Above left and right *Fourteen years separate these two shots of Tom Walkinshaw, encapsulating the transition from fresh-faced race winner to seasoned team boss.*

Left *Peter Warr devoted much of his professional career to Team Lotus, keeping it afloat after the death of Colin Chapman in 1982.*

Top *Frank Williams in charge of team operations at Long Beach, 1981.*

Above *More restricted in mobility, but no less enthusiastic, Frank poses with (from left), Bernard Dudot, Patrick Head and Bernard Casin at the unveiling of the Renault V10 engine used by the team from the start of 1989.*

Right *Walter Wolf was the last of the F1 team owners who bankrolled their operation with virtually no outside funds.*

Left Sweet moment to savour: Jody Scheckter heads for victory in the 1977 Monaco Grand Prix at the wheel of Wolf WR1.

Below John Wyer watches (left), while the great little driver Pedro Rodriguez awaits the return of his JW Gulf Porsche during the 1970 Brands Hatch 1000kms.

Bottom John Wyer presided with autocratic thoroughness over the JW/Gulf Porsche 917s in 1971, and formidable weapons they certainly were. Here Derek Bell dives inside Vic Elford at Paddock Bend, Brands Hatch, during the 1970 1000kms race with Rodriguez, headlights also ablaze, coming up the rise in the background.

23

Eddie Jordan

EDDIE JORDAN TOOK the plunge into Grand Prix racing at the start of the 1991 season with an audacity calculated to amaze even those who had been impressed with his mastery of the junior single-seater formulae. On several occasions during the previous decade, this cheery Dubliner had promised to make the graduation into the sport's most senior category, but many regarded his promises as another dose of his endearing blarney. Yet when he finally made the switch, he did so with what seemed like perfect timing—and with a level of success that took the breath away.

A banker by profession, Eddie's interest in motor sport was sparked by the rallying activities of his uncle, Noel Smith, who drove a Mini-Cooper S to great effect in Irish national events during the mid-1960s. Eddie acquired a 125-cc kart and began to demonstrate his skills at Ireland's Mondello Park track before moving up the steps of the ladder into Formula Ford, then Formula 3 and Formula Atlantic. Then, just as he seemed on the threshold of a professional racing career, Jordan took the bold decision to retire from the cockpit to concentrate on operating his own Formula 3 team, as well as managing the careers of many of those young drivers who drove for him.

In 1983, Martin Brundle drove an Eddie Jordan Ralt to a close second place behind Ayrton Senna in the British Formula 3 Championship. The following year, Brundle moved up into Formula 1 with Tyrrell, leaving Jordan behind. 'It would be great if Martin could wait until 1985 and then come up into F1 with me,' said Eddie longingly, 'but I realise this is not realistic as far as his career is concerned.'

However, as things transpired, it would be another six years before Eddie finally made the move into Formula 1, during which time Brundle's career enjoyed only intermittent success. In the meantime, Jordan's team expanded from being a small Formula 3 operation to one of the fastest developing and most successful private teams operating outside the Grand Prix business.

Jordan was quick to appreciate the possibilities offered by Formula 3000 when the category was introduced to succeed Formula 2 in 1985. Eddie viewed it not only from the standpoint of its pure worth as a racing category, but also as a training ground for drivers signed up with his management company. Belgian Thierry Tassin actually drove EJR's first March F3000 car that season, but it would be another three seasons before consistent success came his way in this category.

In 1987, rising star Johnny Herbert was signed up as Eddie's prime runner in the British Formula 3 Championship, a title he successfully garnered at the wheel of the team's Reynard. The following season, Herbert made the graduation into F3000 along with Ulsterman Martin Donnelly and the team's prospects began to look excellent. Jordan had managed to negotiate Herbert a test drive with Lotus at Monza, during which the young Englishman lapped the unloved Honda turbo-engined type 100T faster than regular driver Nelson Piquet.

More tests were in the pipeline for Jordan's latest protégé, but a few days after that Monza outing Herbert broke both his legs in a major Formula 3000 accident at Brands Hatch. It was a bad setback to Herbert's career, but he would eventually get his Formula 1 break the following year as a member, albeit temporarily, of the Benetton Formula team.

In 1989, Jordan's two key recruits were Donnelly and rising French star Jean Alesi, the young Frenchman winning the International Formula 3000 Championship in one of Eddie's Reynards. Jordan's management company was also shrewdly steering the young French driver's career and, with the help of a mutual cigarette sponsor, helped place Jean with the Tyrrell team mid-season after Italian driver Michele Alboreto left Ken's set-up. Jordan had set up his driver management company in the mid-1980s, effectively investing confidence in a succession of young drivers in exchange for their entering into management agreements with his company for a fixed period of time. It is rumoured that when Alesi signed for Ferrari, Jordan's percentage of the fee was around £600,000.

As was always the case with Tyrrell, Alesi was ostensibly locked into a three-season deal, Ken rightly reasoning that if a young driver was to be given his Formula 1 break at the wheel of one of his cars, then it was only appropriate that he should reap the long-term benefits of his accumulating experience.

In the event, although Alesi stayed through the 1990 season, he was inundated with offers for 1991 that he found difficult to ignore. Jordan had to tread a delicate path through a diplomatic minefield, steering the headstrong Alesi as best he could. In the event, Jean was determined to leave Tyrrell, either for Williams or Ferrari. He finally opted for the latter and a release from his obligation to Tyrrell was duly negotiated. Honour and business expediency were settled all round. Jordan's management company took its percentage of Alesi's reputed $6 million Ferrari fee for 1991, but Eddie emerged from the negotiations a wiser man and more seasoned to the ways of Formula 1.

It was just as well. After spending several years apparently poised to take the plunge, Jordan committed himself to his own Grand Prix operation, aiming for the start of the 1991 World Championship season. He talked long and hard with Ford about the possibility of using their lightweight, Cosworth-made type HB V8. Eventually, Eddie's gift of the gab, which sometimes tends to lay a genial veneer over his fundamental, rock-hard business sense, proved highly fruitful. He convinced Ford that he had finalized sufficient sponsorship to bankroll the £4 million fee required to support the engine programme. Indeed, Ford was not alone on this. Eddie was also convinced he had a firm commitment from a major US sponsor only to find that they were to change their plans at the last minute.

Potentially, this was a nightmare scenario. With budgets committed and manufacture of the first chassis in an advanced state, Jordan found himself 'door-stepping' the recalcitrant sponsor with an energetic indignation that very nearly got him arrested. Amazingly, Jordan not only scraped together the necessary sponsorship, but introduced such high profile investors as 7-Up, the soft drinks brand, and Fuji Film on to the Formula 1 stage.

The new Jordan-Ford was designed by a mild-mannered Ulsterman named Gary Anderson. A one-time McLaren Formula 1 mechanic, he had designed and built his own Anson Formula 3 during the early 1980s before joining Jordan's operation. Now he was being given the opportunity of a lifetime to build a state-of-the-art Grand Prix chassis. Having spent months examining and analysing the opposition, he was confident he could do a worthwhile job and was not even slightly nonplussed about the challenge. Jordan had total confidence in Anderson, even though the whole success or failure of the new Grand Prix team was largely dependent on his efforts.

As things turned out, operating with a staff of barely fifty people against more seasoned organizations with three times the workforce, Jordan Grand Prix proved the most outstanding newcomers to have arrived on the Formula 1 scene for several years. The car was straightforward, uncomplicated, and, by and large, extremely reliable. By the middle of the season Jordan had scored a healthy tally of Championship points and successfully shrugged off the burden of pre-qualifying which every unproved team has to surmount.

Drivers Andrea de Cesaris and Bertrand Gachot had acquitted themselves respectably on the track, although Gachot's behaviour off it had been distinctly less helpful to the team's cause. On his way to a 7-Up presentation in December 1990, Bertrand's over-confident style ended up undermining his entire professional career when he was involved in a minor traffic incident with a London taxi at Hyde Park Corner. In the ensuing exchange, Gachot sprayed CS anti-personnel gas in the taxi driver's face; the result was an 18-month prison sentence.

It was a personal tragedy for Gachot as well as a PR problem that Jordan could well have done without. Such a drama could have had very serious long-term consequences for the team, but such was the degree of competitive momentum built up by Jordan Grand Prix at that stage of the year that it only registered as a slight blip in terms of aggravation.

The real challenge, as Jordan freely admitted, would be the 1992 programme, when the level of expectation focused on the team would be even higher. By keeping his feet firmly planted on the ground, Ireland's first Formula 1 team boss is determined that over-confidence will not be part of the Jordan Grand Prix repertoire during that crucial second season when they enter the first year of a four-season deal to run the works Yamaha V12 engines in their cars.

24

Gerard Larrousse

IN THE EUPHORIA surrounding the emergence of potential Formula 1 stars such as Jean-Pierre Beltoise, François Cevert, and Johnny Servoz-Gavin, the French motor racing fraternity was probably guilty of underestimating the talents of Gerard Larrousse, who developed into one of the country's most versatile and accomplished long-distance drivers. Not only did he share the winning Matra at Le Mans on two occasions, he was also responsible for masterminding the Renault team's sole success at the Sarthe in 1977 before embarking on a career in Formula 1 management that saw him establish his own Grand Prix team at the start of the 1987 season.

Larrousse was born in Lyon on 23 May 1940 and first became attracted to motorsport by an interest in rallying. He took up this pastime in 1966 and his success at the wheel of an Alpine-Renault in 1968 led to an invitation to drive for the Porsche factory team the following year, during which he won the Tour de France and the Tour de Corse as well as finishing second in the Monte Carlo Rally—a feat he repeated in 1970.

His first outing at Le Mans took place in 1969 when he shared a Porsche 908 with veteran German driver Hans Herrmann. They finished second a matter of feet behind the JW/Gulf Ford GT40 shared by Jacky Ickx and Jack Oliver, although it was Herrmann who drove the last stint, leaving Gerard to watch from the pit counter as the far superior Ickx out-manoeuvred him brilliantly in a wheel-to-wheel battle over the final handful of laps. That season also saw him finish fifth in the Austrian 1,000 km at the newly opened Osterreichring, sharing a Porsche 908 with Rudi Lins, sixth in the BOAC 1,000 km race at Brands Hatch (with Gerhard Koch), and fifth in the Nurburgring 1,000 km (with Helmut Marko).

The following year Herrmann would return to win, sharing a Porsche Salzburg 917 with Richard Attwood, but Gerard was second again in a similar car co-driven by Willi Kauhsen. In 1971, at the wheel of a Porsche Salzburg 917, he failed to finish at Le Mans but won at Sebring and Nurburgring in the Martini & Rossi sponsored 917s to round off his competition association with the Stuttgart company. In 1972, he joined the Ford team, racing the classic Cologne Capris in the European Touring Car Championship, but his career really began to blossom the following year when Matra signed him up for a full programme of endurance races.

In 1972 Matra had cut back its sports car racing involvement to encompass only the Le Mans 24-hour classic, a race they felt it was imperative to win above all others. This decision allowed Ferrari total domination of the World Championship for Makes with their flat-12 312PBs; and, since Maranello ducked Le Mans, the two marques never squared up to each other. But once Graham Hill and Henri Pescarolo successfully bagged Matra's first Le Mans victory, the programme was expanded for 1973 and Larrousse was recruited to the line-up.

Gerard was regularly paired with Henri Pescarolo and this new partnership opened its run of success by taking its Matra MS670 to victory in the Dijon 1,000 km before a worrying spate of con-rod breakages threatened to jeopardize the French team's position of superiority over the Ferrari PBs. Thankfully for its management, Matra got things back on an even keel and Pescarolo/Larrousse emerged triumphant at Le Mans, although only after a broken exhaust pipe caused the leading Ferrari of Jacky Ickx/Brian Redman to drop back on Sunday morning.

Larrousse also won the Osterreichring and Watkins Glen races to set the seal on the World Championship, after which Ferrari dropped out of endurance racing to concentrate on revitalizing its Formula 1 programme, leaving Matra free to clean up again in 1974, at the end of which Gerard retired from the cockpit.

Larrousse now turned his attentions to team management as competitions director of Renault Sport, a task which had its long-term objectives firmly fixed on Formula 1. Once Didier Pironi and Jean-Pierre Jabouille had successfully scored their Le Mans victory two years later, the decks were cleared to tackle Grand Prix racing with the first $1\frac{1}{2}$-litre turbocharged engine to make its bow on the Formula 1 stage. It was a difficult and demanding time for all those at the sharp end of the business, for this was no private racing team but a major state-owned organization hungry for success.

Larrousse found his political skills stretched to breaking point on many occasions during 1977–8 as the first Renault Formula 1 turbos continually puffed their way into retirement with worrying regularity and the board of directors wanted to know why on earth this was happening. Gerard, who often projected a rather aloof and austere personal image, found himself patiently explaining, time and again, that success in Formula 1 was not simply a challenge that responded purely to monetary investment and that Renault was pursuing a technical route never before tackled by any constructor.

Eventually, Jean-Pierre Jabouille—one of Gerard's old team-mates from the Matra sports car days—scored Renault's first points in the 1978 United States GP and backed that up the following summer with a brilliant victory in the French Grand Prix at Dijon. The investment was beginning to pay off.

Jabouille won again in Austria the following year, and when Larrousse signed promising youngster Alain Prost at the start of 1981, the results really began to flow. But the Renault management's expectations had increased dramatically and now they wanted a World Championship victory to justify all these years of investment. And in 1983, it seemed as though Larrousse and Renault might just be able to deliver.

However, there were problems developing. Prost felt that the Renault management were not responding to his requests for an acceleration of the engine development programme to combat the increasing competitiveness of the Brabham-BMW driven by Nelson Piquet. Gradually, Renault's mid-season points advantage was whittled away and Prost went into the last race of the year only two points ahead.

'I believe Renault deserves to win the World Championship,' stated Larrousse unequivocally on the eve of the team's departure for Kyalami. Whether through Larrousse's ever-optimistic assessment of the situation, or simply an over-anxious willingness to believe that Renault could get the job done, the French car company ferried dozens of journalists to South Africa to witness what was billed as the Championship clincher. Success advertisements had been booked in most national papers for the following Monday.

Renault failed. Prost retired and Piquet did just enough to take the Championship for Brabham-BMW with a third place finish. BMW even offered to take some of the success advertising space booked by Renault. For Larrousse, it represented a bitter failure, made all the more hard to stomach by the fact that his personal relations with Prost had become totally untenable.

Less than a fortnight after the Kyalami defeat, Prost was turned out on the street. It was a catastrophic misjudgement by the Renault management and, in retrospect, was the beginning of the end for Larrousse's spell at Renault. Prost moved off to McLaren and began a sensational winning streak. Renault would win no more Grands Prix prior to their withdrawal at the end of 1985 and at the end of 1984 Larrousse quit and moved to the rival Ligier team as competitions manager.

Long term, what Gerard wanted to do was to establish his own Formula 1 operation, something he eventually achieved in partnership with businessman Didier Calmels for the start of the 1987 season, using Lola-built chassis with Cosworth V8 engines. It was initially a single-car team for Philippe Alliot, expanded to include Yannick Dalmas later that year. For the 1989 season the team took the ambitious step of switching to Lamborghini engines, but there were problems in the pipeline as Calmels was soon to be arrested and jailed as the result of a shooting incident in which his wife died.

As a result, Gerard was left running the company alone by the start of 1990, forging a new partnership with the Japanese Espo corporation. This lasted only a year before economic problems caused Espo to withdraw and the Larrousse team was forced to its knees when FISA decreed that its points accruing for sixth place in the 1990 Constructors' World Championship were forfeit, accusing him of entering the cars under the Larrousse banner when in fact they were Lolas.

The immediate consequence of this was to threaten the team with pre-qualifying, but a good old Gallic compromise was thrashed out and Larrousse kept running into 1991, using outdated Brian Hart Cosworth DFR engines, but nevertheless occasionally scoring a Championship point to keep pre-qualifying at bay.

25

Guy Ligier

ROBUST, RUMBUSTIOUS, CANTANKEROUS ... all are adjectives that aptly apply to Guy Ligier, a man with an unquenchable enthusiasm for life in general and motor racing in particular, and an amateur racing driver of some distinction before starting his own team. Born on 12 July 1930, this Frenchman's thick set frame testifies to his youthful record as an accomplished international rugby player. His fearsome, table-thumping temper has become familiar around the world's Grand Prix paddocks, but it readily gives way to a mischievious smile, for Ligier loves winding up friend and foe alike. Motor racing Ligier-style has always proved a delightful, idiosyncratic family affair.

A native of Vichy, the provincial French town where his team was based for many years, his enthusiasm for all sports was fired from his school days. From the age of 17 he participated in his country's national rowing championship before switching to rugby, playing as hooker for the Racing Club of Vichy and, later for the French Military team. In 1957, whilst still deeply involved with rugby, he took up motorcycle racing with a 350 AJS and 500 Norton and would eventually win the French 500 cc championship in 1959 and 1960.

In the early 1960s Guy had built up his own civil engineering company that benefited from a lot of public contracts, notably in the area of motorway construction. However, when a change of policy saw Ligier Travaux Public deprived of some prestige contracts on purely political grounds, Guy was outraged. Although by nature a right-winger, he threw as much help and assistance in the direction of a young, ambitious left-wing deputy who was just starting his career in the Magny-Cours/Vichy region. The man's name was François Mitterand; he and Guy became firm friends and that early support would pay off discreetly many years later.

In 1960 he purchased an Elva-DKW Formula Junior car, but was so depressed with its lack of reliability that he promptly retired from racing, not reappearing again until 1963. Then he returned at the wheel of a Porsche Carrera, followed by a 904/4 which he used to make his first visit to Le Mans the following year, finishing seventh with Robert Buchet. He was back the following year in a Ford France-entered GT40, partnering his veteran compatriot Maurice Trintignant, but they were posted as the fifth retirement, lasting little more than one hour before terminal gearbox problems intervened. He also drove a Ford France-sponsored AC Cobra and Formula 2 Brabham.

Having tried his hand briefly at Formula 2, Ligier decided he would make the big leap into Formula 1 at the start of the 3-litre Formula 1 in 1966. He purchased his own private Cooper-Maserati, which he conducted at a leisurely pace towards the back of the Grand Prix fields. No question about it, he was tardy by Formula 1 standards, but he certainly brought a few grins to the faces of his more experienced rivals.

The most embarrassing incident of all came at the 1966 Mexican Grand Prix when the Cooper stopped out on the circuit towards the end of practice. His senior mechanic had been taken ill, so Ligier accompanied him to hospital, leaving his junior mechanic, Jean Mosnier, to sort out the problem. Mosnier began to strip down the engine, convinced that it had seized, only for further examination on his boss's return to reveal it had merely run out of fuel!

Mosnier, who is now a leading Formula 3000 entrant, laughs about the incident today, but recalls that Ligier's mood was not improved at the time. He had no more luck at Le Mans, incidentally, where the GT40 he shared with Bob Grossman again failed to last the distance.

On a personal level, Guy struck up a close friendship with fellow Frenchman Jo Schlesser, the two men sharing a 7-litre Ford Mk2B at Le Mans in 1967. It briefly ran in the top half dozen, only to crash in the hours of darkness; but they had a more successful time together at Reims, winning the 12-hour sports car classic. His association with Ford had a worthwhile business benefit and Guy went into partnership with Schlesser, forming a company called Intersport to market Shelby performance equipment for high-performance Fords. The company operated from smart premises almost within the shadow of the Eiffel Tower, managed by Jose Behra, brother of France's great F1 star Jean Behra who had been killed at Avus in 1959.

In F1, he swapped the Cooper for an ex-works Brabham-Repco and actually managed to score a Championship point for sixth place in the German Grand Prix at the Nurburgring.

In 1968 Ligier began to lay plans to start his own sports car company, although his enthusiasm for motor racing was profoundly shaken when Schlesser was killed in a fiery accident driving the air-cooled Honda RA302 in the French Grand Prix at Rouen. When his first Cosworth-engined sports car appeared two years later it would be designated JS1 to perpetuate the memory of his close friend. All Ligier cars have carried this identification ever since.

The JS1 scored victories at Albi and Montlhery in his first season, but although Guy Chasseuil would manage a morale-boosting victory in the three-hour race staged as an adjunct to the Le Mans test weekend early in 1974, victory in the full 24-hour epic would elude the cars on their five visits to the Sarthe. In 1974 they switched to using 3-litre V8 Maserati engines as part of a deal to produce the commercially questionable Citroen SM sports car on a sub-contracting basis, and Chasseuil would share second place at Le Mans with Jean-Louis Lafosse in 1975, finishing only 14 miles behind the victorious Gulf of Jacky Ickx/Derek Bell.

When the prestigious Matra team withdrew from sports car racing at the end of 1974, having notched up a hat trick of Le Mans victories, their Gitanes sponsorship was now up for grabs. Thus in 1975, Ligier opted for a Grand Prix challenge that eventually made its début the following year, having successfully gained access to supplies of the raucous Matra V12 engines which had been absent from Formula 1 since 1972.

Jacques Laffite was signed to drive for the team, the happy-go-lucky Frenchman enjoying Ligier's congenial surroundings for six seasons, during which time he won a total of six Grands Prix. The team changed to Cosworth V8 power for 1979 and 1980, then switched back to Matra power in 1981 under an arrangement with Talbot that was originally intended to produce supplies of a Matra turbo V6 engine.

In 1983 the team struggled with Cosworth engines once more, failing to gain a single Championship point. But Ligier's old pal François Mitterand, who had been one of the witnesses at the wedding of Guy's daughter Pascale in 1982, helpfully gave the nod to Renault to supply its highly competitive turbo V6 engines to Guy for the next three seasons. The team began the slog back to competitive form, aided immeasurably by the return of Jacques Laffite for 1985. Sadly, Jacques's Formula 1 career ended when his Ligier-Renault became involved in a first corner pile-up in the 1986 British Grand Prix at Brands Hatch. Guy's most faithful campaigner broke both his legs in the smash and would never race a single seater again.

For 1987, Ligier turned to Alfa Romeo for the use of its brand new 4-cylinder turbo. However, a few ill-timed critical remarks from René Arnoux following a pre-season test session at Imola gave the Italian company a tailor-made escape route from the imminent embarrassment of having their name on a singularly uncompetitive engine. Claiming Arnoux's remarks constituted a fundamental contractual breach, they withdrew from the deal. Ligier sued, but meanwhile did a quick deal to install Megatron-BMW engines in the cars. A catastrophic season ensued.

Since then, Ligier has bumped along in the Formula 1 ruck, a midfield runner at best; but he always looks on the bright side and, at the start of 1989, moved his team into a brand new, purpose-built factory at the new Magny-Cours circuit. With convenient access to what amounts to their own personal test track, and a supply of Renault V10 engines arranged for 1992, Guy's team can at least be expected to perform well now that the French Grand Prix has moved to this venue.

26

Brian Lister

BRIAN LISTER'S ENTHUSIASM for motor racing was tempered by sound judgement and a shrewd business sense. Combining all three of these personal facets resulted in his family firm, based in the university city of Cambridge, conceiving, building, and racing some of the most exciting and competitive sports racing cars to appear on the British racing scene in the 1950s.

At the end of the decade, Lister withdrew from the sport, bruised and dejected by the tragic deaths of two of his works drivers within a year of each other, but his conscientious endeavours earned the Lister marque a highly respected niche in motor racing history.

The Lister family ran an engineering business which, during its time, manufactured everything from wrought iron gates to bridges to sports racing cars. The company had its roots in a partnership established by Brian's grandfather George way back in 1890, but in 1919 it became George Lister and Sons after his other partners gradually retired from the business and his two sons joined him. Brian was born in July 1926, the son of Horace Lister who took over sole control of the company after the early death of his brother Alfred and father George.

It was understandable, bearing in mind his background, that Brian Lister should serve an engineering apprenticeship, followed by two years in the RAF just as peace started to break out in Europe during the late 1940s. He was very much a child of his age, an enthusiastic jazz fan who played the drums and vibraphone with gusto, and to a respectable standard, with a number of bands in the Cambridge area during his spare time.

By 1948 he had turned his hand to motor racing at the wheel of a Morgan 4/4, later moving on to a home-brewed Cooper-MG which he extensively modified off his own bat. At around the turn of the 1950s, George Lister and Sons were approached by fellow fledgling sports car constructor John Tojeiro to fabricate some components for his forth-coming new cars. Brian Lister was intrigued, and began thinking privately along similar lines.

Lister and Tojeiro developed a special powered by a 1,100-cc JAP-engine—dubbed the 'Asteroid Tojeiro'—and a fearsomely precarious beast it proved to be. Brian Lister raced it during the first half of 1952, but openly conceded he 'had too much imagination' to make a decent driver, and stepped down. The man he invited to take over at the wheel was Archie Scott-Brown, a remarkable little man from Paisley, almost the same age as Brian Lister. Almost forty years later, the names of Scott-Brown and Lister remain synonymous with the best qualities of British motor racing during the 1950s.

Brian Lister realized that running cars made by other people was really a waste of time, given the resources available to the family company. He took a deep breath and proposed to his father than the firm's engineering capabilities could be promoted in a uniquely effective manner by building their own racing machine.

Predictably, Horace Lister reacted with extreme caution to his son's suggestion, but agreed to think it over long and hard. He gave the green light to the project, only on the understanding that the budget was limited to £1,500 and that Brian was allowed six months to prove the idea would work.

On 3 April 1954, Archie Scott-Brown drove the first prototype 1.46-litre Cooper-MG at the team's local circuit—Snetterton—and won two races. Horace Lister was convinced and the first seeds of a motor racing legend were sown.

Brian Lister had enormous faith in Scott-Brown, with whom he developed a close friendship, never ceasing to marvel at the little Scot's ability behind the wheel. Archie achieved miracles despite the fact that he had been born with a deformed right hand that was little more than a vestigial stump. Blindingly quick behind the wheel of a racing car, displaying tremendous acuity and balance, Scott-Brown was also imbued with considerable daring.

It was always Brian Lister's intention that they should sell replicas of their racing machines to private owners. Although the racing prototype had an MG engine, a 2-litre Bristol engine was soon fitted and Scott-Brown really put the marque on the map with a splendid televized victory in the unlimited sports car race that supported the 1954 British Grand Prix at Silverstone. From that moment onwards, Horace Lister was an absolute convert to the business of motor racing.

Although the Lister-Bristols were successful enough in 1955, and Brian would later dabble in the single-seater market with a Formula 2 project for 1957, it was the Jaguar-engined sports cars that really made the Cambridge company's name. They would take on and beat the mainstream Jaguar D-types in just about every British event of consequence and, although Lister's detractors shrugged them aside as precocious special builders, there was never any doubt about the engineering integrity which Brian Lister insisted was applied to the manufacture of all their cars.

Brian Lister was extremely safety orientated, not merely because he was a conscientious engineer in his own right, but because he never allowed himself to forget the fundamental rationale behind their involvement in motor racing as manufacturers. The bottom line was always that the Listers were out there racing to promote and enhance the good name of George Lister and Son, not merely to sell racing cars at as big a profit as possible. Lister left nothing to chance in this respect.

It was towards the end of 1956 that the idea of a Lister-Jaguar was prompted through an approach from North London diamond merchant Norman Hillwood, who had been racing and developing his own racing specials for several years. He approached the company to buy a Lister-Bristol chassis frame into which he would insert a C-type 3.4-litre engine.

Brian Lister admits to being a little dubious about the whole project, but almost before he knew it the team's fuel supplier, BP, were nudging him in a similar direction for the works team. BP's racing manager, Bryan Turle, was quick to point out that the Shell-contracted Jaguar works team had just withdrawn, leaving the British sports car scene apparently a personal playground for Aston Martin and Ecurie Ecosse—both of whom ran on Esso. Lister wasn't really convinced, but eventually went ahead. It was to be a brilliant decision.

Scott-Brown and the works Lister-Jaguar took the 1957 British sports car racing scene by storm, beating Aston Martin's DB3S and a host of private Jaguars almost wherever he went. Similar cars were sold into private hands, notably to US entrant Briggs Cunningham, and Archie was also dispatched on a successful winter tour to the Tasman races in New Zealand at the end of the year.

Scott-Brown's physical disabilities had resulted in his RAC competitions licence being suspended back in 1955. Although a successful lobby was mounted that saw its return after only a few weeks, continental race organizers were generally reluctant to accept his entry. But after racing successfully in New Zealand, Sweden, and North America, there were strong signs that European promoters were finally relenting when his works Lister-Jag was accepted for the sports car Grand Prix de Spa on 11 May 1958, the same day as the F1 Monaco Grand Prix.

Tragically, it was to be the great little man's last race, and the saddest day in Brian Lister's racing career. After a mesmeric battle with Masten Gregory's Ecurie Ecosse sister car, Scott-Brown crashed heavily approaching La Source and the works car burst into flames. The accident had taken place at precisely the same point on the track as that which claimed the great British driver Dick Seaman some twenty-nine years before. And, tragically, the outcome was the same.

Brian Lister had been so convinced that his friend was not going to die that he set off for home. But en route he heard the devastating news on the radio that Scott-Brown had succumbed to his injuries. It was a monumental body blow, and Brian Lister confesses that his initial response was to quit racing on the spot. But the company had on-going contractual responsibilities and emotion had to be thrust to one side. Lister continued racing.

Just before Archie's death the works Lister team had been defeated by Gregory's Ecurie Ecosse car in a straight fight at Silverstone, so it was to Brian's great satisfaction that BP arranged for Stirling Moss to drive the works car at the British GP meeting. Predictably, 'Stirl' did the job and Gregory shunted in a big way trying to keep up ...

For 1959, Lister developed a revised Jaguar-engined car with slippery bodywork designed by Vanwall aerodynamic genius Frank Costin. The works team drivers were now Ivor Bueb and Bruce Halford, both of whom performed superbly well, but when Ivor died following injuries sustained in a Formula 2 race that also saw Halford hospitalized, for Brian Lister it was the final straw.

He announced the immediate withdrawal of his company from motor racing and that was an end to it. But Lister-Jaguars would race on in private hands for several years and, to this day, they happily grace the starting grids of historic sports car events on both side of the Atlantic. And George Lister and Sons still continue their respected engineering business in Cambridge, with Brian Lister running the show.

In 1990, to celebrate the centenary of the birth of George Lister—Brian's grandfather—the company revived memories of its halcyon racing days by laying down a production run of 25 '1958–spec' Lister-Jaguars, as identical as possible in terms of materials used and manufacturing methods, to the original machines.

27

Sir William Lyons

THE WAY IN which William Lyons built Jaguar into one of the greatest names in the history of the British motor industry from humble beginnings as a sidecar manufacture based in Blackpool is the stuff of automotive legend. Since the immediate post-war years Jaguar's name has been synonymous with performance motoring at a remarkably modest price tag; and, in the palmy days of its ascendancy, the company embarked on an international racing programme that saw its cars win Le Mans on no fewer than five occasions during the 1950s.

Born on 4 September 1901, William Lyons would grow into a motor industry mogul who combined a somewhat austere outward demeanour with a genuine and deep-rooted concern for the well-being of his employees. Although he quickly developed a tremendous enthusiasm and feel for motor racing, his business, first and foremost, was that of car maker. Racing and other motorsport competition served as a useful adjunct by which means his company could develop its engineering ability and promote its wares.

The son of a musician, Lyons hailed from Blackpool, where he founded the Swallow sidecars business, the seed from which Jaguar would eventually grow, in partnership with William Walmsley. On leaving school he had been on the point of taking up an apprenticeship in the Vickers shipbuilding yards in Barrow, but at the last minute his father's contacts ensured that he opted for a grounding in engineering with Crossley Motors at their Gorton, Manchester, works. Unfortunately, while Crossley were extremely successful at the time of Lyons's association—towards the end of the First World War—the young Lancastrian was already developing an independent, resourceful streak which, he judged, had no real place in a large organization. He returned to Blackpool, keen on motorcycling as a hobby, but with no specific ambition in mind. Only when the Walmsley family moved into a neighbouring house and the son of the family, William, began building a few motorcycle sidecars in the garage did Lyons have the first inkling of the career route that would lead him to fame and fortune.

The two men would eventually go into business together manufacturing sidecars, from which Lyons's path into the motor industry proper would proceed via special-bodied Austin Sevens into the manufacture of elegant saloon and sports cars in the 1930s carrying the SS Jaguar ('SS' for Swallow Sidecars) designation. The company moved from Blackpool to Coventry in 1928 and when William Walmsley left in 1935 to concentrate on other business interests, Lyons continued to pursue his ambitions alone.

The events of the Second World War made it tactful to drop the SS designation and, in the early months of 1945, the company changed its name to Jaguar pure and simple. Competition activity in various rallies, trials, and minor races, notably with the SS100, had been part of the marque's history in pre-war years, William Lyons himself proving a dab hand behind the wheel; but Jaguar's great racing achievements would run hand-in-hand with its rise to commercial prosperity in the post-war era.

Much early publicity was gained by the Lyons's son-in-law Ian Appleyard at the wheel of his famous Jaguar XK120 'NUB 120' on the rallying front, while young racing star Stirling Moss cemented the factory's decision to go motor racing by winning the 1950 Tourist Trophy at Dundrod in a similar machine owned by motoring journalist Tommy Wisdom.

These were heady times for the Coventry based firm. The graceful lines of the XK120 had taken the lucrative US export market by storm, and for 1951 Lyons sanctioned the preparation of the XK120C, essentially a development of the road car but fitted with an elegant, wind-cheating body designed by Jaguar aerodynamicist Malcolm Sayer. At the wheel of one such machine, Peter Walker and Peter Whitehead won the marque's first victory at Le Mans, the success repeated in 1953 by Tony Rolt and Duncan Hamilton. The following year saw Sayer produce the classic D-type which Rolt and Hamilton took to an heroic second place in the French classic, a last ditch spurt in stormy, torrential conditions just failing to catch the Ferrari of Froilan Gonzalez and Maurice Trintignant.

The D-type Jaguar is still widely regarded as the most coveted, classic machine the Coventry manufacturer ever produced, yet in 1955 its foray to Le Mans was associated with the biggest motor racing tragedy in history. Mike Hawthorn, jousting for the lead with Fangio's Mercedes 300SLR, swung abruptly across the traffic flow into the pit lane, triggering off the accident that saw Pierre Levegh's 300SLR vault into a packed spectator enclosure, killing more than eighty onlookers.

The Mercedes team was later withdrawn, allowing Hawthorn and Ivor Bueb to score a somewhat hollow victory. William Lyons, however, was burdened with his own private grief; on the way to Le Mans, his son John had been killed instantly when the Jaguar Mk 7 saloon he was driving hit an army lorry just outside Cherbourg as he was travelling to the race. It was a devastating personal blow to Lyons and his wife, who displayed great dignity and fortitude in coming to terms with this dreadful loss.

Jaguar would win again with the D-type in 1956 and 1957, on these occasions thanks to the efforts of the Edinburgh-based Ecurie Ecosse, run by former racing driver David Murray, but the onset of a 3-litre limit at the Sarthe circuit decided Jaguar against further development of the car beyond 1958. The company was approaching possibly its most successful period, with the splendid compact Mark 2 saloons just about to be launched onto the market, to be followed shortly afterwards by the striking Mark 10 and stupendous E-type.

William Lyons may have been keen on motor racing, but he never let expenditure on competition programmes run wildly out of control, either in financial or manpower terms. He was a very conservative and conventional man, inevitably referring to even his senior executives by their surnames, and expected to be treated with due formality and deference. Most of his employees called him 'Sir', a handful 'Mr Lyons' (or Sir William after he received his knighthood in the 1956 New Year Honours List). Nobody in their right mind would ever have had the temerity to call the boss by his Christian name ...

The early 1960s would see Jaguar Mk 2 saloons racing in private hands with spectacular success, while E-types, notably those entered by that great American enthusiast Briggs Cunningham, would keep the Jaguar flag flying briefly at Le Mans. By the mid-1960s, however, Sir William Lyons's company was thriving on past motor racing glories, and while the tide of commercial success was still running their way, the firm's co-founder was approaching 70 years old and Jaguar's long-term future just had to be assured.

In 1966, Jaguar was merged with the British Motor Corporation. Two years later Sir William relinquished his title of Managing Director of the Jaguar Group, but stayed on as Chairman and Chief Executive. That same year the company lost its independence when it became a component within the vast British Leyland Motor Corporation, an entity which would become more unwieldy and financially precarious throughout the decade that followed.

In 1972, Sir William handed over the reins of office to 'Lofty' England, his former racing manager who himself was 60 years of age. Two years later he was succeeded by BL nominee Geoffrey Robinson, effectively bringing to an end the William Lyons era.

Sir William Lyons happily lived to see the rejuvenation of his company as a privatized operation under the dynamic leadership of John Egan, a man in whom he recognized qualities similar to those that had motivated himself in the pioneering years of his business. He died at Wappenbury Hall, his home in Warwickshire for almost fifty years, on 8 February 1985 at the magnificent age of 83 years, content that Jaguar was in safe hands for the future.

It was forty years, almost to the month, that the SS tag had been dropped and Jaguar as we know it today started out towards building its brave new world.

28

The Maserati Brothers

THE GREAT IRONY about the story of the Maserati brothers is that the company bearing their name enjoyed its most spectacular international successes after passing out of their control in the immediate post-war years. Today many still regard the Maserati name as being right up there with Ferrari in terms of prestige and international charisma; but while Maserati has a much longer history than its famous rival, it was a truly tiny company before the Second World War, producing only a handful of cars each year.

Rodolfo Maserati was a railway engineer from Piacenza who fathered seven sons; Carlo (born 1881), Bindo (1883), and Alfieri, who died as a baby in 1885. That name was perpetuated by his next son, the second Alfieri, who was born in 1887, followed by Mario (1890), Ettore (1894), and Ernesto (1898). From an early age Mario pursued his artistic inclinations, but the remaining five brothers all steered towards an engineering career with considerable drive and enthusiasm.

By the end of the century, Carlo Maserati had developed a motorcycle engine and began racing it in 1899. In 1903 he became a test driver for the newly established Isotta-Fraschini company and was later a works motorcycle rider for the Bianchi team. Sadly, he died suddenly in 1910, by which time Alfieri had already won a major race for Bianchi at Dieppe and also moved across to join Isotta Fraschini, where he would eventually be joined by both Bindo and Ernesto.

Alfieri and Ettore were sent off to Argentina in 1912 to build and service racing cars on behalf of the factory, staying away for two years. Alfieri Maserati was ambitious, shrewd, and intelligent. Amongst the brothers, he was the driving force, the visionary, the man who got things done. In 1914 he established his own company—the Societa Anonima Officine Alfieri Maserati—which was effectively put on ice, ticking over in the hands of young Ernesto when the elder Maserati brothers were called up at the start of the First World War.

At the end of the war, Alfieri Maserati turned his company's attention to the serious business of car manufacturing. Operating from their base at Pontevecchio, facing the Via Emilia on the eastern edge of Bologna, Alfieri contested some of the early post-war Italian races, recruiting Ernesto as his riding mechanic. Initially, they used Isotta Fraschini machinery, but the rival Diatto firm was so impressed by the Maseratis' efforts that it effectively delegated its entire racing operation to their small preparation company.

In 1926 Maserati manufactured the first car bearing its own name; but only six years later, on 6 March 1932, the company was dealt a major body blow with the death of Alfieri at the early age of 44. He had recently undergone an operation following a major accident at Messina. This unhappy event had a far-reaching effect on the business, for whilst Bindo was prepared to move from Isotta Fraschini to join Ettore and Ernesto, the company's motivating force was now gone. Although the Maserati brothers seemed capable of sustaining their momentum over the next few years, a collective lack of commercial confidence would eventually prove to be their undoing.

Maserati produced sixteen cars in 1934, seventeen in 1935, but shrank back to only nine in 1936 after a season of poor results. The Maseratis were now getting extremely nervous, being engineers and enthusiasts who knew little about the ways of commerce or the realities of economics. Although production climbed again to fourteen cars in 1937, with Carlo's death and Ettore's retirement, Ernesto and Bindo decided to accept an offer from the Modena-based Orsi family and sold control of the company that Alfieri had founded just over twenty years earlier.

Adolfo Orsi and his son Omer were wealthy and successful industrialists whose business empire ranged from steel mills to the manufacturer of agricultural machinery. Their involvement was initially extremely subtle. Knowing that the Maseratis had a good name and image, Adolfo Orsi initially remained in the background, retaining the Maserati brothers on a ten-year contract. To the outside world, it was as if nothing had changed. Yet gradually, and understandably, the Orsis began to take a firmer hand in the day-to-day management of the company.

During the war plans were laid for a move into road car production and Adolfo Orsi recruited both Alberto Massimino—who had designed the eight-cylinder '815s' for Enzo Ferrari's fledgling Auto Avio Construzione concern—and Vittorio Bellentani to head up the design side in a move which effectively undermined Ernesto Maserati's position. The tensions inevitably increased and, in 1947, the Maserati brothers decided to go their own way, returning from the operation's new base in Modena to the familiar surroundings of Bologna where they started the Osca company.

Throughout the 1950s the surviving Maseratis produced a succession of splendidly engineered and highly competitive 2-litre sports cars which performed with distinction on the Italian national scene, in the hands of such talents as Eugenio Castellotti and Giulio Cabianca. By the early 1960s, however, Osca was merged with de Tomaso who would, ironically, go on to acquire the Maserati company as well in the post-Orsi era and keep the famous name in existence to this day.

The Orsi family would take the Maserati name to great success, notably with the splendid 250F, which was to become hailed as possibly the most romantic front-engined Grand Prix car of all.

Its exploits in the hands of Juan Manuel Fangio and Stirling Moss are now part of Formula 1 legend, but they were Maseratis in name only. The blood line extending back to the pioneering day of Alfieri Maserati's dreams was bound up with the Osca company.

29

Raymond Mays

IF THE LIKES of Colin Chapman and Ron Dennis can be held up as the embodiment of technical and commercial savvy in the post-war motor racing age, then Raymond Mays helped construct the foundations on which those achievements were built. Britain's role as a significant motor racing force owes a great deal to this well-heeled gentleman from Lincolnshire whose vision, whilst admittedly often clouded, produced both the pre-war ERA voiturettes and the post-war BRM, which eventually won the World Championship in 1962.

Mays was born just prior to the turn of the century in Bourne, Lincolnshire, where he lived in Eastgate House for his entire eighty-one years. His father was a wealthy and successful wool merchant and young Raymond grew up with all the social trappings implicit in such financial security. Educated at Oundle, he gained a commission in the Grenadier Guards and briefly saw action in the closing months of the First World War before going up to Cambridge. He once explained that, since commissioned officers were permitted to live outside barracks, his mother generously rented him an apartment at the Savoy. It made life away from home much more bearable for a young man ...

Mays's father had the distinction of owning the first car in the county of Lincolnshire and quickly became a keen motorist, passing this enthusiasm on to his son. At the age of 20, while still at Cambridge, he cajoled a local Hillman dealer into selling him a 1500-cc sports model on particularly favourable terms and actually won his first race at Brooklands in the car. His studies took very much a back seat during this period and, legend has it, his lecturers only really came to know who he was when his name started popping up in these early English race results!

Throughout the following decade, Mays became a master of the hillclimb and sprint technique, swapping the Hillman for the first of two Brescia Bugattis. The second such car was presented to the Englishman by Ettore Bugatti's factory in recognition of his achievement in smashing the outright record at Shelsley Walsh at the wheel of the Hillman.

Throughout this period Mays's cars had been tuned and developed by his old friend Amherst Villiers, and this partnership continued as he competed with AC and Mercedes-Benz machinery through to 1928, when Mays acquired a 3-litre TT Vauxhall. Villiers had earlier supercharged this machine for one of its previous owners, Humphrey Cook, and it was quickly dubbed the Vauxhall Villiers. At around this time two other friends, Peter Berthon and Tom Murray Jamieson, joined the Mays team to help Villiers in his development programme.

Mays continued to dominate the British motor racing scene into the early 1930s, using Invicta and Riley machinery in addition to the trusty Vauxhall Villiers. But it was the development of a $1\frac{1}{2}$litre Riley 12/6 special that sowed the seeds of a longer-term plan to manufacture a purpose-built racing car to contest the well-supported 1.5-litre voiturette category, which was proving a popular attraction for European race promoters at the time.

Although Mays filled the role of the high profile public face behind this new venture, its driving force and financial support came from the taciturn Humphrey Cook from whom Mays had originally purchased the TT Vauxhall. An extremely wealthy young man who had inherited his father's successful wholesale drapery business at the age of 12, Cook was left with the means to do precisely what he wanted for the rest of his life. His great passion had been cars from a very early age and he made the approach to Mays that resulted in the formation of English Racing Automobiles Ltd in November 1933.

From a factory in the grounds of Eastgate House, Bourne, the technical lessons learned from the Riley Special were incorporated into the design of the first distinctive square-cut ERA single seater. After taking in some preliminary British domestic races during the 1934 season, Mays sallied forth onto the Continent the following season to win his first voiturette event, the Eifelrennen at the challenging Nurburgring. Unfortunately, through a combination of poor preparation and ill-starred attempts to squeeze excessive power from the 4-cylinder engine, Mays did not win again at the wheel of an ERA for another two seasons.

However, the marque's name was sustained in the forefront of European racing success by the exploits of several famous customers who beat a path to ERA's door, either to purchase one of the machines or pay for a 'works supported' drive. Earl Howe, Tony Rolt, Pat Fairfield, Dick Seaman, band leader Billy Cotton, Prince Bira and Humphrey Cook himself acquitted themselves well over the next few years, although by the time the clouds of war were gathering at the start of 1939 Mays had split with ERA, taking Berthon and engineer Ken Richardson with him. Disappointed and disillusioned, Cook closed down the company.

In the late 1940s, Mays continued to be a formidable hillclimb and circuit racing contender, even though he was by now approaching the age of 50. The continued role of ERA in the rebirth of post-war international motor racing stood as a fine monument to the imagination and foresight of those who had founded the company over ten years earlier. Indeed, Humphrey Cook re-established ERA Ltd in 1946, but by this stage Mays and Berthon had formulated more ambitious long-term plans.

Mays circulated a letter to all the captains of British industry, detailing his ideas for a $1\frac{1}{2}$-litre supercharged 'national British' Grand Prix car. The idea was to project the country's technical prestige on the international racing scene but, while this was a fine idea on paper, the project was fraught with technical and administrative problems. Administered by a trust the $1\frac{1}{2}$-litre supercharged V16 BRM project ran at least two years late and the car eked out a twilight existence in British club events after the formula for which it was built had been abandoned for World Championship races in 1952.

If it had been ready for competitive action in 1950, things might have been dramatically different.

Eventually the BRM project, still with Mays and Berthon, was taken over by Sir Alfred Owen, head of the industrial empire that carried his family's name. Under the patronage of the Owen Organization, BRM was streamlined and formed into a more tightly knit team, but it was not until 1959 that Jo Bonnier won the marque its first Grand Prix. By the start of the $1\frac{1}{2}$-litre Formula 1 in 1961 Sir Alfred and his family were becoming impatient for success, but the splendid little V8-engined car stole the 1962 World Championship in Graham Hill's hands and the team's future was assured.

Mays himself had retired from the cockpit at the end of 1949 and devoted much of his remaining life to championing the BRM cause, the team retaining and expanding the base at Bourne that had been home to all his cars since he first took up motorsport over forty years before BRM finally won the Championship. Over half a century of effort on the British motor racing scene was duly recognized in 1978 with the award of a CBE.

Two years later, on his death bed in hospital at Stamford, this spruce, nimble and suave life-long bachelor expressed a desire for a tin of watercress soup—from Fortnum and Mason. Right to the very end, Raymond Mays sustained the capacity for relish and discernment that had been a hallmark of his long and happy existence.

30

Bruce McLaren

ONLY TWELVE YEARS separated Bruce McLaren's arrival on the European international motor racing scene from his sudden death in a testing accident at Goodwood. Yet twenty years after that tragic fatal accident, his name lives on attached to one of the most prestigious teams Grand Prix racing has ever seen.

Bruce would have liked that, for even if the ascetic atmosphere that prevails at McLaren International in the '80s and '90s might not have been to his lighthearted taste, he would have keenly appreciated the high quality professionalism they have brought to bear on the business of Formula 1. One can only speculate how the McLaren team might have evolved if its founder had survived to this day.

Born in the comfortable Auckland suburb of Remuera on 30 August 1937, Bruce Leslie McLaren found himself absorbed into a world of cars and motorsport almost from the cradle. His father was a highly regarded member of the New Zealand motorsports milieu, the owner of a successful garage business who imbued Bruce with a sound technical grounding which was to prove invaluable in the years to come. In fact, Bruce was to light a torch for his country's involvement in international motor racing, pioneering a path that has been followed by a succession of optimistic racing stars. Yet only his compatriot Denny Hulme, World Champion in 1967, would eclipse McLaren in terms of achievement.

Bruce grew up with a sunny and relaxed personality which a skirmish with Perthes disease, a complicated hip condition, failed to dim. He had pulled through this potentially debilitating problem with equanimity by the age of fourteen, although he was left with one leg shorter than the other and a perceptible limp as a consequence. He cut his competitive teeth on an Austin Seven Ulster, originally bought for his father to drive, and from there the transition via an Austin Healey through to an ex-Jack Brabham centre-seat Cooper sports racer set the tone for a professional career in the cockpit.

In 1958, Bruce won the Driver to Europe scholarship promoted by the New Zealand International Grand Prix Association, thanks to some sterling performances at the wheel of his own privately run Formula 2 Cooper. That car was shipped across to England, where the still 20-year-old McLaren fully lived up to the predictions of his fellow antipodean Jack Brabham. A succession of promising Formula 2 performances in his own car brought promotion to the Cooper factory team for 1959, first in Formula 2 and later in Formula 1. By the end of 1959 he had won his first Grand Prix, the US event on the bumpy Sebring airfield circuit in Florida, on the day that Jack Brabham clinched his first world title.

Bruce opened the 1960 season on a similarly successful note, winning his second Grand Prix on the trot after surviving to finish first in the heat of Buenos Aires. He continued his unobtrusive supporting role in the Cooper Formula 1 team as Brabham reeled off the wins to take his second straight title, Bruce winding up second in the World Championship points table.

Young McLaren seemed to have become every bit as essential a component as Brabham in the Cooper equation, but nothing lasts for ever and as Cooper's star faded, both men eventually cast around for fresh pastures. Brabham quit at the end of 1961 to start his own Grand Prix outfit, and while Bruce would stay on until the $1\frac{1}{2}$-litre Formula 1 expired at the end of 1965, by the time he left it had been clear for a couple of seasons that his long-term plans revolved round his own racing team.

When Charlie Cooper, the company's ageing, penny-pinching, and autocratic patriach, refused to sanction the preparation of two special single seaters for the prestigious 1963/64 Tasman Championship, Bruce decided to go it alone. He formed Bruce McLaren Motor Racing and ran the cars himself, duly clinched the Championship, and used this as a springboard to acquire the 'Zerex Special', a central-seat Cooper sports with which American Roger Penske had flattened the opposition in the 1963 August Bank Holiday Brands Hatch sports car race. Revamped and redubbed a Cooper-Climax, in part to mollify old Charlie Cooper, who was becoming increasingly unnerved by his number one driver's freelance activities, this was effectively the first McLaren sports car, precursor of the range of highly successful machines that would dominate the lucrative Canadian-American (Can-Am) Challenge Cup series in the late 1960s and early 1970s.

That Tasman adventure at the start of 1964 also had its tragic side, for Bruce's gifted young team mate, Timmy Mayer, was killed in practice for the final round of the Championship at Longford, Tasmania. However, Teddy Mayer—who had abandoned a career in law to manage his younger brother's career—became involved as a founder-director of McLaren Racing, bringing some much-needed finance as well as considerable mental dexterity and an equally appreciated appetite for hard work. The other two key directors from those early days were Tyler Alexander, Timmy Mayer's one-time mechanic, and Phil Kerr, Bruce's keenest rival from the Austin Seven days back in Remuera.

McLaren Racing was as a breath of fresh air in the mid-1960s, a group of genial, motivated youngsters set on challenging the establishment, Mayer's high pressure business aggression tempered by Bruce's easygoing tolerance. It was a well-balanced organization that thrived on hard work and a no-nonsense approach. McLaren was always keen on recruiting suitable New Zealanders to the team and a job on the team guaranteed entry to an exclusive Antipodean outpost within the heartland of British motor racing.

After winning the 1962 Monaco Grand Prix for Cooper, six years would pass before Bruce triumphed again in a World Championship Grand Prix. Then it would be at the wheel of a Cosworth-propelled car bearing his own name, in the 1968 Belgian Grand Prix at Spa. By now his compatriot Denny Hulme had been recruited to drive alongside him in the team, and while Bruce was content for him to set the Formula 1 pace, the domination exerted by the rumbling, ground-shaking McLaren-Chevrolet sports cars were such as to make the Can-Am series their own private domain. Bruce scooped the rich pickings that went with the title in 1967 and 1969, Hulme ensuring a McLaren team hat-trick by winning it in 1968.

By the start of 1970, Bruce McLaren had established himself as a respected and prosperous businessman as well as an accomplished racing driver. The team was launching an assault on the Indianapolis 500, his plans for an exclusive high performance road car were nearing fruition, and he was happily married with a young daughter, Amanda. Although not the fastest driver of his time, he had consolidated a reputation for absolute consistency and dependability. At the age of 32, rumours abounded that he was on the verge of quitting Formula 1 in order to devote more time to the expanding business, as well as to test and development driving, a task which he relished.

In May, Denny Hulme suffered serious burns at Indianapolis, an event that concerned Bruce greatly. Then, on 2 June, Bruce was out at Goodwood testing his M8D Can-Am contender in preparation for the forthcoming summer series. The end came with terrible suddenness.

The rear bodywork covering the Chevy V8 had been improperly secured. Hurtling out onto the Lavant Straight, the engine cover flew back, lifting the rear wheels clear of the track surface for a fleeting second. Pitched out of control, the car slammed into a disused marshals' post, killing motor racing's mild-mannered hero instantly. If this sport could claim Bruce McLaren, then anyone and everyone was vulnerable.

31

Leo Mehl

TYRES ARE LARGELY taken for granted in Grand Prix motor racing. The technology that goes into their development is so sophisticated that they generally only hit the headlines in the sporting press when something goes wrong. Nigel Mansell's spectacular tyre failure when he was apparently on course for the World Championship, two-thirds of the way through the 1986 Australian Grand Prix in Adelaide, is a classic case.

Foremost amongst the Formula 1 tyre makers is Goodyear, the Akron (Ohio)-based corporation which celebrated its 250th Grand Prix victory two races into the 1991 World Championship season. The man who can take much of the credit for that sustained level of achievement is Leo Mehl, the company's Director of International Racing.

Mehl's craggy visage is permanently creased in a welcoming smile, accurately reflecting his sunny personality. One of the most influential and powerful of Grand Prix trade barons, he enjoys enormous personal popularity in the paddock. This level of appreciation has worked very much in Leo's favour over the years, for even when delivering the bitter pill of Goodyear rejection to a competing team, he can couch it in such a kind and diplomatic manner that the let-down comes gently.

More significantly, Leo Mehl is no corporate automaton. He is a man who has grown up with motor racing and is passionate in his belief that it can do his company—any company—a great deal of good. He has argued Formula 1's case energetically to the Goodyear board for more than twenty years with a persuasive dexterity that has almost always won the day, even against those sceptics amongst the senior management who would like to see the money spent elsewhere.

Born in 1936, Mehl's entire working life has been spent at Goodyear. After graduating from university in 1959, he even spent a short time working for the company before serving his mandatory three years' national service with the USA Air Force.

Picking up his career proper with the company, he quickly became involved with the laboratories at Akron, concentrating on the chemical aspect of racing tyre development, before gaining his first practical experience in the field working on the NASCAR stock car racing programme. Later he worked on Shelby Cobras in US national sports car events and first crossed the Atlantic as part of the tyre support programme for the Ford GT40 project at Le Mans in 1964 and 1965.

Mehl had his first taste of Formula 1 when Jack Brabham did some preliminary testing on the Akron rubber; but although Goodyear made a serious commitment to Formula 1 at the start of the 1965 season, it would be another two years before Leo came back to Europe. He spent two years working as a compounder on the crucially important Goodyear Indianapolis development programme before taking charge of Goodyear's European Formula 1 operations in 1967.

By this time, Goodyear was riding high on a wave of Formula 1 success. Richie Ginther had won Akron its first Grand Prix with the Honda at Mexico City in 1965, then Jack Brabham and Denny Hulme grasped successive World Championship titles during the next couple of seasons. Mehl's relaxed, no-nonsense dealings with drivers and team owners balanced cordial civility with just the right amount of corporate pressure. With Leo, everybody knew where they stood.

He was more than the man who supplied the tyres and negotiated the contracts. He took a very personal interest in and fought tenaciously to uphold the interests of his employers. On one memorable occasion, Jack Brabham headed off to compete in the Tasman Series only to discover that the Goodyear tyres he'd been supplied with were just not sufficiently competitive.

Jack got in touch with Akron and advised Leo that, in his team's interests, he might be forced into making a switch to Firestone for one particular race in Australia unless some revised compounds were forthcoming. Mehl cabled back that Brabham should do no such thing, and that a special delivery of revised specification tyres was being dispatched immediately. Brabham's crew duly arrived at Sydney airport—to find Leo himself marching through customs with the new set of tyres virtually clutched under his arms!

For the 1971 season, Mehl helped engineer the deal which got Jackie Stewart and the Tyrrell team running on Goodyears, an achievement which not only saw the Scot win his second World Championship that year, but also enabled Akron to harness Stewart's fluent, outgoing personality as a tremendously effective public relations tool. Small wonder, under the circumstances, that Mehl returned to Akron at the end of 1971 to assume the role of Director of International Racing. To the Formula 1 world, it seemed nothing less than his rightful reward.

Goodyear enjoyed a tyre supply monopoly in Formula 1 between Firestone's withdrawal at the end of 1974 and the serious arrival on the scene of the French Michelin company at the start of 1978. Michelin would enjoy considerable success, none more significant than supplying the all-conquering McLaren-TAGs which won 12 out of the season's 16 races in 1984.

Towards the end of 1984, McLaren team chief Ron Dennis approached Leo asking whether it would be possible to arrange a

Goodyear tyre contract for 1985. Mehl naturally jumped at the chance of gathering Formula 1's top team on to the Akron bandwagon and a deal—very lucrative for McLaren—was duly concluded.

Shortly afterwards, Michelin announced its intention to quit Formula 1 at the start of the 1985 season. Under the circumstances, it was not altogether surprising that some people in the pit lane believed that Dennis had prior warning of their departure and engineered his Goodyear deal with that knowledge in his mind. Ron denied this and Leo took him at his word.

Dennis was too shrewd an operator to have misled Goodyear, and Mehl too clever to voice any trace of a suspicion. In his view, if Ron had been acting on an inspired hunch, then good for him: that was what business was all about. He looked on happily, secure in the knowledge that McLaren was likely to add considerably to the tyre company's victory tally. And so it has proved.

Nevertheless, anybody who imagined that Leo Mehl might be a soft touch was allowing themselves to be misled by his outgoing and avuncular demeanour. During 1980, Grand Prix racing became embroiled in a power struggle between the Formula One Constructors' Association—the car owners—and the sport's governing body FISA. On this occasion, Mehl had no hesitation in executing the instructions of his board to withdraw from Formula 1. Although he knew the benefits involved, it was a reflection of just how badly the situation was perceived by the outside world that a company so committed to racing as Goodyear decided that it did not wish to be associated with Formula 1 throughout that period.

Paradoxically, although the withdrawal lasted only a little more than six months, Leo felt it strengthened his case for Formula 1 involvement even more. 'After our withdrawal there were a number of happy executives who had never believed in the racing programme. Now the extra money was available, but what should we do with it? As things transpired, we found it impossible to get an equal "bang for the buck" as we derived from racing in any other activity. Any doubts as to the value of the programme were quickly removed!'

At the start of the 1987 season Leo Mehl found his diplomatic qualities taxed yet again, at a time when Goodyear was subjected to a hostile takeover bid on the US stock market. In order to sustain a presence in Formula 1, Mehl brought the message to Europe that there would be just a standard specification 'control' tyre made available in 1987—and that it would have to be paid for. It may have been unfortunate, but it was a *fait accompli*.

Generally, Mehl makes three or four visits a season to Formula 1 Grands Prix, but his genial presence is generally taken as a tacit indication that top-line negotiations may be underway. It may be time for one of the top teams to renew its tyre contract, or simply the opportunity for a wide-ranging discussion on Goodyear's future Formula 1 strategy.

Either way, with Leo Mehl overseeing their racing efforts, Goodyear has an accumulation of general respect—even affection—amongst all Formula 1 competitors. His relaxed and sympathetic style has reaped more dividends than could ever be achieved by investments of cash alone.

32

Max Mosley

IT IS TEMPTING to speculate just how Max Mosley might have handled a career in the House of Commons had not the shadow of his father's extreme political views understandably fallen across his path at an early age. Most people who met him through the motor racing fraternity have concluded that he would have done outstandingly well, for his affable and eloquent public persona was backed up by tremendous determination and ability to concentrate on complex matters whilst never quite losing his underlying sense of humour.

Max's father, Sir Oswald Mosley, was one of Britain's most able Labour politicians of his day before his career took a wrong-turn in the early 1930s when he established the British League of Fascists. Max was the second son of his much-publicized marriage to Diana Guinness, one of the famous Mitford sisters, who hit the headlines when she left her first husband, the Hon Bryan Guinness, for Sir Oswald in 1933. Max was born in 1940, a few weeks before his mother was interned in Holloway prison. He and his brother Alexander enjoyed a privileged, if not exactly settled, upbringing in the immediate post-war years as the Mosley family moved first to Ireland and later to France, where Sir Oswald and Lady Diana finally settled for the rest of their lives.

Max's education was understandably cosmopolitan, in France and Germany, but he concedes that he was never a terribly committed student, although additional coaching enabled him to catch up sufficiently at the last moment to gain a place at Christ Church, Oxford. He read physics and law, and at one point seemed a likely candidate for President of the Oxford Union. In fact, he got as far as Secretary before his surname debarred him from any further progress. Although at this time Sir Oswald was approaching seventy years of age, he still attempted to reactivate his political career, the last remnants of his old party thinking now reconstituted in the Union Movement. Fleetingly, Max acted as one of his right-hand men and, when the old man was knocked down by a mob on his way to address a meeting in London during 1962, the possibility of serious injury was only averted by Max's prompt and brave intervention.

Max continued to become a barrister, specializing in the complexities of patent and trademark law; but even by the time he qualified, motor racing had drawn his attention. Whilst at Oxford, he visited a race meeting at Silverstone. Max found it utterly hypnotic and fascinating. 'From that moment, I realized I absolutely had to do it,' he said later.

Soon after being called to the Bar in 1964, he tried his hand at clubmans sports car racing, an extremely well-supported category in the mid-1960s and early 1970s. His fast and immaculately prepared U2 clubmans machine raced to a succession of wins and lap records at circuits all over southern England throughout 1966 and 1967. He even entered it in the 1967 Crystal Palace Whit Monday Formula 2 International, although this was more a symbolic effort than anything else.

Nevertheless, Max determined that he would try for the big time. In 1968 he ordered a brand new Formula 2 Brabham BT23C and teamed up with former kartist Chris Lambert in a similar car under the London Racing Team banner. It proved to be a wearing season. Lambert was killed in a controversial accident at Zandvoort and Max found the going harder, perhaps, than he had imagined. Undaunted, he ordered a Lotus 59 F2 car for 1969, but after it had dumped him in the scenery at the Nurburgring following a suspension breakage, he called it a day. By this stage it had become clear to Max that he was never going to become a World Champion and, anyway, there were more exciting business developments in the wind.

Together with Robin Herd, Alan Rees, and Graham Coaker, Max founded March Engineering at the end of 1969. The new company started with a small Formula 3 special, largely built out of Lotus components, but on the back of its race début the new company announced grandiose plans to build cars not only for this highly competitive category, but also for Formula 1, Formula 2, Formula Ford, and the Can-Am sports car classes.

Their arrival on the scene was perfectly timed, for March seemed to catch the mood of the moment and, as international motor racing blossomed into the early 1970s, March would ride the crest of a commercial wave of success. That the company projected a far more confident outward mood than perusal of the accounts might have justified was largely down to Max's persuasive patter. Not for nothing would he become known as 'Silver Tongue' in the years that followed.

Max did a fine job creating the illusion that March had substantial private backing from a 'secret sponsor'. It all seemed so plausible at the time. After all, Max was on the fringes of the mega-wealthy Guinness family, socially well connected and, for all we knew, extraordinarily well off in his own right. Although it had long been rumoured that Max had inherited the royalties from his authoress aunt Nancy Mitford on her death in 1973, it was not until Sir Oswald's death in 1980 that he did have any substantial independent means and March ran through most of the 1970s on a financial knife edge, its survival aided substantially by some extremely generous banking facilities.

Whilst Robin Herd was in charge of the technical side of the company's development, it was Max who romanced and cajoled the sponsors, sweet-talked the drivers, and gradually became heavily involved in the political side of Formula 1. As Bernie Ecclestone grew to prominence in his role as President of the Formula One Constructors' Association, so Max gradually assumed the role of informal legal advisor, Bernie's right-hand man in effect. Almost on first acquaintance, Max recognized Bernie as one of his few intellectual equals amongst Formula 1 team principals. To this day, their joint influence on the international motor racing scene remains considerable.

By the end of 1977, however, Max was tiring of his role as March director. By this stage the Grand Prix team had gradually run downhill and was existing on a diet of sponsored drivers, Ian Scheckter and Alex Ribeiro generally struggling to qualify for a start. It was a long way from 1970, when Jackie Stewart, François Cevert, Chris Amon, Jo Siffert, and Ronnie Peterson had burst onto the Formula 1 landscape at the wheel of Robin's first Grand Prix creation.

At 37 years old, Max decided he'd had enough of attempting to run a Formula 1 team and was tired of the annual round of sponsorship chasing. 'The business no longer really had any need for me,' he explained, 'and I'd really run out of enthusiasm for it ...'

At the end of the year, he sold his shareholding to Robin and moved off to pursue new interests. His position as Ecclestone's legal sounding board intensified as Grand Prix racing lurched towards the FISA/FOCA wars of the early 1980s. Max played a key role in drafting the regulations for the World Federation of Motorsport 'rival' Championship, which FOCA supported as part of its complex game of poker with FISA President Jean-Marie Balestre.

Max had seemingly inherited his father's instinctive attraction towards politics and, in the early 1980s, talked long and hard with various senior members of the Tory party as to whether he might stand for Parliament. But Sir Oswald's activities half a century earlier still cast a political shadow across Max's path and it was concluded that the Mosley surname still represented a considerable electoral handicap.

He thus focussed his considerable talents on the political side of motor racing, gaining the post of President of the Manufacturers' Commission, representing the world's motor manufacturers on the World Motor Sport Council.

Everybody could see what was coming next. Max was perfectly positioned for a challenge to the FISA Presidency. With superb timing and judgement, he took on Balestre in the October 1991 elections and won commandingly, 43 votes to 29.

A new era of international motorsport administration thus dawned.

33

Alfred Neubauer

SHORTLY AFTER THE end of the Second World War, Enzo Ferrari received a visit from Alfred Neubauer, former manager of the Mercedes-Benz Grand Prix team which, along with Auto-Union, had exerted such dominance on the international racing scene during the 1930s. Ferrari recorded in his memoirs just how gaunt and haunted Neubauer looked, a shadow of his former rotund self.

A few years later, Ferrari observed that his German colleague had regained much of his lost girth, speculating that if that country was recovering its stature at the same rate as Neubauer was making ground in the avoirdupois stakes, then perhaps Germany was preparing for a Third World War!

Alfred Neubauer was the man who virtually invented the business of motor racing team management, but that didn't mean he fulfilled a subordinate role to the drivers under his command. Far from it, for Neubauer was a shrewd organizer and a man with a well-honed theatrical sense.

Clad in a double-breasted suit, and with a Homberg perched atop a head which seemed too small for his gargantuan frame, Neubauer stamped his identity on Mercedes-Benz's motor racing history over a period of four decades. Yet if his outward countenance looked stern and unbending, it was a penetrable façade. On duty, he might well have chased unwanted photographers and journalists out of the Mercedes pit, but off duty, with a twinkle in his eye and a glass in his hand, he was an enchanting social companion with a splendid sense of fun.

Alfred Neubauer was born in 1891 in the region of Czechoslovakia then known as Northern Bohemia. Having served in the Austro-Hungarian armed forces during the First World War, he was offered a job in the road test department of the Austro-Daimler company, ironically by Professor Ferdinand Porsche who would go on to design the Auto Unions against which Neubauer's Mercedes would later race.

Initially, Neubauer wanted to be a driver. He achieved this aim with Austro-Daimler and Mercedes-Benz, although in subsequent years he was the first to admit that he wasn't in the front rank. At the time, his fiancée, seeking to speed him up, commented that he drove 'like a nightwatchman'. That was a pretty crushing rebuff, particularly coming from his future wife, but Neubauer clearly got the message.

Following the 1924 Italian Grand Prix, where Louis Zborowski crashed fatally, Neubauer swapped the steering wheel for the stop watch and virtually invented the job of team manager simply to keep himself in the racing business that he loved so fervently.

He assumed the role of team manager as early as the 1924 Solitude Grand Prix, at the same time carving himself a distinctive niche within Mercedes-Benz and becoming a lifelong supporter of the legendary Rudolf Caracciola, who began racing for the German team in the mid-1920s. At the end of the 1930 season, the depressed economic climate saw Mercedes withdraw from motor racing, which concerned Neubauer greatly. Not only could he see his own position in jeopardy, but he was also worried that if Caracciola was allowed to slip through their fingers, should Mercedes ever return to racing they would have lost one of their biggest assets for good.

Neubauer thus approached the Mercedes management with a proposition that the company should loan Caracciola an SSKL sports car for him to race on an independent basis throughout 1931. Neubauer, naturally, proposed that he operate as team manager, and while the arrangement proved extremely successful, with Caracciola winning many races, Mercedes felt there was no way they could continue such an arrangement.

This was a heart-rending situation for the devoted Neubauer, whose commitment to Mercedes was matched only by his enthusiasm for racing. Shortly afterwards, Auto Union offered him a post, only for Daimler-Benz Managing Director Dr Wilhelm Kissel to intervene with the hint that the company did in fact have a racing future and would eventually be back on the scene, probably for 1934.

This was great news for Neubauer, but to his considerable dismay, Caracciola crashed heavily during practice for the 1934 Monaco Grand Prix and it was not until the middle of 1935 that his close friend and protégé returned to the scene, his recovery set back further by the shattering loss of his wife Charly in a skiing accident earlier that year.

Happily for Neubauer, Caracciola found his old form and stormed away to win the 1935 European Championship; but the Mercedes manager found himself forced to assume the role of diplomat and politician as he balanced the wider interests of the team's success with his private regard for Caracciola. There is no doubt that Rudi was a bit of a handful to deal with, suspecting that his team-mates were attempting to undermine his number one position in the team.

During the period of Caracciola's convalescence from the Monaco accident, Neubauer had found himself forced to look outside Germany for suitable driving talent. With apparent reservations about hiring either Achille Varzi or Tazio Nuvolari, Neubauer opted for Luigi Fagioli—probably as much to keep Caracciola as for any other reason. Either way, Caracciola didn't care much for Fagioli, who proved somewhat undisciplined, and Neubauer breathed a sigh of relief when he left at the end of 1936.

Not that this was the end of his problems with Caracciola, for while Rudi got along well enough with the aristocratic Manfred von Brauchitsch, he didn't care for the way in which former mechanic Hermann Lang began performing rather too successfully for his ease during 1937. But by this time Neubauer's shrewd judgement had also resulted in the arrival of an Englishman in the Mercedes ranks in the person of Dick Seaman.

Of course, the driver selection process operated by a top team such as Mercedes-Benz was dramatically different in those days. Imagine, if you can, Ron Dennis inviting thirty youngsters to turn up at Silverstone for some preliminary tests at the wheel of a Porsche 959. Then, having killed one of them and badly injured another, whittling down the list to a handful who would be allowed behind the wheel of a McLaren-Honda.

Not very likely, is it? Yet this was precisely the method Neubauer employed at the Nurburgring in late 1936, a huge collection of hopefuls effectively running riot round the place in a fleet of 2.3-litre Mercedes sports cars. The two ripe plums to emerge were Seaman and the Swiss driver Christian Kautz, and while recruiting Britain's top international driver was a major political coup for Mercedes—enjoying the personal approval of Adolf Hitler—it was just another complex factor for Neubauer to take into account in his dealings with Caracciola.

Eventually, Caracciola's truculent attitude towards Lang would erupt during the 1939 season, first at Tripoli in a dispute over who was to race the new 1.5-litre 'voiturette' and later at the Eifelrennen over how much fuel was necessary to top up the cars' tanks at a routine pit stop. Caracciola decided that Neubauer was against him, and the dispute got so serious that it was placed before the Mercedes-Benz directors for consideration. They told everyone involved not to be so stupid, to sort it out on their own, but Caracciola was always rather cool towards Neubauer, the man who had championed his cause for so many years, from that moment onwards.

The 1939 season saw Lang win the European Championship for Mercedes before the storm clouds of war engulfed the world and motor racing ceased for the duration. Yet Neubauer returned to its racing department. Headed by Neubauer, three 1939 Mercedes-Benz W163s were shipped to Argentina to contest a series of races that year, but they were no longer winning propositions and were forced to give best to Jose-Froilan Gonzales at the wheel of a Ferrari 166.

The way back to serious international racing lay via the splendid Mercedes 300SL sports car with which Hermann Lang and Fritz Riess won the 1952 Le Mans 24-hours. Two years later the three-pointed star was back in Formula 1, carried proudly on the sensational 2.5-litre W196s which helped Juan Manuel Fangio to his Championship titles in

1954 and 1955. Neubauer was also instrumental in recruiting Stirling Moss to drive alongside the great Argentinian in 1955 and, just as he had presided over Dick Seaman's historic victory in the 1937 German Grand Prix, he watched with pride eighteen years later as young Moss pipped Fangio to win the British Grand Prix at Aintree.

By then, catastrophe had intervened in the shape of Pierre Levegh's terrible accident at Le Mans, the wreckage of his 300SLR cutting a swathe through the crowded spectator enclosure to leave over eighty onlookers dead. The Daimler-Benz directors not only withdrew their cars from the race, but, soon after, took the longer-term decision to quit motor racing altogether.

Thirty-four years later, a sleek silver Sauber-Mercedes, carrying the three-pointed star on its nose cone, would win once more at Le Mans, reviving the image of those early pioneering days. By then slick pit stops, with ultra-efficient tyre changes and refuelling procedures were taken for granted, techniques pioneered by the portly giant with the wide-brimmed hat and the dominant manner.

Alfred Neubauer had died in 1980 at the grand age of 89 years, a Mercedes man to the last, but his ghost must have been stalking the pit lanes as the descendants of his beloved Silver Arrows wrote another chapter in motor racing history.

34

Jack Oliver

KEITH JACK OLIVER was born in Romford, Essex, in April 1943, the son of a prosperous and successful businessman. Although his personal ambitions as a driver were to take him as far as Formula 1 by the middle of 1968, he never gained significant success in the sport's most exalted category. Subsequently, as Managing Director of the Arrows team, he would continue to chase Grand Prix success from the pit wall, but at the time of writing his team seems as far as ever from finally achieving that elusive first victory.

In his youth, Oliver was confident to the point of cockiness. He certainly had ability, but his bouncy self-assurance could rub people up the wrong way. The passing of the years have tended to soften those asperities. Oliver was a typical example of the 1980s thrusting entrepreneurial spirit; motor racing has made him undeniably rich, if not as successful as his competitive spirit would have liked.

Oliver's position as a Grand Prix team chief represents a long haul from his maiden competition outing in 1960. His first event was a sprint meeting at Snetterton at the wheel of a Mini in which he successfully established fastest time of the day in his class. He continued with this machine before scraping up sufficient money to purchase a Marcos sports car, but a later visit to the Norfolk track was rather less successful. He lost control at the Esses and reduced the car's wooden chassis to a pile of splinters at the side of the circuit.

He then graduated via a Diva sports racer through to one of the very first racing Lotus Elans to be released into private hands mid-way through the 1964 season. It was typical of the way in which Lotus operated at the time that the car was delivered late, only being finished on the eve of the first British Grand Prix to be held at Brands Hatch.

In the supporting sports car race Oliver was well satisfied to finish in third place behind Jackie Stewart and Sir John Whitmore. The original car was duly replaced by the uprated Elan S2 model in which he set about toppling many sports car lap records in British domestic events.

For the 1966 season, Jack moved up into single seaters with a Brabham F3, and while this proved less than totally successful, a chance outing at Snetterton enabled him to get a drive behind the wheel of a works-backed Charles Lucas-Team Lotus type 41. The Lucas team was busy testing rally driver Andrew Cowan—a pal of Jim Clark's—at the time, but Oliver made his indignation felt to Lotus Engineering Director Jim Endruweit. He felt that those earlier successes with the Elan should have at least earned him the merit of some consideration for a Lucas drive. This rather aggressive approach worked and he did in fact earn some drives in the Lucas team before racing one of the first Lotus 47s—a racing version of the Europa coupé—at the 1966 Boxing Day Brands Hatch meeting.

With support from Lotus Components, which manufactured the company's range of proprietary racing cars, Oliver moved up into Formula 2 in 1967 at the wheel of an uprated F3 Lotus 41 powered by a Cosworth FVA engine. The car did not prove particularly reliable, but Jack used it to enhance his reputation as a future single-seater talent.

For the 1968 season, Oliver continued in Formula 2 with an ex-works Lotus 48, earning the distinction of attracting one of the few non-industry sponsors to be involved on the racing scene at that time. The support came from the Herts and Essex Aero Club and a promising season beckoned. However, within a few months, Jack Oliver was to find himself propelled to the forefront of international attention by a tragedy that rocked the Grand Prix world. On 7 April 1968, Jim Clark was killed at Hockenheim, driving a Lotus 48 similar to Oliver's, and Jack found the door unexpectedly opening for him to take a works Lotus Grand Prix drive.

Of course, what was on offer wasn't just any old Formula 1 seat, it was a place alongside Graham Hill in the second Gold Leaf Team Lotus 49. This was a big break for the young lad from Romford and he almost fluffed it on his very first outing. Despite Chapman's urgent entreaties that he keep out of trouble at Monaco, he collected Lodovico Scarfiotti's Cooper and Bruce McLaren's McLaren going through the tunnel on the opening lap.

Chapman was so livid that Jack found himself fired on the spot, but the Lotus boss relented and he was back in the team for the Belgian Grand Prix at Spa, where he finished fifth. Oliver's confidence received another major knock when he destroyed another Lotus 49 in a high-speed shunt during practice for the French Grand Prix at Rouen-les-Essarts; but he bounded back to lead the British Grand Prix at Brands Hatch until the transmission failed just after half distance. Had he won that crucial race, his entire racing career might well have been different.

Oliver makes no bones about the fact that he didn't quite get the personal support from Chapman that he really needed. After Jimmy's death, there was a perceptible change in the Lotus chief's attitude. He was in no way hostile, merely distant. Clark had been his absolute idol and it seemed unlikely that any other driver would ever replace him in Chapman's affections. Either way, it certainly wasn't to be Jack Oliver and, after rounding off the season with a strong third place in the Mexican Grand Prix, his contract was not renewed for the 1969 season.

Nevertheless, those races for Lotus had done wonders for Oliver's marketability. At the start of 1969 he was signed up by BRM, with whom he spent the next two seasons. The first year he had a difficult time, living in the shadow of team leader John Surtees, who, he felt, was always trying to steamroller him into a subservient position. It wasn't a satisfactory situation and the equipment wasn't up to much. In 1970, with the new Tony Southgate-designed BRM P153, Oliver's form was better, but the machinery was still fraught with unreliability. As a result, he dropped out of Formula 1 for three years.

For 1971, Oliver was signed on to partner Pedro Rodriguez as a member of the JW/Gulf Porsche 917 squad, but he angered team boss John Wyer by quitting mid-season to contest the US-based Can-Am Championship. This would lead to his becoming involved with Californian-based entrepreneur Don Nichols, owner of the Shadow Can-Am cars, and in 1973 Oliver would return to Grand Prix racing in the first of the team's Formula 1 machines.

It wasn't a particularly successful curtain call. The first Shadow DN1 wasn't notably competitive and Oliver was increasingly spending his time on the business side of the operation, tying together sponsorship deals and so on. For 1974 he dropped out of Formula 1 again, but continued driving their F5000 and Can-Am cars on the other side of the Atlantic.

In 1977, Jack had his final Formula 1 outings when he drove the Shadow DN8 in the Brands Hatch Race of Champions and Swedish Grand Prix, thereafter dropping out to concentrate all his time on administrative matters. Behind the scenes, however, he and team manager Alan Rees were becoming increasingly disenchanted with Nichols's style of management and determined to set up on their own at the start of the following year.

Along with ex-Shadow designer Tony Southgate they set up the Arrows team in time for the second race of the 1978 season, but soon found themselves in very serious legal hot water, having used designs for the Shadow DN9 for the first Arrows chassis. Although the Arrows beat the new Shadow on to the tracks by over a month, it was clear that the two cars were virtually identical and Nichols pursued the matter to a hearing in the High Court which he duly won. It was an extremely embarrassing and highly publicized episode from which Arrows emerged with their credibility apparently unscathed.

Thereafter, Oliver concentrated on operating the business side of the team, attracting a wide variety of sponsors from differing areas of business throughout the 1980s. Riccardo Patrese would get closest to winning races for the team during their early years, but the Italian eventually left to join Brabham at the start of 1982. Subsequently, drivers such as Thierry Boutsen and Gerhard Berger used Arrows as the first step on the ladder of Formula 1 opportunity, but although Oliver generally managed to come up with the necessary finance, the team's on-track performance never rose to a level calculated to sustain the drivers' interest.

Nevertheless, in 1990, Oliver and his colleagues sold a controlling stake in the company to the Japanese Footwork corporation, thereby raising the necessary finance to commission Porsche to manufacture a bespoke 3.5-litre V12 for their exclusive use. Unfortunately, the engine proved a major disappointment when it appeared at the start of 1991, being withdrawn for further development after only six races.

If the disappointments taxed Oliver's patience, he didn't let it show. Resilient and streetwise, he continues to project the unruffled, rather distant confidence of one whose self-belief continues to sustain a burning sense of ambition.

'Our organization has improved greatly over the last twelve months,' said Oliver at the start of 1991. 'Alfred Neubauer started professional motor racing organization in the 'thirties and Ron Dennis of McLaren has finished it off. We have tried to model ourselves on their example.'

On the strength of the Footwork-Porsche team's showing over the weeks immediately following that remark, Jack Oliver and his colleagues clearly had some way still to go.

35

Sir Alfred Owen

IF RAYMOND MAYS was the man responsible for planting the seed of hope for a British national Grand Prix car in the form of the BRM, it was Sir Alfred Owen who nurtured the plant to full flower and he should thus be accorded due recognition for this not inconsiderable feat. Sir Alfred was head of the giant Owen Organization, one of Britain's most successful and wide-ranging industrial giants of the post-war era, and took over the failing BRM project from the British Motor Racing Research Trust in 1952. Ten years, and much heartache, later, the team achieved its aim and won the World Championship.

The Owen Organization had been founded by Alfred Owen's hard-working and diligent father Ernest, in partnership with J. T. Rubery, back in 1893, at Darlaston, Shropshire, where the group's headquarters remained for many years. He died at the relatively early age of 61 leaving a fortune in excess of £1 million. Shrewd management and careful financial husbandry enabled the Owen Organization to ride out the post-First World War slump, ensuring that his sons Alfred and Ernest, and daughter Jean, inherited a thriving industrial empire.

Sir Alfred Owen's brother-in-law, Louis Stanley, would later run the BRM racing organization in partnership effectively with his wife Jean. Stanley was one of the more controversial, larger-than-life personalities on the post-war Formula 1 racing scene for twenty years starting in the mid-1950s, and has made some perspicacious observations on the way the team was operated in relationship to its parent company. Amongst other remarks, he has said that 'had the BRM project coincided with his [Ernest Owen Senior's] heyday, success would have come twice as quickly at half the cost'.

This in itself provides a telling insight into Sir Alfred Owen's personal *modus operandi*. As the eldest of Ernest Owen's offspring, he assumed the chairmanship of the family firm by the mutual consent of his brother and sister. Although an incredibly astute businessman, he was kind and warm-hearted to the point of over-indulging those who worked for him. There was a strong paternalistic streak in his character, a deeply ingrained awareness of his obligations as an employer. Critics have said he was too soft.

Ernest Owen Snr had been fascinated by motor racing, both from the sporting standpoint and for its potential as a valid engineering exercise.

Alfred inherited that enthusiasm and, when Raymond Mays was casting round for financial support to get BRM off the launch pad in 1947, he came in on the ground floor as one of the key members of the trust. When in 1950 it was decided that a more manageable, smaller committee should be formed to direct the project, he was appointed to the BRM Executive Council in company with bearing magnate Tony Vandervell, Lucas boss Bernard Scott, Mays, and his colleague Peter Berthon.

Amidst the mechanical chaos and uncertainty surrounding the development of the troublesome $1\frac{1}{2}$-litre BRM V16, these industrial chiefs attempted to impose more rigid disciplines on the operation, but expecting such high-powered tycoons to agree on any set course of action proved too much.

By the time the $1\frac{1}{2}$-litre supercharged BRM V16 was developed to a competitive pitch, the category for which it had been conceived had all but died on its feet. Shortage of suitably competitive machinery had obliged the sport's governing body to decree that the 1952 World Championship would be for Formula 2 contenders. The V16 was thus left to potter around in national British, non-championship libre events. It was hardly surprising that the whole project was put up for sale later that year. Sir Alfred decided that the Owen Organization would buy BRM and try to make something of it alone.

Throughout the 1950s, BRM struggled to field a competitive $2\frac{1}{2}$-litre machine for the new Formula 1 regulations that had been instigated at the start of 1954. Sir Alfred Owen sanctioned what, by the standards of the times, was a simply massive investment in the team, but it was not until the 1959 Dutch Grand Prix that Jo Bonnier finally notched up that elusive first victory.

At the start of the $1\frac{1}{2}$-litre Formula 1, Sir Alfred authorized the development of a brand new V8 engine, but since all the British-based teams prevaricated when the CSI announced these new regulations at the end of 1958, BRM found itself unprepared when the new engine regulations came into force at the beginning of 1961. The V8 was not ready to race seriously until the following year, by which time even the placid Sir Alfred was running out of patience.

He informed the team management that, unless they managed to score at least two race victories in 1962, the BRM team would be closed down. Graham Hill duly managed his first win with the V8 at Zandvoort, after which designer Tony Rudd felt sufficiently confident about the future to write to Sir Alfred raising the subject of planning for 1963. But the Owen Organization chairman meant what he had said; back came a letter by return, reminding Rudd that two wins were necessary to secure the team's long-term future. Hill subsequently obliged with further wins at the Nurburgring, Monza, and East London to clinch what was to be the marque's sole World Championship.

Yet for all his enormous enthusiasm for motor racing, Sir Alfred

Owen attended Grands Prix only infrequently, his religious beliefs leaving him a mite uncomfortable about attending sporting events on the Sabbath. His brother Ernest, meanwhile, kept in the background, reluctant to trespass on his elder brother's personal domain, so an increasing amount of responsibility for the team's operations fell to Jean and Louis Stanley.

'Big Lou' was not always the easiest of customers to deal with, but many share his widely published views that Sir Alfred was just too nice and over-tolerant with the workforce at Bourne. Stanley has written: 'he showed unbelievable patience, sometimes to the point of weakness, and there were occasions where stern actions would have produced results ... but he was reluctant to upset the ties of friendship.'

Of course, Sir Alfred's business commitments were wide and varied, extending all over the world. He was an extremely conscientious man who carried a heavy load—more contemporary jargon would have labelled him a 'workaholic'. One man who knew him extremely well was Reg Parnell's son Tim, who rose to take over the BRM F1 team manager's job at the start of 1969.

'Sir Alfred was quite the most amazing and remarkable man I have ever met in my life,' Tim told me. 'He was the chairman of over 1000 subsidiary companies, all round the world, yet he also found time to be a committed Methodist lay preacher, a great family man, and worked on many public boards and charities ... Dr Barnardo's, the YMCA ... the list was incredible. He had an army of secretaries keeping tabs on his appointments and work programme which used up every minute of his day. People talk about workload ... but my goodness, he was absolutely unbelievable. He was an extremely nice man and, of course, my family knew him well from the time that my father drove for the team. Then in the mid-1960s I managed the BRM Tasman team for three consecutive years and Reg Parnell Racing ran what was effectively a 'B' team for the BRM factory with people like Richard Attwood, Piers Courage, and Chris Irwin ... but if I ever had to see him on business, it was usually a few moments squeezed into the back of a taxi while he was en route between board meetings ...'

Criticism of Sir Alfred's weaknesses notwithstanding, Tim Parnell believes he was extraordinarily shrewd, with the happy knack of being able to pick the right man for the right job at the right time. Yet he is equally certain that this whirlwind business schedule was directly responsible for hastening the stroke suffered by Sir Alfred in 1969 which brought his business life to an effective close.

Sir Alfred Owen died on 29 October 1975, at least spared the embarrassment of BRM's F1 death throes a couple of seasons later. The industrial empire his father had founded passed on intact into the custody of his sons David and John and still thrives to this day.

36

Reg Parnell

REG PARNELL WAS a shrewd wheeler-dealer from Derby who, but for the Second World War, might have matured into one of Britain's top-line Grand Prix drivers. A garage owner and farmer, he stock-piled unwanted racing cars in his barn throughout the hostilities. After his retirement from driving he would become a highly respected team manager for the Aston Martin sports car and Formula 1 programmes and later established his own private Grand Prix team for 1963.

He also ran a road haulage business, the Standard Transport Company, which was involved in official duties during the war, and its far-sighted owner often conveniently dovetailed those trips with the opportunity to collect a wide variety of competition cars for his own personal Aladdin's cave, either purchasing for himself from owners who felt there would never be much future use for such 'luxuries' or simply storing them for friends and colleagues. Amongst the machines moth-balled in this way were the Alfa Romeo Bi-Motore, Reggie Tongue's Maserati 4CLT, and a selection of ERAs.

As a result of these enterprising activities, in the post-war years Parnell was able to make a tidy profit selling these machines to a wide variety of customers when interest in the sport began to perk up once again.

Parnell began racing in 1935, at the age of 24, at the wheel of a tiny MG at his local circuit, Donington Park. Just before the outbreak of war he acquired a 1.5-litre ERA voiturette—chassis R6B—which he converted to 1100 cc, and actually took part in the 32-mile RRC Imperial Trophy at Crystal Palace on 26 August 1939. He finished fifth, but this was the last motor race in Britain to be held before the outbreak of hostilities and the car was tucked away in his collection.

After the war Parnell picked up the threads of his own motor racing career, selling his first ERA to Leicester garage owner Bob Gerard and replacing it with a similar car acquired from Earl Howe. He had a few promising outings in a 1.5-litre Maserati, but in 1947 he really got into his stride with a victory in the Jersey International road race and was third behind Luigi Villoresi and Louis Chiron in the Nîmes Grand Prix.

The following season saw him tackle an international *grand épreuve* for the first time, taking fifth place in the Italian Grand Prix at Monza, and in the years that followed he became acknowledged as one of Britain's most reliable and successful international drivers. By now he was in his late thirties, with considerable experience under his belt, and when BRM's ambitious $1\frac{1}{2}$-litre V16 programme began to gain momentum, it was only natural that the British team should look towards Parnell as a likely candidate for a drive.

Although the BRM was not ready for serious international competition at the start of 1950, the first year of the 'official' World Championship, Parnell drove it to morale-boosting victories in the Woodcote Cup and Goodwood Trophy races held at the Sussex circuit early in the season. By today's standards they were trivial little club events, but the news-starved media hyped them up beyond belief with the result that Parnell's modest achievements attracted coverage that was quite out of proportion to the significance of the meeting.

Nonetheless, it all helped Reg's growing credibility and, when the all-conquering Alfa 158s arrived to do battle in the British Grand Prix at Silverstone, Parnell was invited to drive a fourth works car. The Englishman fully justified his inclusion in the team and got onto the front row of the grid in company with his exalted team-mates Farina, Fangio, and Fagioli. Parnell finished fourth in a race distinguished, if that is the correct word, by the BRM's continuing unpreparedness. The glorious-sounding V16 did a few tentative demonstration laps in the hands of Raymond Mays, but was not considered ready to race.

Twelve months later, in the British Grand Prix that saw Froilan Gonzalez score Ferrari's first World Championship Grand Prix victory, the dogged Parnell wrestled the BRM to fifth place, on the verge of collapse with his feet blistered by the furnace-like conditions in the British car's under-cooled cockpit. Earlier that year he had scored a satisfying victory in the rain-shortened Silverstone International Trophy at the wheel of Tony Vandervell's $4\frac{1}{2}$-litre Thinwall Special Ferrari, and also used this machine to triumph in the Festival of Britain Trophy at Goodwood and a formule libre race at Winfield, in Scotland.

Throughout the 1950s Reg would also fulfil a key role in the Aston Martin sports car racing programme, having first been suggested to team manager John Wyer by George Abecassis, the man who later married Angela Brown, daughter of Aston Martin boss David Brown. Wyer conceded that he had not given Parnell much consideration, feeling that he was more of a single seater racer, but duly took him on.

Reg adopted a totally pragmatic approach to his motor racing. It gave him a great deal of satisfaction and enjoyment, but he made no bones about the fact that it was also a highly profitable hobby that was enabling him to accumulate funding for his pig farm in Derbyshire. That's not to say he was mercenary—far from it—but he was hard-nosed about his motor racing in a way that perhaps set him apart from the ranks of gentlemen enthusiasts with whom he had rubbed shoulders at Donington in those pre-war days.

His sports car record proved respectable; second at Sebring and fifth in the Mille Miglia during 1953, a wasted season persevering with the unsuccessful V12 Lagonda in 1954, and a couple of prestigious national British wins in the Aston DB3S the following year. In the summer of 1956 he had one hell of a shunt at Crystal Palace whilst driving Rob Walker's Connaught. Reg survived with superficial injuries and a sharp awareness that, at the age of 45, it was perhaps time to call it a day.

With John Wyer's imminent promotion to the post of Aston Martin Lagonda General Manager, the moment was ripe to offer Parnell the post of Aston Martin race team manager. He accepted wih alacrity, slipping into the post with a relaxed ease and familiarity that rather contrasted with the brisk formality of John Wyer's regime.

Reg had a sure hand with the drivers, even if he was not one for paperwork. But David Brown's racing team was no less successful in his custody than it had been in the past and Reg duly presided over its 1959 Le Mans triumph and victory in the World Sports Car Championship. In 1960 he left the team to run a private team of Cooper Formula 1 cars for Yeoman Credit, this evolving into the Bowmaker equipe for 1962 and then into Reg Parnell Racing at the start of 1963.

Having invited John Surtees for a test drive in an Aston Martin DBR1 as early as 1957, Parnell had a shrewd knowledge of the former motorcyclist's potential and acted as guide and mentor to the serious young man over two seasons (1961 and 1962) as he honed his craft as a Grand Prix driver. In 1963, that tutelage would pay off when Surtees took over as Ferrari team leader.

Parnell's next protégé would be the 19-year-old New Zealander Chris Amon, who cut his F1 teeth on the ex-Bowmaker Parnell team Lolas throughout 1963. But Reg never had the satisfaction of seeing the second of his lads make it to a Ferrari Grand Prix drive.

In January 1964 Reg Parnell went into hospital for a supposedly routine appendectomy. Complications set in, and he died at the early age of 53. The entire British motor racing community was shattered at the tragic news.

37

Roger Penske

NOW A MULTI-MILLIONAIRE, for two decades the patrician Roger Penske has been a pivotal personality on the US motor racing scene. Not only does he head a corporation that made a dramatic impact on his country's truck leasing and retail automotive scene during the 1980s, but his Indy car team is statistically the most successful of all time with 53 wins to its credit by the start of 1991.

British race fans may recall seeing Penske in action behind the wheel in the summer of 1963 at Brands Hatch. This 'unknown' American won the Guards Trophy race in something called a Cooper-Zerex. This machine would later be sold to Bruce McLaren and, in effect, became the first McLaren Can-Am car, the first twist on a convoluted path that would lead Penske and McLaren into becoming racing rivals in North America.

Two years later Penske was to retire from the cockpit. He worked as general manager of a Chevrolet dealer in Philadelphia and now decided to buy the business. He was told that his personal insurance premiums would go through the roof if he continued to race, and so he quit on the spot, never to look back. Since then, his cars have won eight Indy 500s and the Indy Car National Championship seven times.

In the late 1960s he fielded Lola T70s and a Ferrari 512M in both Can-Am and international sports car events; then in 1972 he took custody of the Porsche factory Can-Am efforts and won that prestigious series with Mark Donohue driving.

Penske then graduated to Formula 1, again with Donohue driving, but the American driver tragically died after crashing in the team's March 751 and suffering severe brain injuries during practice for the Austrian Grand Prix. Saddened at the loss of his close friend, Penske nonetheless continued the F1 operation, recruiting Ulsterman John Watson to take Donohue's place.

Watson won the 1976 Austrian Grand Prix with the elegant Cosworth-engined PC4 before Roger abruptly quit to consolidate his commercial activities back home. His business interests were burgeoning in the USA, so he decided to concentrate his focus on Indy car racing as a high-tech promotional vehicle for his sponsors, many of which did plenty of off-track business with the Penske Corporation.

Thus was Penske able to satisfy his fiercely competitive passion for motor racing with a programme that made sound commercial sense. Yet at a time when FISA, the sport's governing body, became increasingly paranoid about the possibility of the CART Championship expanding outside the USA, Penske would retain a clear perspective on Indy car racing. In his view, it was a booming national formula that in no way posed any sort of threat to F1. By the end of the 1980s, however, he was not discounting the possibility that he might get involved in Grand Prix racing again, having once described it as 'unfinished business'.

'Certainly, I would like at some time to look at coming back into F1,' he says firmly. 'We've got a few things still to do here in the USA, but now that we're involved with Detroit Diesel and General Motors, we've bought into an international business with over 120 dealers outside of North America—major distributorships in Europe, the Middle East, Africa and Pacific Asia—so there are some business reasons which would make some sense to be in F1.

'That's one of the reasons, of course, that I've focused so completely on North America because the benefits we get out of racing here is a common thread throughout all of our companies. At the time we withdrew from Formula 1 I think we were trying to do too much, tackling F1 and Indy cars racing, so it was simply a case of deciding where I could get the best value from my dollars.

'However, from the standpoint of being competitive, I think the moment you decide to go F1 racing you've got to commit 100 per cent of your efforts and assets to it. I'm not ready to do that today, but I sure feel that there could be something there in the future once the new naturally aspirated engine regulations have settled down and we see how things are progressing. I'm certainly not ever going to get out of motor racing and Formula 1 is a challenge we'd like to have.'

However, while Penske's own team has proved consistently successful at the highest level of US motor racing, his biggest single contribution to the sport has been in reshaping the face of Indy car racing from an administrative standpoint. When Championship Auto Racing Teams Inc (CART) was formed in 1978 as a breakaway group from the ultra-conservative United States Automobile Club (USAC), which then controlled the Indy car racing scene, Penske, along with fellow car owner Pat Patrick, was right at the sharp end of the action.

At the time, many people saw Penske as assuming the sort of domineering role exercised by Formula One Constructors' Association tsar Bernie Ecclestone. But he shrugs that notion aside.

'I think that's probably something of a misnomer,' he responds thoughtfully, 'because I'm just one of a nine-man Board of Directors. CART runs like any other business. Of course there are always some factions within any organization who approve or disapprove of the way things are going, but, taken as a whole, we're pretty proud of how far we've come in the last ten years.'

Of course, Penske is correct. CART has come a long way. Yet this high-profile entrepreneur is playing down his own perceived status within that racing *demi-monde*. A decade ago CART was established in an attempt to inject more owner participation into an area of the sport which, it is commonly agreed, was being stifled by USAC's stuffy, outmoded approach to the business of motor racing.

When USAC tried to block CART's ambitions, the fledgling organization responded by saying it would run its own series of races. USAC, however, sanctioned the Indianapolis 500, the jewel in the North American racing crown, and came up with what they reckoned was a whip hand response. They voted to reject the 1979 Indy 500 entries from Penske Racing, Patrick Racing, Chaparral Racing, Team McLaren, and Dan Gurney.

Penske then initiated court action to have the teams reinstated and was successful. CART never looked back. He is understandably satisfied with the way in which CART has developed as a prestige American domestic formula. It is a pride shared with every team owner, driver, and mechanic involved in the business. He shrugs aside rumours of any potential conflict of interests with F1, feeling there is more than enough room for both categories.

Penske corporations also control the race tracks at Michigan and Nazareth, both of which host successful Indy car events. Penske's two regular drivers, Rick Mears and Danny Sullivan, earn relatively small retainers, but if they do well they can more than double their money during the course of a season. 'You can only pay what you can afford,' Penske says, with just the trace of a twinkling smile, reflecting acknowledgement, perhaps, of a reputation for hard bargaining in the area of driver retainers. 'In Formula 1 there are obviously much larger sponsorship programmes involved and, obviously, those sponsorships are subsidising the drivers' compensation.

'Our drivers share in 45 or 50 per cent of our cars' earnings and, in the first six months of this year, we've probably earned $1.6 million, including winning at Indianapolis. So we've paid something like $800,000 of that back out to our drivers. So yes, with Rick winning Indy and Danny perhaps taking the championship, they could have earned more from their winnings than their basic retainer.

'This is a results-orientated business. I don't think that's wrong. The incentive works both ways. We feel it's been a good way to compensate our drivers, but on the other hand we're obviously prepared to pay what a good driver is worth. I don't want them feeling that I'm taking advantage of them. And, of course, we've had very good drivers in Sullivan, Mears, and Al Unser. And a very good relationship with them all.'

By the mid-1980s, Penske was leading a whirlwind business existence presiding over his corporation's three business groups dealing with transportation services, retail automotive, and automotive performance.

In December 1987 he pulled off a particularly successful coup, forging a partnership with General Motors in the Detroit Diesel Corporation as well as revitalizing the Hertz truck leasing business in which he became involved back in 1982. He talks about these and other business activities with every bit as much relish as he brings to bear on the racing team.

'Hertz/Penske was originally a fifty-fifty deal,' he enthuses, 'but I bought out the other half and we're now free to use the Hertz name for another ten years. We have now merged that organization with GE Capital's Gelco truck leasing company and formed what is now Penske Truck Leasing. We hold 69% per cent of the equity, General Electric 31 per cent ...'

Hertz Penske by now had some 55,000 trucks and 22,000 tractors, on lease or rental, nationwide. They had come from nowhere in six years and were now second only to Ryder in this field. In 1989 he was predicting that this arm of his business empire would do $800 million worth of business.

There are one or two other details as well. Like the Penske Auto Center of New York and Penske Cadillac in Downey, California. 'Between them, we are the largest single Cadillac dealer in the US,' he remarks somewhat casually. Oh yes, and he'd forgotten Longo Toyota in California. That happens to be America's largest Toyota dealership.

The Penske Corporation has an annual turnover in excess of $2 billion and employs upwards of 9,500 people at 383 facilities in 37 states. He and his family live amongst 25 acres of waterfront real estate in Red Bank, New Jersey, an enclave of the seriously rich, a mere 15 minutes from downtown New York by company helicopter.

Penske sets a bruising business schedule and expects his key executives to show a similar level of single-minded commitment. Whether criss-crossing the USA in one of the corporation's two Learjets, or focusing his mind on being first to the ski-lift whilst out on the piste in sun-drenched Colorado, Roger Penske is typical of that distinctive breed of compulsively driven, self-made men who finds it almost impossible to relax.

38

Ferry Porsche

ALTHOUGH THE PORSCHE company was founded as engineering design consultants by Professor Ferdinand Porsche in 1931, it was the great pioneer's son of the same name who was at the helm, building the family firm up to a level of achievement and status matched only by Daimler-Benz and BMW in the German automotive community. Throughout Ferry Porsche's professional career, motor racing and engineering excellence have been two inextricably entwined facets of the Porsche company's development, ensuring a splendid competition tradition.

Ferdinand Anton Ernst Porsche was born in the Austrian town of Wiener Neustadt on 19 September 1909 at a time when his father was working as technical director of the Austro-Daimler company. It was perhaps a portent of how significant a role motor racing would play in his future life that his father actually won his class in the Semmering hillclimb, near Vienna, on the day 'Ferry', as the new baby would become known within his family, was born.

In 1923 the Porsche family moved to Stuttgart where Professor Porsche took up an appointment as technical director of Daimler-Benz. Young Ferry commenced working with his father when the Professor established his own independent design office, the first project for which was the development of a 2-litre car for the German Wanderer company. The success of this machine led the newly established Auto-Union company, which had incorporated Wanderer, to commission Professor Porsche to design a Grand Prix car conforming with the newly established 750-kg regulations.

The Auto-Union not only became famous for its heroic battles against rival machines from Mercedes-Benz, it also established new design parameters for single-seater racing cars. With its 16-cylinder supercharged engine, installed behind the driver, it was years ahead of its time inasmuch as it set a trend that was not widely adopted by Formula 1 teams until the Cooper/Lotus technical revolution of the late 1950s.

One less well-known fact to arise from this period is that young Ferry Porsche carried out much of the initial test and development driving on the Grand Prix Auto-Union until his father intervened to prevent him, remarking 'I have enough drivers, but only one son.' Turning his hand to the technical side, in 1936 Ferry Porsche was responsible for the introduction of a limited-slip differential—a design facet that was to give their top driver Bernd Rosemeyer a considerable performance advantage that year, and something that is now taken for granted on all competition cars.

In 1935 Ferry Porsche married the then Dorothea Reitz, whom he had met when he came to Stuttgart; they would be together for fifty years up until her death and had a family of four sons. Then, shortly before the war, Porsche designed possibly their most significant car of all, the Volkswagen 'people's car', which would form the basis of the first proper Porsche sports car over a decade later.

The war itself hit Ferry Porsche's life very hard indeed. The company moved from Stuttgart to Gmund, in Carinthia, in 1943, but from 1945 the company had effectively to start from scratch, initially keeping the wolf from the door with the manufacture and repair of farm machinery.

Much of the responsibility for the Porsche company's survival at this dark time fell squarely on Ferry Porsche's shoulders as the Professor was held in custody by the French through to 1947.

This was a confusing, stressful period in Ferry's life. In August 1945, Professor Porsche had been interned in a castle near Frankfurt in the immediate aftermath of the war as part of a programme whereby the credentials of many prominent German personalities were exhaustively investigated by the Allies. Ferry, his Austrian brother-in-law Anton Piech, and several other members of the Porsche organization were also briefly held.

In November 1945 Professor Porsche was approached by the French with a commission to, in effect, design a national Volkswagen for them. No conclusion was reached before the Professor, Piech, and Ferry Porsche were again arrested on instructions of the French Justice Ministry. Ferry was released after a few months, but both the Professor and Piech were imprisoned for almost two years. This was destined to have an appalling effect on the old man's health, contributing to his death in January 1951. In those immediate post-war years the Porsche company took a lucrative commission to design a rear-engined single-seater racing car for the Italian Cisitalia concern, the fees going towards paying what the French described as bail—but was in fact little more than a crude ransom demand—for the release of Professor Porsche.

Ferry Porsche then pursued his ambitions to build a light, compact sports car based on available proprietary components—which in post-war Germany during the 1940s meant Volkswagen components. The concept was to match good acceleration with matchless braking and high standards of road holding. As Porsche Junior said at the time: 'If I build a car which gives me satisfaction, then there must be others with the same sort of dreams who would be prepared to buy such a car.'

The first car to bear the Porsche name was the type 356, the first example of which was delivered on 8 June 1948. The following year, in order to ensure its continued production, Ferry Porsche arranged a new component supply contract with VW chief Heinz Nordoff. Additionally, the Porsche company was appointed consultant engineers to Volkswagen and were awarded a royalty on every Beetle produced—at a time when the cars were leaving the Wolfsburg production line every seven seconds throughout each working day!

Since then, Ferry Porsche committed his life's work to enhancing the family company's products, notably by accelerating the process of product development through motor racing. They first went to Le Mans in 1951, achieving a class win on this maiden outing, since which time the name Porsche has become a watchword for motorsporting success. Porsche would subsequently win the World Sports Car Championship 14 times and, since 1970, has won Le Mans outright on a record 12 occasions.

In 1972, Dr Ing. h.c.F. Porsche AG—the firm's official title—became a joint stock company, after which Ferry Porsche became Chairman of the Supervisory Board. This was a year after he had expanded the design consultancy side of the Porsche business by opening the world-famous engineering centre at Weissach.

This now carries out research and development for a wide number of other manufacturers as well as overseas governments and for NATO. One of its most highly publicized and successful sub-contracts was the design and manufacture of the TAG turbo V6 Grand Prix engine, used by the McLaren International team to win two Constructors' Championships and three drivers' titles between 1984 and 1987.

Fêted with all manner of academic and engineering awards, the Porsche company's father figure reached the splendid age of 80 years in September 1989, still consumed with absorbing interest in the company that still carries the family name, still propounding the engineering excellence that stimulated his father's efforts more than three generations ago.

'The Porsche, as I have always regarded it,' says Ferry Porsche, 'is more than simply an automobile; it embodies my philosophy of freedom of individual progression—serving mankind without burdening it.'

159

39

Lance Reventlow

LANCE REVENTLOW WAS the son of Woolworth heiress and social butterfly Barbara Hutton by her marriage to the irascible and short-tempered Danish nobleman Count Court Haugwitz-Reventlow. Spoilt and pampered in his youth, almost smothered some might say by his family's vast wealth and taste for over-indulgence, he grew into a chubby, good-natured young man who seemed somehow faintly embarrassed by the role he was destined to play in his five times married mother's shadow.

Almost as if to emphasize his own identity, Reventlow's early enthusiasm for cars and motor racing prompted him to launch what still stands as the USA's most serious onslaught on Formula 1 with his front-engined $2\frac{1}{2}$-litre Scarabs at the start of 1960. Tragically, they were over a year too late on the Grand Prix scene and completely eclipsed by the contemporary breed of agile rear-engined F1 contenders and the project was quickly abandoned. Yet by trying, Reventlow guaranteed himself a distinctive and individualistic place in motor racing history.

Born to this great wealth in London on 14 February 1936, Lance went to live with his mother in the USA at the early age of four. He was only 19 when he drove his Mercedes 300SL road car in a production car event at Santa Barbara airfield in California, but the racing bug bit hard and the following year, 1956, saw him purchase an 1,100-cc Formula 3 Cooper and win no fewer than ten US domestic races.

In 1957 he made his first foray to Europe where he purchased a 2-litre Maserati. The highlight of this trip was a big accident at Snetterton and he also tried his hand in an F2 Cooper before returning to the US with the repaired Maserati.

Buying other people's cars, reasoned Reventlow, was not the way to go, so he decided to build his own. In 1958 he established Reventlow Automobiles Incorporated in Venice, California and commissioned established chassis specialists Troutman and Barnes to produce him a space frame sports car from a design penned by Warren Olson.

The first Scarab sports car was powered by a 4.94-litre Chevrolet V8 later bored out to 5.56 litres, in which form it allegedly produced in the order of 380-bhp at 6,000 rpm. Reventlow's racing partner Chuck Daigh evolved a Hilborn-Travers fuel injection system for the car and the Scarab finally made its racing début in Lance's hands at Palm Springs during April 1958. It had originally been intended that the Scarabs should contest the World Sports Car Championship, but the instigation of a 3-litre capacity limit scuppered that idea even before the cars were ready to run.

On the US sports car racing scene the Lister-Jaguars fielded by wealthy fellow Californian Briggs Cunningham were the cars to beat, and Reventlow finally dished out a defeat to his rival on the airport circuit at Montgomery, New York, in August that same summer. Daigh drove the second car regularly and they rounded off the year with Lance winning the Nassau Cup, and Chuck the Nassau Trophy, in the annual speed week held in Bermuda at the end of the year.

The Scarab sports cars would race on in private hands, but Reventlow now cleared the deck for what he regarded as the serious business— building an American Grand Prix car that would be capable of taking on Europe's finest. Leo Goossen, the man whose Offenhauser 4-cylinder supercharged design ruled the roost at Indianapolis, and now working for the Meyer-Drake company that had taken over Fred Offenhauser's concern, was brought in as design consultant.

Drawing on his Indianapolis experience, Goossen produced a light alloy, 4-cylinder engine with a bore and stroke of 82.25×85.73 mm, equipped with twin overhead camshaft that actuated the desmodromic valve gear. Conceived originally with water-cooled brakes and other esoteric technical subtleties, the Scarab RA1s were supposed to be ready in 1959, which would have been almost too late but perhaps would have given them a slim vestige of a chance. As it was, by not arriving until 1960 they were hopelessly outclassed and buried by the opposition.

Having attempted to make the grid at Monaco in 1960, then having to withdraw at Zandvoort, where Daigh qualified quite well, Reventlow and his team-mate finally squeezed into the line-up at Spa-Francorchamps for the Belgian race; but the inexperienced drivers in their ponderous, albeit immaculately crafted, machines were on a hiding to nothing. They retired early and, after a further unsuccessful attempt at qualifying for the French Grand Prix at Reims, where Richie Ginther took Reventlow's seat, the whole project was wound up.

A subsequent half-hearted attempt to revive the programme for the emergent 'Intercontinental formula' fell flat on its face after a couple of races, and while Daigh raced on in his own right, Reventlow returned to the US and quit racing, a decision in which he was encouraged by his young first wife, actress Jill St John, allegedly with some collusion from Lance's mother.

Shy and retiring he might have been, but Lance Reventlow could still push the boat out when it came to hospitality and partying, as a group of his racing friends discovered when they were invited to a lavish bash at his Beverley Hills mansion over the weekend of the 1960 United States Grand Prix at Riverside.

Food and wine flowed in abundance, guests were garlanded with flowers freshly flown in from Hawaii, the place was packed with starlets and, by the end of the evening, the swimming pool was filled with jostling, naked bodies. Yet while his guests let their hair down in the biggest possible way, Reventlow never really joined in, keeping himself to himself on the fringes of all the fun.

Having abandoned motor racing, Lance Reventlow turned his attention to skiing and polo, sports in which he became extremely accomplished, during the remaining twelve years of his life. On 24 July 1972, en route to a skiing outing, he was a passenger in a single-engined Cessna 206 that crashed into a wooded slope amidst the Rocky Mountains in Colorado during a heavy storm. None of its occupants survived.

40

Carroll Shelby

THIS GENIAL TEXAN'S trademark was the distinctive bib-style overalls that gave him a swashbuckling Casey Jones-like appearance throughout a distinguished racing career, the high point of which was sharing the winning Aston Martin with Roy Salvadori at Le Mans in 1959. Later, after retiring from the cockpit, he was one of the most significant personalities in the development of Ford's multi-million dollar sports car racing onslaught in the 1960s, his name perpetuated on such contemporary high performance machinery as the Shelby American Cobra and the Shelby Mustang GT350.

Born in Leesburg, Texas, on 11 January 1923, the son of the town's postmaster, young Shelby's family moved to Dallas when he was a child. Despite being diagnosed as suffering from a slight heart murmur at the age of 10, he served as a flight instructor with the USAAF during the Second World War, dabbling in the truck business before turning his hand to chicken farming, unsuccessfully, in the late 1940s.

In 1952 he started to gain recognition with some promising outings at the wheel of a borrowed Jaguar XK120, switching the following year to a fearsome Allard-Cadillac. It was that year, for an event at Eagle Mountain Air Station, near Fort Worth, that he first appeared in his distinctive striped overalls. Legend has it that he'd just spent a hard day working on a nearby farm and almost forgot he was due to compete—however difficult that may be to believe.

It was a hot afternoon, so the story goes, and he didn't bother to change. In his own words: 'I found the overalls cool and comfortable and, since I won the race, I sorta' became identified with them ... so I started wearing them all the time!'

In the 1954 Buenos Aires 1,000-km race, Kleenex heir Jim Kimberly had donated a cup for the best performance by an amateur driver. The Allard-Cadillac duly made the trip, Shelby co-driving with airline pilot Dale Duncan, a useful connection who helped arrange air freight the machine to Argentina.

Shelby's first competitive appearance outside the USA was memorable, to say the least. They finished tenth, despite a carburettor fire during a pit stop that had to be extinguished by the simple expedient of Duncan urinating on the engine. More significantly, Aston Martin driver Peter Collins introduced Shelby to John Wyer. Both Collins and

Wyer had been impressed by the Texan's handling of the wild and woolly Allard; a deal to drive an Aston Martin in Europe was spoken about.

In the event, Carroll was invited to drive that year's Sebring 12-hour event, sharing the third works DB3S with Chuck Wallace, but failing to finish. The plan was then that Shelby would come to Europe where Texan oil man Guy Mabee planned to buy him a DB3S, apparently as a prelude to a more ambitious plan to manufacture a world-beating American sports racing car. This ambitious project never got off the ground, nor did Mr Mabee's tentative agreement to purchase an Aston Martin for Shelby to race in the meantime.

When Carroll reached England there was a blue and white DB3S all ready for him to race, but no money with which to purchase the machine. Nevertheless, Shelby found himself absorbed into the Aston Martin team operation, first helping with servicing on the Mille Miglia, before returning to England where he finished second to Duncan Hamilton's Jaguar C-type at Aintree, his first outing with the blue and white DB3S.

John Wyer graciously declined Shelby's over-ambitious offer to fulfil the outstanding financial obligation on the new car, inviting him to drive at Le Mans with Paul Frere, where the car retired, and the Supercortemagiore 1,000 km at Monza, with Graham Whitehead, where they finished fifth. Another ride at Silverstone followed before Carroll headed back to the USA and his family.

For 1955 Shelby, in his own words, 'vacillated between Europe and the States', trying to balance his racing ambitions with the demands of a growing, teenage family. He had crashed badly practising an Austin Healey for the Carrera Panamericana, but was sufficiently recovered to share wealthy enthusiast Alan Guiberson's Ferrari with Phil Hill at Sebring.

Shelby stayed racing at home in Ferraris for the equally wealthy Tony Parravano and John Edgar. Surviving a very serious crash at Riverside in September 1957—four vertebrae needed fusing together and he also underwent minor plastic surgery—he then rejoined the Aston works team in 1958, staying through to score that memorable victory with Salvadori at Le Mans with the shapely DBR1.

Like most of those who drove for Aston Martin in the 1950s, Shelby simply loved the team's ambience and never really seriously considered fleeting, and possibly empty, offers to join Maserati or Ferrari. His Texan penchant for straight talking occasionally made David Brown wince; telling the Boss that the DBR2 handled like 'ten pound of shit in a five-pound bag' was pretty strong stuff for a hired hand in the mid-1950s. In Shelby's own words again: 'He got pissed off at that, turned round and walked away.' Understandably so.

Along with Roy Salvadori, Shelby also handled the DBR4 Grand Prix Aston Martins, which had arrived on the scene too late. At the start of 1960 Shelby suffered serious chest pains that alerted him to a potential heart condition and, despite attempting to control the situation by driving with nitroglycerine pills under his tongue throughout a 1960 season of US domestic sports car racing, Shelby quit the cockpit at the end of the year.

After retirement he stayed in the racing business, establishing the Carroll Shelby Driving School at Riverside and becoming a distributor for Goodyear tyres. Still personally keen on the idea of a US sports car, he approached the English AC company on hearing that their supply of Bristol engines had dried up towards the end of 1961. He suggested they consider installing a lightweight US V8 engine and, while his initial thoughts tended towards General Motors products, he eventually turned to Ford to use their latest 4.7-litre V8, successfully romancing key senior Detroit executives into appreciating the potential benefits of such a link-up.

His new company, Shelby American Incorporated, ironically made its original base in the workshops at Venice, California, previously occupied by Lance Reventlow and his Scarabs. However, by getting the mighty Ford Motor Company to back his efforts, Shelby's project was aimed in a more specific direction.

The Shelby Cobras were homologated as GT cars by the end of 1962 and began racing in earnest during the 1963 season, essentially pitched against the Ferrari GTOs and Chevrolet Corvettes in national US sports car racing, and against the Italian machines in particular in the GT categories of major international sports car events. They were clearly not going to be potential winners against the faster sports prototypes, a fact which Ford had difficulty coming to terms with, but when Peter Bolton and Ian Sanderson finished seventh overall at Le Mans that year it was clear that the car had potential.

By this stage, however, Ford had invested around $3 million in Shelby's programme and were starting to get a little nervous about the whole thing, more through a thwarted sense of over-optimism than anything else. They accordingly engaged the man who'd given 'Shel' his big chance in Europe a decade earlier, John Wyer, to head up an English-based prototype group working with Eric Broadley's Lola company with a view to manufacturing a front-line prototype that would be able to take on Ferrari head to head. This step would lead to the birth of the Ford GT40.

In 1965, however, the Shelby Cobras won the FIA Manufacturers' Championship for GT cars, wresting the title from Ferrari. Moreover, in 1966 and 1967, Shelby-managed teams won Le Mans and by 1970 Carroll was diversifying into other business ventures outside motor racing.

It was not until 1982, when his friend Lee Iacocca offered him the opportunity to serve as a performance consultant to Chrysler, that he returned to the motorsporting business. He also operates two of his own major California-based businesses, the Dodge Shelby Performance Centre in Santa Fe Springs and his own Shelby Autos company at Whittier.

41

John Surtees

THE ONLY MAN to have won the World Championship on two wheels as well as four, John Surtees was a highly accomplished performer who might have achieved considerably more in car racing than he did had he simply concentrated more on his work behind the wheel instead of attempting to become involved in all the other facets of racing team operation. That said, in several cases during his career he had little choice in this respect, but it was sad that the time spent operating his own Grand Prix team produced such disappointing results prior to the point when it closed its doors at the end of 1978.

Born on 11 February 1934 in Tatsfield, Kent, Surtees grew up in a household deeply involved in the motorcycling business. His father, Jack, was in the motorcycle trade and featured among the most keen and accomplished grass track riders of the pre-war era. The family had quite a struggle through the war years, but when peace returned Jack Surtees re-established himself in the motorcycle business and his eldest son quickly became a devoted and loyal disciple of the family racing cause.

Initially, John passengered for his father on his combination, but his individual racing career really got under way when he became apprenticed to Vincents and acquired a single-cylinder Grey Flash motorcycle. It was on this machine that he won his first race, at Brands Hatch in 1951, and he would go on to earn the title of uncrowned King of the Kent circuit which he would retain right through his career on two wheels until the end of 1960.

One of Surtees's great qualities was his mechanical knowledge, the ability to work on his machines as well as the mechanics who later serviced his bikes during his professional career. He was brought up with a strong family instinct and retained an unswerving affection for and loyalty to his parents—an undeniably attractive quality in a man who gained a reputation for being something of a loner amongst his peers.

He later bought a Manx Norton and was invited to join the works team in 1955, clinching his reputation as one of the sport's most gifted rising stars with a memorable victory over Geoff Duke's Gilera at Silverstone at the end of that season. Unable to persuade Nortons to continue with a works effort in 1956, despite attracting potential sponsorship from a major British national newspaper, he switched to the

Italian MV Agusta team from 1956 and set about writing his name into the motorcycle racing history books.

Despite crashing heavily in the German Grand Prix at Solitude, Surtees clinched his first two-wheel world title with the 1956 500 cc crown, and the following year was spent developing the MV Agustas to a point where they could seriously compete with the more competitive Gileras and Moto Guzzis. It was therefore with some disappointment that Surtees found himself in 1958 without this opposition to measure himself against, as the other Italian factories withdrew from international racing, leaving MV to dominate the stage.

In the three seasons up until the end of 1960, when he quit professional motorcycle racing for good, Surtees won both the 350 and 500 World Championships as well as the Senior and Junior Isle of Man TTs in 1958 and 1959, plus the Senior again in 1960. Yet he was always disappointed at Count Domenico Agusta's increasing reluctance to field bikes in non-championship and British domestic events, or to permit Surtees to use his own private Nortons in these events.

This lack of flexibility on Agusta's part led Surtees to supplement his 1960 programme with a diet of car racing after he had pointed out to the Count that, while his contract may have debarred him from racing any other motorcycles, there was nothing to prevent him competing on four wheels.

John's interest in car racing was sparked by Reg Parnell, who invited him to try an Aston Martin DBR1 sports car at Goodwood late in 1959. He also received a lot of encouragement from Vanwall team chief Tony Vandervell and from Mike Hawthorn, who had become the first Englishman to win the World Championship in 1958.

Surtees made his Formula Junior debut at Goodwood in a Ken Tyrrell-entered Cooper-Austin in April 1960, only narrowly being defeated by Jim Clark's Lotus. In short order he was approached by Colin Chapman to drive for Team Lotus in Formula 1 whenever his motorcycle commitments allowed, proving his world class by finishing second in the British Grand Prix at Silverstone and taking pole position for the Portuguese race at Oporto.

At the end of the season, Chapman tried to play ducks and drakes with his driver line-up, offering Surtees a deal to run alongside Jim Clark for the following year despite already having a contract with Innes Ireland. Surtees, unwilling to jeopardize Ireland's position, withdrew from the negotiations and joined the Reg Parnell-run Yeoman Credit team instead. Ethically, he had done the right thing, but it was certainly the wrong turn as far as his career was concerned.

In 1962 Yeoman Credit became Bowmaker Racing and, armed with the new Eric Broadley-designed Lola Mk 4, Surtees began to establish himself as a consistent front runner. But real Formula 1 success would not come his way until he switched to Ferrari at the start of 1963 and played a crucial role in the Italian team's racing renaissance in the mid-1960s.

The attraction of driving for the Prancing Horse team was easy to see. Surtees had come to love Italy during his time with MV Agusta and admired the way the Italians operated. Yet, despite the success that would come his way, in Enzo Ferrari he found the same sort of stubborn, self-absorbed, autocratic character as that of Count Domenico Agusta. Despite this, an air of mutual respect would bind the two men together until their much-publicized split at the start of 1966.

Surtees won his first car Grand Prix at Nurburgring in 1963 with the Ferrari 156, but would have to wait until the same event the following year to score his second victory. By then he would be in the Ferrari 158 V8 which took him all the way to a somewhat fortunate World Championship, only resolved on the final lap of the Mexican Grand Prix when Jim Clark's Lotus retired with engine trouble and Surtees slipped through to take the crucial second place he needed.

After this success, the 1965 season proved highly disappointing, yielding no Formula 1 victories, and in late September John was gravely injured when he crashed his own Lola T70 in practice for a sports car race at Mosport Park, near Toronto. After lingering close to death for several days, he forced the pace of a quite remarkable recovery from his multiple injuries and returned to the cockpit of a Formula 1 Ferrari for the start of the 1966 season.

By this time Surtees's position at Maranello was being undermined by the political machinations of team manager Eugenio Dragoni and, despite winning the Belgian Grand Prix, he eventually left the team in the wake of a row about driver pairings at Le Mans. The reasons behind the rift have never been satisfactorily explained to this day, but they were certainly mutually destructive as far as the subsequent winning potential of both driver and team were concerned.

Surtees first went briefly to Cooper, for the balance of the 1966 season, then spent two years struggling with Honda during which he won the last of his six Grand Prix victories, the 1967 Italian race at Monza. A stint with BRM in 1969 reduced him to the depths of depression, so he decided to take the plunge and build his own Surtees Formula 1 car for 1970.

The early Surtees TS7s, TS9s, and 9Bs were highly competitive Cosworth-engined machines which twice came close to winning a World Championship Grand Prix. John himself nearly won the 1971 South African event, thwarted only by engine failure in the closing stages, while Mike Hailwood was on the verge of dislodging Jackie Stewart's Tyrrell from the lead of the same race the following year when a front suspension link failed.

Surtees himself bagged a couple of non-title Formula 1 victories in the Oulton Park Gold Cup (1970 and 1971) and the team performed well enough for Mike Hailwood to win the 1972 European Formula 2 Championship. Subsequently, investments made on the basis of agreed sponsorship that never materialized blighted Surtees's Formula 1 efforts and, despite a brief resurgence with the pretty TS19 driven by Alan Jones in 1976, the team gradually slipped off the pace and closed its doors at the end of 1978.

Several of his drivers recall Surtees as too much of an interventionist with an inability to delegate or accept that his ways or methods might be wrong. John would see it differently, clearly believing that personal attention to detail and involvement with every facet of the racing operation was the only realistic way for a Formula 1 team owner to operate. He blames lack of finance for Team Surtees's gradual eclipse as a potential Formula 1 force. Yet even he now agrees that if he had only concentrated on driving, far more success than his single World Championship probably would have come his way.

On a personal level, Surtees could be a prickly customer who found it difficult to forgive those with whom he crossed swords. Only after his retirement from active involvement in the sport did he really mellow, with the onset of middle age and the arrival of his own children, as he says himself, perhaps rather late in the day.

42

Ron Tauranac

RON TAURANAC SPENT the first ten years of his career as a designer on the European racing scene in the shadow of his famous compatriot Jack Brabham, masterminding the design of the cars that helped put his fellow Australian's name in lights, both as a driver and a constructor, through to his retirement from the cockpit in 1970.

Thereafter, the taciturn and introspective Tauranac would emerge from behind a cloak of relative anonymity to become a successful and wealthy racing car constructor in his own right using the marque name Ralt, which had originally been applied to a 500-cc Formula 3 machine he had constructed himself back in Australia at the turn of the 1950s.

Brabham and Tauranac came from similar backgrounds, both with family roots in Britain and both having served in the Royal Australian Air Force in the last few months of the Second World War. Jack had joined the RAAF as a flight mechanic at the age of 18 in 1944, while Ron trained as a pilot flying Harvards on a course in Canada, switched to Wirraways on his return to Australia, and was just spared an involvement in battle when Japan capitulated after the atom bombs were dropped on Hiroshima and Nagasaki.

Ron was in fact born in Gillingham, Kent, but his family emigrated to Australia when he was just over three years old, in 1928. He grew up in Fassifern, a rural community between Sydney and Newcastle, a 'real backwoods' kid' by his own admission. He got his first job just before the outbreak of war as a jig and tool draughtsman with the Commonwealth Air Corporation, and when he was finally demobbed he took a job with a chemical company.

Together with his brother Austin, Ron conceived the first Ralt Formula 3 car from technical know-how culled from investigative sessions in the local public library. It went quite well and he gradually refined the concept to the point where Ron raced it with considerable distinction, finishing second in the 1953 New South Wales Hillclimb Championship before winning it the following year. Third and second respectively in these two contests was Jack Brabham ...

By 1955 Jack had made tracks for England in pursuit of a professional career that would lead him into the Cooper factory Formula 1 team en route to consecutive World Championship titles in 1959 and 1960. During his early years in Europe, Jack corresponded frequently with his old friend Ron, from time to time asking for advice on some aspect of Cooper engineering technology, and Tauranac used to oblige with helpful sketches which Jack sometimes fed into the team's design process.

By 1959, Jack had his own ideas about setting up as a commercial racing car manufacturer in the junior formulae and invited Tauranac over to help with the project. By this time Brabham had established his own successful motor business in Chessington and Ron found himself hurled into the task of installing Coventry-Climax engines into Triumph Herald road cars by day and designing the racers by night.

Together the Australian duo founded Motor Racing Developments with the share capital split 60/40 in Jack's favour. Initially, the cars would be called MRDs, but those initials had an unfortunate French connotation, so eventually they were dubbed Repco Brabhams.

From the outset, Tauranac's designs gained a reputation for being uncomplicated and straightforward to set up from the chassis viewpoint, a particularly attractive feature for the inexperienced private customers who flocked to MRD in ever-increasing numbers as the 1960s rolled on. It was just as well that Jack decided to quit Cooper and go it alone in 1962, for Charlie Cooper, the autocratic old patriarch who founded the company, was becoming increasingly irritated as Brabham sales chipped steadily away at what once had been a market flooded with Cooper products.

Once again, Tauranac applied his practical design skills to produce an uncomplicated space frame chassis into which Brabham installed a Coventry-Climax V8 in time for the 1962 German Grand Prix. But Jack was either shrewd or tight, depending on which side of the fence one viewed any deal into which he entered. Dan Gurney, who drove loyally for him from 1963 to 1965, described him to me as 'tighter than a bull's ass in fly season' and there were times when Tauranac must have echoed those sentiments.

Brabham established a separate company, Brabham Racing Developments (BRD), away from MRD's production car business, to manufacture the Grand Prix machines. They were then passed over to the Brabham Racing Organization, the racing team itself, for £3,000 per car. So Tauranac found himself in a position where the company in which he had a partnership—MRD—did not earn any of the profits generated from the Grand Prix cars.

Understandably, Ron quickly tired of such an arrangement and advised Jack at the end of 1965 that he didn't really want to design any more Grand Prix cars—'it was getting to be a case of a lot of effort for no real interest'—and Jack eventually took his point. The company was restructured in a way that saw MRD take control of the Formula 1 side from Brabham Racing Organization, which is why Tauranac was present at far more races during the 3-litre Formula than he had been previously.

For the rest of the decade, Jack and Ron would travel the world together, successfully presiding over the 1966 and 1967 World Championships using Repco V8 engines. Ron continued to produce agile, forgiving F1 chassis, just as he had done for the junior formulae, and this now-contented business partnership came to an end in 1969 when, in anticipation of retirement, Jack sold out his MRD shareholding to Tauranac.

Jack had hoped to lure the dynamic Jochen Rindt back into the Brabham fold for 1970, but despite his and Goodyear's best efforts, Lotus boss Colin Chapman made it crystal clear that he would outbid anybody to keep the Austrian. So Jack shelved his retirement plans for another twelve months, staying on to drive—effectively just as an employee—for a final season.

Then he quit for good, leaving Tauranac with the responsibility for the commercial development of the team as well as the engineering side. But F1 was changing fast as the 1960s gave way to the 1970s. The whole scene was becoming more overtly commercial and fast-moving. 'I was really not much good at getting sponsorship,' Ron recalled, 'and even though Goodyear was paying the lion's share of the budget in 1971, it still represented a £100,000 gamble which I could ill-afford at a time I was still paying Jack back the money he lent me to buy his shares.'

Eventually he began to talk to Bernie Ecclestone about the possibility of a partnership. Bernie wasn't over-anxious about that idea, but he would buy Brabham if Ron wanted out. Tauranac agreed and Bernie took over at the end of 1971. Ron stayed on for a bit, but eventually moved off to take up a succession of freelance engineering posts. The Brabham team now went forward to embrace a successful future with neither of its co-founders at the helm.

One of the by-products of Bernie's acquisition was that Brabham soon dropped out of the customer racing car market to concentrate exclusively on Formula 1. March, Chevron, and Modus filled the void for a time, but in 1975 the Ralt name was propelled onto the British domestic scene as Tauranac went back into business under his own steam manufacturing practical, down-to-earth racing cars in much the same way as he had done for Brabham over a decade before.

Was he successful second time round! Even more so. From that moment until the present day, Ralt has never looked back, winning everything that was around in Formula 3 and Formula 2. In September 1988, the Ralt shares owned by Ron and his wife Norah changed hands for £1.15 million when March Group plc, parent company of their one-time rivals March Engineering, bought them out.

It was a brilliant deal. Ron still runs Ralt, doing what he loves, but without the day-to-day business worries that necessarily went with a business generating a profit of £750,000 a year.

43

Ken Tyrrell

THERE IS NOBODY in motor racing more capable of keeping a secret than Ken Tyrrell. Early in 1985 the author found himself amongst a group of fellow writers on a plane heading for Paris for the launch of the new Formula 1 Renault RE60. By apparent chance, on the same plane was Ken Tyrrell. It was at the height of the turbo era when Ken's team was still struggling with a naturally aspirated Cosworth V8 engine. He desperately needed a turbocharged engine.

'Suppose you're off to Renault to sort out some turbos,' we all chortled. Ken smiled benignly, yet gave nothing away. On arrival at Charles de Gaulle airport we went our different ways. Little did we know that, chatting with Tyrrell on the aircraft, we had hit the nail absolutely on the head. But Ken's cool reaction had thrown us off the trail. We agreed we wouldn't have wanted to play poker with him.

Some people find Tyrrell a grumpy old stick-in-the-mud. Others reckon he's good value. Truth be told, he's both—often, unwittingly, at the same time. But he is an absolutely passionate enthusiast who loves Grand Prix racing dearly and has been on and around the motor racing scene for 39 years.

Ken served with the Royal Air Force during the war as a teenage navigator and his yarns about these aeronautical exploits have listeners splitting their sides. One favourite is how their Halifax bomber, piloted by a former bank manager, managed to overshoot the runway at its Yorkshire base, slithered across a road or two before coming to rest in a field. It must have been absolutely terrifying at the time, but somehow Ken makes it sound like some sort of comedy routine.

Football was Ken's game in those immediate post-war years, but when his local soccer club organized a day trip to a Formula 1 race at Silverstone he tagged along. He was instantly attracted by the 500-cc Formula 3 cars and contested his first such race at Snetterton in 1952.

The 500-cc F3 was a closely contested category throughout the late 1940s and early 1950s, spawning such rising stars as Stirling Moss, Peter Collins, and Stuart Lewis-Evans. While Ken became one of the stalwart supporters of this category, he never became a front-line ace, although he did manage to win an international event at Karlskoga in Sweden and was given a test drive for Aston Martin before retiring from the cockpit at the end of 1958. In motor racing circles he assumed the nickname

'Chopper' for his cars carried the emblem of a woodman's axe in recognition of the Tyrrell family's Surrey-based timber business.

For 1959 he ran the works F2 Coopers in partnership with Alan Brown and Cecil Libowitz, then struck out on his own, fielding the factory Formula Junior cars.

In 1965 he fielded the highly promising young American Timmy Mayer in the latest Formula Junior machine. After Mayer's tragic death at Longford, Tasmania, in January 1964 Ken found himself casting around for a first-rate driver to lead the Cooper works team into the 1-litre F3 category that was initiated that season.

Goodwood track manager Robin McKay had seen the young Scottish driver Jackie Stewart turning some superb lap times in an elderly Ecurie Ecosse Cooper-Monaco and recommended Tyrrell get in touch with him. After a brief telephone conversation, Ken invited Jackie down to Goodwood for another test session, this time with Bruce McLaren setting a bogey time at the wheel of the new Cooper F3 car.

Stewart proved quite capable of matching anything McLaren could pull out of the bag, so Tyrrell signed the Scot there and then. It was the start of a relationship that would lead to three World Championship titles over the next decade.

Predictably, young Jackie totally dominated the 1964 F3 season and disappeared into Formula 1 with BRM the following year. Tyrrell moved up into Formula 2 with a series of progressively less competitive Coopers before switching to French Matras. Jackie Stewart used these to increasing effect in Formula 2 throughout 1966 and 1967, and when the new Keith Duckworth-designed Cosworth-Ford DFV V8 burst onto the Formula 1 scene in 1968, Ken began toying with the prospect of Formula 1.

After three largely disappointing seasons, Jackie was keen to leave BRM, so Ken put together a deal whereby Matra would loan his team a Formula 1 chassis while he supplied the engines, running costs, and general operation. Thus Matra International came into being at the start of 1968, the season in which Stewart took over the mantle of Formula 1 pacemaker after Jim Clark's death at Hockenheim.

Using the Matra MS10, Stewart won the Dutch, German and United States Grands Prix, only just losing out to Graham Hill in the quest for the World Championship. The following year Tyrrell and Stewart couldn't miss; Jackie won five races to clinch his first title. But there were problems on the horizon. Although undeniably impressed with the manner in which Tyrrell had operated its MS80 chassis, the Matra company was committed to using its own V12 engine in 1970. The message to Ken was simple: use our engine, or we go our separate ways.

Rightly, Stewart and Tyrrell considered the future belonged to Cosworth's DFV. Long-term, the only option was for Ken to build his own car, but for now he found himself having to buy the unproven March

701s as a stop-gap expedient for the first half of the 1970 season. The first Tyrrell was developed in conditions of tremendous secrecy at a cost of £22,500, a massive sum set against the March 701s at £6,500 apiece. But the new car was ready in mid-summer 1970, and proved just the ticket.

Although Stewart failed to win a single race in the second half of 1970, he stormed away with the Championship in 1971 and would probably have scored a hat trick of Championships through to the end of his career had his 1972 title challenge not been blighted by a gastric ulcer. Jackie had developed a rather neurotic side to his character, burning the candle at both ends as he tried to dovetail too many business commitments in with his racing programme. Throughout this troubled period, Tyrrell handled his star driver with care and consideration, making it very clear that he had to sort out these problems on his own while at the same time giving him all the support he could muster.

After Stewart's retirement at the end of the 1973 season, Tyrrell's team continued in Formula 1 although it never again really looked like scaling the heights of achievement it had enjoyed during the Scot's heyday. Instead, Tyrrell increasingly fell into the role of grooming stars of the future, the likes of Jody Scheckter, Michele Alboreto, and, latterly, Jean Alesi building their F1 reputations behind the wheels of his cars.

Fundamentally, Ken Tyrrell loves his motor racing and has always been an enthusiast. He has a gruff exterior and is sometimes accused of being over-paternal in his attitude to his young charges. He can shout, argue, and splutter with the best of them—during the early 1980s, if you felt like having a right royal shouting match, you only had to seek out Ken Tyrrell and ask his opinion about turbocharged engines. He remains a man with trenchant opinions and the lung capacity to ensure that they are heard.

But the best single thing about Ken Tyrrell is that he can disagree with you, have a blazing argument, and then forget it ever happened. He is not a man who bears grudges.

44

Tony Vandervell

GUY ANTHONY VANDERVELL was a self-made industrial magnate who sprang from a mould similar to that which produced Enzo Ferrari, Colin Chapman, and Bernie Ecclestone. The main difference was that he was born to comfortable circumstances, his father, Charles Anthony Vandervell, having founded the successful CAV electrical empire. Born in 1899, young Tony Vandervell was educated at Harrow but grew up to be a self-reliant, enterprising, if rather wayward young man who raced cars and motorcycles at Brooklands before settling down to a spectacularly successful business career of his own.

In 1926, Charles Vandervell, finally despairing that his independent-minded son would settle down and toe the family line if he inherited his business empire, sold out CAV's electrical interests to Joseph Lucas Ltd. Tony Vandervell did not take to working under the new regime and soon fell out with the management, leaving to establish his own company which became pioneers in the manufacture of quality electric radiograms.

However, in 1930, young Vandervell made a discovery that was to start him on the road to wealth and prosperity. By chance, he learned that a new replaceable car engine bearing was being manufactured in the United States. Quickly appreciating its implications for reducing cost and easing the manufacture of production car engines, he hurried to the United States and concluded a deal with the Cleveland Graphite Bronze Company, who had invented this new technique, for the British licence. With the enthusiastic financial advice and assistance of his father, Tony Vandervell now established a new company, Vandervell Products Ltd, based on a purpose-built factory in Western Avenue, Acton, on London's western fringes.

Vandervell Products' production of 'thinwall' bearings made an extremely significant contribution to Britain's war effort between 1939 and 1945, after which the immensely patriotic Tony Vandervell became involved as one of the consultant directors to the BRM project for a British national Formula 1 car. He fully appreciated the benefits motor racing could offer both as a technical test bed and a vehicle for projecting the country's international prestige, but soon became impatient with the unwieldy and ponderous 'management by committee' which handicapped this ambitious and over-complex racing programme.

It soon became clear to Vandervell that the $1\frac{1}{2}$-litre V16 **BRM** project was going to run hopelessly late, so he broke away and decided to start his own racing programme with a long-term view to perhaps building a Grand Prix car off his own bat. Initially, in 1949, he purchased a $1\frac{1}{2}$-litre supercharged Ferrari 125 which was raced under the 'Thinwall Special' banner as a competitive test bed for the Vandervell Thinwall bearings, later superseded by a $4\frac{1}{2}$-litre non-supercharged car early in 1951.

Vandervell's two green liveried Ferraris did sterling service in the hands of Reg Parnell, Peter Collins, and others, but by the start of 1952 it gradually became clear that the company had more ambitious long-term plans. Tony Vandervell had originally become involved with the BRM Trust in order to facilitate the production of a worthwhile British Formula 1 contender 'to beat those damned red cars', as he referred to the Italian Alfa Romeos, Maseratis, and Ferraris that were dominating the immediate post-war international motor racing scene. But now, step by step, he was laying plans to achieve that aim with his own racing cars.

Gruff and autocratic, Vandervell was enough of a practical realist to employ the right people for the right job and look after them to the best of his ability. Although his word was law within his business empire, he learned the art of delegation in a way that was perhaps not emulated by the likes of Chapman, Ecclestone or even Ferrari. While they were in the motor business, Vandervell had built up a broader based industrial empire and knew precisely what was required to succeed in the wider business world, outside the restricted confines of a sport so introspective as motor racing.

By 1955, the second season of the $2\frac{1}{2}$-litre Formula 1, the Vanwalls, as the new cars were named, had started to show genuine promise. After experimentation with chassis frames designed by Cooper, Tony Vandervell commissioned Lotus chief Colin Chapman to produce a new chassis clothed in a distinctive body conceived by aerodynamics expert Frank Costin.

Mike Hawthorn was duly signed to race for the team, but when 'Old Man' Vandervell ruined the clutch of one of the cars driving it from Spa to the circuit at Francorchamps, the two men fell out and harsh words were exchanged on the spur of the moment. There was clearly going to be no future for this particular relationship and Hawthorn duly left the team almost before he had started, the unhappy partnership being put down to experience by both sides.

By 1956 the Vanwall had improved to the point where it was a really serious contender, and when the Franco-American Harry Schell got in amongst the Ferraris battling for the lead of the French Grand Prix at Reims, the message was writ large on the wall. Britain at last had a top-line, home-grown Grand Prix team and it was a measure of Stirling Moss's confidence in Tony Vandervell's operation that he signed up to drive a Vanwall in 1957.

Three glorious moments arrived in quick succession. Moss and team-mate Tony Brooks shared a Vanwall to win the British Grand Prix at Aintree, Stirling following this up with two more splendid triumphs. The first was at Pescara, the second in Italy's motor racing heartland at Monza. A Vanwall had won the Italian Grand Prix, beating off the Ferrari and Maserati opposition. For the large man in the white alpaca jacket and wide-brimmed hat standing in the pit lane, it was a long-held ambition finally realized.

But there was more to come for Tony Vandervell and his Vanwalls. In 1958, Moss and Brooks between them won five Grands Prix to clinch the Constructors' Championship for Vanwall, capping a glorious period of British motor racing history. Yet for Vandervell, the price exacted for this success was too high. In the final race of the season, the Moroccan Grand Prix at Casablanca, Stuart Lewis-Evans, the team's highly talented number three driver, was badly injured when his Vanwall crashed and caught fire.

Flown home to England in Vandervell's chartered airliner, Stuart was admitted to the burns unit established at East Grinstead hospital named in memory of Sir Archibald McIndoe, the surgeon who had carried out valuable pioneering skin graft techniques on airmen burnt during the Second World War. Sadly, Lewis-Evans succumbed to his injuries despite a tremendous fight.

The impact of the young English driver's death on Tony Vandervell cannot be underestimated. Although this outwardly rather brusque and grumpy man may have given the impression of being hard and uncaring to those who didn't know him, the reality could not have been further from the truth. He was inwardly devastated by Stuart's death and it was this, not his declining health, that caused him to withdraw the Vanwalls from full-time competition from that moment onwards.

Tony Vandervell died in 1967. He was only 68 years old, but worn down by a lifetime of enterprise, enthusiasm, and sheer hard work. A Churchillian figure, he had inspired all those who came in contact with him and had laid down standards of British motor racing dominance that would be emulated by others through the decades that followed.

45

Rob Walker

AN IMMACULATE GENTLEMAN with a fund of hysterical anec-
dotes from years gone by, Rob Walker secures a place in motor racing
history as one of Formula 1's most prestigious and successful private
entrants. For almost two decades his dark blue cars with their white nose
bands raced with the best of them throughout the world, with Stirling
Moss's achievement in the last four seasons of his personal Grand Prix
career being the most outstandingly memorable phase in the history of
Rob's equipe.

Born in 1917, a member of the Johnny Walker whisky dynasty, Rob
was attracted to the world of planes and motor cars at a suitably early
age. On his 21st birthday, his mother bought him a drophead Delahaye
coupé that had formerly been owned by Mrs Leslie Hore-Belisha, the
wife of the Minister of Transport after whom the pedestrian-crossing
beacons were named.

At the time he was pursuing a degree course at Cambridge where the
Delahaye, with its Cotal electrically-operated epicyclic gearbox, fulfilled
a key role in many jolly japes around that university city. One such
escapade involved Rob capitalizing on the Delahaye's four speeds in
reverse, upending the car and breaking a fellow undergraduate's arm as
an unfortunate consequence. The car survived remarkably intact.

Whilst supposedly studying for his finals, Rob found himself strolling
down Park Lane when a $3\frac{1}{2}$-litre Delahaye racing two-seater caught his
eye in the French firm's showroom. Priced at £400, it was a full £40 more
than the annual allowance provided by his family for his spell at
Cambridge, but the salesman quickly introduced young Walker to the
intricacies of hire purchase. The necessary forms were signed and the car
changed hands!

Rob drove the Delahaye at Le Mans in 1939, sharing an eighth place
finish with Ian Connell, before reporting to the Fleet Air Arm base at
Yeovilton where his instructors reported he was an outstandingly adept
pupil, grasping the principles and techniques of aviation quicker than
anybody they could recall. What Rob didn't tell them was that he'd
learned to fly a few years earlier, but after an impromptu lunchtime
demonstration at a point-to-point meeting, where he flew a Tiger Moth
round the course a few feet off the deck, vaulting the jumps, he had been
reported to the Air Ministry and had lost his licence for life.

By the time racing got underway again after the war, Rob had married Betty Duncan and promised his new wife that he would not participate in circuit races, although he continued to take part in sprints and hillclimbs for several more years. He now turned his hand to becoming an entrant, a role in which he was to flourish in the years ahead.

Tony Rolt and Guy Jason-Henry drove the Delahaye at Le Mans in 1949, Rob subsequently realizing that its retirement after about twelve hours with ruined bearings might have something to do with the fact that he hadn't changed the oil for ten years!

The blue Delahaye became something of a celebrity in its own right the following year when Jason-Henry, who had taken it abroad for several races, was apprehended by Customs at Newhaven and found to be smuggling 3,000 watches in a dummy fuel tank. Needless to say, Rob knew nothing of this subterfuge, but the car was confiscated and Walker found himself having to buy it back from Customs and Excise following a prolonged court case!

Throughout the 1950s, Rob became increasingly involved with a wide variety of cars, but it was not until 1958 that he hit the big time. Vanwall boss Tony Vandervell agreed to release Stirling Moss to drive his Cooper-Climax in the Argentine Grand Prix at Buenos Aires, where Vanwall was not competing, and in sweltering conditions 'Stirl' ran through non-stop without changing tyres to score an historic victory, the first for a rear-engined machine in a World Championship-qualifying event.

This was the beginning of the end for the front-engined $2\frac{1}{2}$-litre Grand Prix car, and Walker's team helped drive another nail into their coffin when Maurice Trintignant scored a second—albeit fortuitous—victory at Monaco the same year.

After Vanwall's withdrawal at the end of 1958, Stirling Moss switched to Rob's dark blue Coopers for 1959, finishing second in the World Championship, while a switch to a Lotus 18 the following year saw Moss win at Monaco to notch up the marque's maiden Grand Prix success. Rob and Stirling had an absolutely splendid relationship, based on mutual trust, admiration, and personal affection, so when Moss's career tragically came to an end after his Goodwood accident on Easter Monday 1962, it was not surprising that Rob found it difficult to get excited about running Trintignant and Jo Bonnier in the immediate aftermath. Moreover, the 1962 season brought more tragedy when both Ricardo Rodriguez and motorcycle ace Gary Hocking were killed at the wheel of Rob's Lotus 24s, at Mexico City and Natal respectively.

However, in 1963 the young Swiss driver Jo Siffert moved into Formula 1 with his own Lotus 24, switching to a Brabham for the following year, and it was not long before Rob took him under his wing, effectively partnering Bonnier in a two-car Brabham line-up for 1965.

Bonnier is remembered as a great gentleman by many, but he could be quite arrogant and self-opinionated, losing his temper with Rob after the 1965 Brands Hatch Race of Champions when he blamed a lack of pit signals for the fact that he failed to win. Walker told the bearded Swede, in no uncertain terms, that if he didn't like the way the team was run, then he could always leave ... Bonnier stayed.

The onset of the 3-litre Formula 1 in 1966 meant that Grand Prix racing would become considerably more expensive, so Rob decided to run a single Cooper-Maserati. Typically, Bonnier expected it would be for him, so when Rob informed him that there would only be a single entry, he instinctively asked 'What are you going to do with Siffert?' Rob replied, with superb timing, 'I'm going to have him drive my car ...'

By the end of 1967, however, it became clear that the Cooper-Maserati was no longer a competitive proposition, so Rob invested heavily in a brand new state-of-the-art Lotus-Cosworth 49 for Siffert to drive the following season. Disastrously, 'Seppi' crashed it in the rain during practice for the Brands Hatch Race of Champions. If that wasn't bad enough, as the wreckage was being stripped down in Rob's Dorking racing base, a stray spark ignited the fuel vapour. In the ensuing blaze, the remains were burnt out, Rob's ex-Dick Seaman ERA-Delage was gutted, and all his priceless archives were destroyed.

It was a devastating body blow. Rob thought it was the end of the road. But he had reckoned without the fabulous generosity of his brother-in-law, the late Sir Val Duncan, Chairman of the giant Rio Tinto Zinc Corporation. He immediately wrote out Rob a cheque for £10,000 to keep him in the racing game. A new Lotus 49B was ordered— and delivered just in time for the British Grand Prix at Brands Hatch.

The rest is history. After the works Lotus 49Bs failed, Siffert's dark blue Walker entry held off Chris Amon's Ferrari to win Rob's final Grand Prix victory, the first time one of his cars had triumphed in his home Grand Prix. It was an historic moment to savour, the last occasion on which a true private entrant, using an 'off-the-peg' racing car, would emerge victorious in a World Championship Grand Prix.

Rob would continue as an entrant in his own right through to the end of 1970, gradually winding down with a series of co-sponsorship deals. Still a respected member of the Formula 1 community, having been a regular contributor to the American magazine *Road and Track* for 25 years, Rob Walker's debonair charm serves as a reminder of more gentle and civilized times that have long been consigned to the pages of motor racing history.

46

Tom Walkinshaw

TOM WALKINSHAW HAD much the same effect on international sports car racing in the 1980s as Ron Dennis had on Formula 1, raising the competitive stakes by setting fresh standards of professional intensity which saw his TWR empire take Jaguar back to the winner's podium at Le Mans after a 31-year absence. It was almost two decades since this tough and gritty Scot had set out with bright ambitions to make the grade as a single-seater star, yet a combination of opportunity and circumstance would see him establish one of the most formidable business empires within the motor racing business.

Born in 1948, Walkinshaw came from a farming family near Prestonpans, on the banks of the Firth of Forth to the east of Edinburgh. He started out racing Formula Fords in 1968, winning the 1969 Scottish Championship in a Hawke before briefly acquiring his own Formula 3 Lotus 59, which he contrived to upend in the rain at Snetterton early the following year, before being recruited to drive for the fledgling works March F3 team.

In retrospect, any single-seater talent Walkinshaw might have possessed was being masked by the limitations of his machinery. The March 703 was a difficult mount and, after struggling hard, Tom was rewarded only with a couple of broken ankles when he rolled the device going into Paddock Bend during practice for an event at Brands Hatch. This wrote him out of the action for the rest of the season, but he returned in 1971 to make the graduation to Formula 2, again with a March but now under the Ecurie Ecosse banner. Little success attended his efforts during a season that was punctuated by a serious road accident, and in 1972 his single-seater career took a significant wrong-turning when he became involved with the ill-starred GRD team and had only a handful of Formula 2 outings in their cars. Then he made the switch to saloon cars, forging a fruitful relationship with Ford as a works-backed Capri driver that lasted through until 1976, when he switched his allegiance to BMW.

That season saw Walkinshaw notch up one of his most significant victories, sharing the winning BMW CSL coupé in the Silverstone six-hour endurance event with John Fitzpatrick; it was a dramatically close finish which saw them fend off the Kremer Porsche of Hans Heyer/Bob Wollek by little more than the length of the Woodcote chicane. It was typical of the pace at which Walkinshaw was now conducting his life that he left Fitzpatrick alone on the rostrum to collect the trophy, flying immediately to Thruxton where he scored his second victory of the day in a round of the British saloon championship, this time for Ford in a Capri.

During the early 1970s, Tom had shrewdly come to realize he had a happy knack for test and development work. His reputation in this sphere grew to the point where many private owners were only too willing to pay the Scot a daily fee to sort out their own saloon racer. He was also ambitious, with a ready eye for business opportunities, so he set out to market his technical abilities. He felt it was only logical that this talent should be channelled into a commercial application and, in 1976, Tom Walkinshaw Racing was established on an industrial estate at Kidlington, near Oxford.

TWR initially forged its reputation by preparing and operating a fleet of 3-series BMW saloons in the County Championship during 1979 and 1980. At the same time he would conclude a deal with Mazda to prepare an RX7 that was destined to win its class in the 1979 British Championship; he also produced the Audi 80s that Stirling Moss and Martin Brundle drove in 1980. On the face of it, Walkinshaw's business operation looked like producing an irreconcilible conflict of interests, but individual projects for rival manufacturers were separated with a meticulous, almost surgical precision that satisfied all concerned.

In 1980 TWR was also charged with the responsibility of fielding the works Rover 3.5-litre V8s in the British Championship, this machine eventually winning the title outright in 1983 thanks to the efforts of Steve Soper. Tom wasn't stinting in his own efforts behind the wheel either; in 1981 he shared the winning Mazda RX7 in both the Spa 24-hours and the Silverstone Tourist Trophy. But the best was yet to come, for 1982 saw TWR forge what was to be a long-standing partnership with Jaguar.

Walkinshaw had taken a long look at the 5.3-litre V12-engined Jaguar XJS coupé and concluded it would make a worthwhile European Touring Car Championship contender under the latest Group 2 regulations. Introduced to Jaguar's dynamic new boss John Egan, Walkinshaw recognized an ambitious kindred spirit. He sold Egan, and Jaguar technical chief Jim Randle, the feasibility of using the XJS as a worthwhile racing tool and the company gave Tom the green light to go ahead.

With sponsorship from Motul oil, and with Jaguar looking on with detached, paternalistic interest, the TWR Jaguar XJS won four major races in its first season, including the prestigious Nurburgring six-hour epic in BMW's back yard. Not surprisingly, this led to official works backing for a two-car team in 1983 when only a few minor setbacks prevented Walkinshaw himself winning the Championship.

In 1984, now fielding a three-car team, Tom surged to the European Touring Car Championship title almost unchallenged. The high spot of the season came when he shared the winning car with Win Percy and his old rival Hans Heyer in that year's Spa 24-hours. It was Tom's second victory in this challenging event, the first for Jaguar in a major 24-hour race for 27 years. But not their last.

Jaguar was now extremely anxious to sustain the momentum of its motorsport programme and the only realistic way forward was a return to the sports car racing arena. In the USA longtime Jaguar campaigners Group 44 had provided a hint of what could be done by producing its own V12-engined XJR5 prototype in conjunction with the factory. It proved successful in IMSA sports car events and would race, unsuccessfully, at Le Mans in 1985. Suitably encouraged, Jaguar now gave the green light to Walkinshaw. What followed was an intensive three-year programme of high technology development that saw TWR steadily raise the competitive tempo of sports car racing with their splendidly crafted XJR prototypes. In 1986 they won a single race, the Silverstone Six-Hours, in 1987 they won the Championship with eight wins out of ten races, and, finally, in 1988 they won Le Mans. By this stage Walkinshaw's wide-ranging business activities had expanded to the point where TWR had become just one component in a larger group of more than twenty companies producing a total annual turnover of £100 million.

Although Tom swapped his driving overalls for a business suit at the end of 1984, he remains as much the boss as ever before. Unquestionably, he has an intimidating presence and has been known to make famous international drivers quake with apprehension with his steely gaze.

Derek Warwick and Eddie Cheever recall horsing around in the TWR motorhome at one sports car race in 1986, believing Tom to be away at another European event. The motorhome was festooned with flame-proof overalls and underwear, amongst other more general debris, when the door suddenly opened and Walkinshaw appeared on the step.

He looked around the interior with a thunderous expression, then announced he would be back in a few moments and closed the door. Warwick and Cheever transformed those fleeting seconds into a whirl-wind of activity to clean up the mess, trembling lest their employer returned before the task was completed. Walkinshaw runs a first-class operation, pays top dollars for the job, but never lets his drivers forget they are, at the end of the day, his employees!

It had long been imagined that Walkinshaw would eventually make a bid to become involved in Formula 1, so it was no surprise when it was announced in the summer of 1991 that the TWR would take an initial 35-per cent stake in the Benetton Formula team. This share was scheduled to be expanded to 50 per cent in due course, with Walkinshaw having total control over the technical side of the operation. With brilliant young German Michael Schumacher scheduled to drive for the team in 1992, alongside Walkinshaw's personal favourite Martin Brundle, it would be fascinating to see how the burly Scot's graduation to F1 developed.

47

Peter Warr

WHEN PETER WARR left Lotus in the middle of the 1989 season, the once proud British Formula 1 team had sunk to its lowest ebb since the death of its founder, Colin Chapman, almost seven years earlier. Yet to judge Warr's achievements on the basis of the performances produced with an off-the-shelf Judd engine during the final weeks of his tenure would be to take an unrepresentative picture of this bespectacled, scholarly-looking man's contribution to Lotus fortunes over the years.

As far as his place in motor racing history is concerned, Warr must be regarded as an energetic keeper of the Chapman flame amongst those outside the boss's family circle; his efforts on their behalf over two decades were not only considerable but, in the main, highly productive. He had first worked for Lotus Engineering as long ago as 1958 when, at the age of 20, he had turned up at the young company's North London premises at Hornsey as assistant sales manager.

A knee injury had previously brought about a premature end to his national service with the Royal Horse Artillery and, following the death of Lotus general manager Norman 'Nobbie' Clarke from a sudden heart attack, he took over running the sales for Lotus Components, the division of the company specializing in building racing and kit cars.

Peter nurtured his own racing ambitions and eventually purchased the Lotus 7 that had been specially built up for Graham Hill to run at the Boxing Day Brands Hatch meeting at the end of 1959. He raced it enthusiastically for a couple of seasons before switching to Formula Junior single-seaters.

It was an exciting, not to mention exhausting, time. Not only was he working all the hours imaginable at the factory, but he would then rush off on Friday evening, towing his car, to get to a race on the Continent and be back in time to start work again on Monday morning. Behind the wheel, Warr achieved some modest success and certainly travelled widely. He won the Formula Junior Eifelrennen at the Nurburgring at the wheel of a Lotus 20 and made two trips to Japan for races at Suzuka, winning one with a Lotus 23B.

By the early 1960s, Lotus had moved to new premises at Cheshunt, in Hertfordshire, but quickly outgrew them. By the time Warr retired from the cockpit in 1964 Chapman was making even more elaborate plans for a move to Norfolk and an ambitous new factory at Hethel.

Although extensively involved in the detailed planning for the move to Norfolk in 1966, when it came to the crunch Peter didn't want to go. Privately, he really wanted the job of Team Lotus Formula 1 manager, but since that had already fallen to his colleague, Andrew Ferguson, Warr decided to move off on his own, in his own words, 'to see whether I could make it outside Lotus'.

For three years he would run a model and hobbies import business, a challenge he found to be enjoyable, but it wasn't on the same level as working for Lotus in terms of pure 'buzz' and satisfaction. In the back of his mind, he wanted to find a way back into the sport.

One day in 1969 he received a telephone call from Andrew Ferguson, tipping him off that there would soon be a vacancy at Team Lotus. Ferguson was leaving. Warr quickly got in touch with Chapman and a deal was done. Peter was back in the Lotus fold and would stay there as team manager for the next seven years.

His first race for the team was at Watkins Glen in 1969, the fateful day Graham Hill crashed heavily and broke both his legs, while Jochen Rindt won the first Grand Prix of his career in the Lotus 49. What followed was a golden phase of Team Lotus history, moments of great success punctuated by some inevitable tragedies. Warr was there, as Chapman's loyal lieutenant throughout, sharing the triumph and the tension.

Warr managed the team through the halcyon years of the Lotus 72, suffering the tragedy of Rindt's death at Monza in 1970, and then presiding over the team's rebirth in 1972 when Emerson Fittipaldi became the sport's youngest-ever World Champion. This level of dominance continued through 1973 with Ronnie Peterson joining Fittipaldi in the team, but then in 1974 the team's fortunes began to wane slightly and Peter's efforts were hampered in the spring of 1975 when he broke both legs in a road accident.

Into 1976, Warr started to feel that Chapman was beginning to use him as something of a whipping boy if things went wrong. 'Colin seemed to get all the glory when things went well, but I felt increasingly under pressure when things fell apart,' he said, although that view in no way undermines his high opinion of Chapman as an extremely generous employer in every way.

At the 1976 British Grand Prix, Warr suddenly found himself presented with a golden opportunity. He was approached by Austro-Canadian oil magnate Walter Wolf who had taken over the assets of the bankrupt Williams team. Unfortunately, Walter Wolf Racing was busy going nowhere on the strength of its 1976 performance, so Walter wanted to start with a clean sheet of paper the following year. He wanted Peter to mastermind the whole project as his team manager.

For all his outward bluster, Chapman retained a keen perception of Warr's contribution to Team Lotus and was very disappointed when

Peter explained that he wanted to leave. The Lotus team manager could be tart and didactic on occasion, displaying a brusque approach that could rub people up the wrong way. But he was immensely loyal to the Lotus cause, conscientious and meticulous about the way in which the team was operated. Colin bade him good fortune and suggested he look on his detour to Wolf as 'temporary leave of absence'.

Warr's brief was effectively to set up a new Wolf Racing operation from the ground up. With Harvey Postlethwaite as chief designer and Jody Scheckter signed up to drive for the single-car team, their assault on the 1977 Championship was as impressive as it was unexpected. Under Warr's steady guidance, Scheckter won in Buenos Aires, Monaco, and Canada to come within an ace of taking the Championship title. The following year saw Wolf produce an ambitious ground effect car, the WR6, and although Jody did not win another race for the team he remained a consistent front runner.

Wolf had assumed the financial burdens of those two seasons almost exclusively, but it was clearly something he was not prepared to handle indefinitely. Sponsorship from Olympus cameras brought James Hunt into the team at the start of 1979, but the English driver's interest and commitment was flagging and he retired before mid-season. That left Warr scurrying to find a new driver. The man he selected was then driving for the Carl Haas/Paul Newman Can-Am team. His name was Keke Rosberg.

At the end of the year, Wolf decided to withdraw, paying all his bills and dropping out of Formula 1. Warr was left with over thirty people in the Reading factory and looked for a means whereby the operation could survive. The answer was a merger with the Fittipaldi team, but this was the prelude to a depressing decline in which Warr's personal relationship with the Brazilian double World Champion was but one of the casualties. In the middle of 1981, Chapman contacted him again. It was time to return to Team Lotus.

Warr found it a very different operation from the one he had left five years earlier. His first meeting with Colin's new protégé, Nigel Mansell, did not augur well for the future. The two men didn't hit it off and things did not improve after Chapman's tragic death in the early hours of 16 December 1982.

The death of the Lotus chief made a profound impact on Warr and his colleagues. It was Peter who had to drive down to where the team was testing at Snetterton that morning and break the terrible news. He also had to motivate them as best he could, galvanizing them to the reality that life must continue, that the team still had a role to play in Formula 1.

Warr was faced with the challenge of extending his influence. Now he had to be a motivational force, stepping into the shoes of an employer he had long admired. Difficult times lay ahead, but although Peter would subsequently be blamed for the downward spiral into which Team Lotus became locked towards the end of the 1980s, he had little choice but to make the decisions he did.

More to the point, he made some tremendously bold and successful decisions. For the 1985 season, it was Warr who recruited Ayrton Senna, the driver who put Team Lotus back in the winner's circle for the first time since before the death of the 'Old Man'. He also acceded to Senna's pressure to make a pitch for Honda engines in 1987, ironically a move that would result in Lotus losing the gifted Brazilian, along with the Japanese V6 turbos, to McLaren the following year when the aerodynamic limitations of the Lotus 99T chassis were shown up in a bad light alongside the rival Williams FW11B.

After a disappointing season with Honda in 1988, Lotus lost their engine deal and sank to the status of Judd-propelled also-rans in 1989. By mutual agreement, Warr left the team in the middle of the season. It looked as though he had been made the fall guy for the team's dwindling fortunes.

With the benefit of hindsight, the problems clearly lay elsewhere and, had Peter Warr stayed on at the helm of Lotus, it is fair to say that many of the pitfalls that eventually brought this once-proud racing team to its knees might have been avoided.

Warr was appointed secretary of the British Racing Drivers Club, based at Silverstone, in the summer of 1991.

48

Frank Williams

FRANK WILLIAMS'S ENTHUSIASM, commitment, and utter singlemindedness have established his team as one of the very best in the Grand Prix business, earning him as much respect in the 1980s as Colin Chapman was accorded in the two preceding decades. Yet, highly regarded as Williams is for building a Championship-winning Grand Prix team, the way in which he fought back from a crippling road accident early in 1986, adapting himself to life in a wheelchair, has produced an even more telling index of the man's unquenchable determination.

By any standards, Frank came up the hard way. He was born in 1942 amidst the harsh industrial surroundings of South Shields on Tyneside, his father left for the war when he was a few months old, and his mother subsequently took him to live near Nottingham. He grew up with a fiercely independent streak, developing an early interest in cars and motor racing that was fuelled by an arduous programme of hitch-hiking round the country to various race meetings.

Having left school in 1960, he enrolled on a management trainee course with a local motor distributor, working on commercial vehicles. It was a hard life, but instructive none the less. By now he had a keen ambition to be a racer. Finally, with some financial assistance from his mother, he achieved his ambition.

He acquired an ex-Graham Hill Austin A35, which he entered for his first race at Oulton Park in April 1961. He was on his way. The A35 duly gave way to a faster, slightly more modern Austin A40 for 1962, by which time the gregarious youngster from Nottingham had forged a strong friendship with well-heeled aspiring racers Jonathan Williams (no relation) and Piers Courage, heir to the famous brewing dynasty.

All of them were desperately attempting to carve out a niche in motor racing whilst ostensibly preparing for more serious careers approved by their parents. Frank was captivated and, over the next few months subjected all his efforts to go single-seater racing. He became a part-time tenent of a famous motor racing flat in Harrow which Williams and Courage shared with other young blue-bloods, including Charlie Crichton-Stuart and Charles Lucas. Initially as a mechanic, and later as a driver, Frank latched onto that wandering band of nomads who trailed round Europe contesting Formula 3 races at remote circuits where a

fistful of prize money and a decent meal would help them muddle
through as far as the next weekend's event.

It was a great proving ground for future driving talent, but Frank
gradually came to the conclusion that his forte did not lie behind the
wheel, much to his disappointment. But he did have considerable
commercial acumen and, by 1967, had started a business selling new and
used racing cars from cramped premises at Slough. At the end of that
season he entered a Formula 3 car for Piers Courage for the first time
and, one thing leading to another, wound up as a full-blown entrant in
1968 running a Formula 2 car for Piers in the prestigious and hotly
contested European Championship.

By his own admission, Frank was still slightly overawed by the whole
motor racing business. He worked to no grand plan, just making his
arrangements by thinking on his feet, working out how to tackle the next
challenge as it came. This spontaneous approach led him into Formula 1
in 1969, now fielding Piers in a dark blue, ex-works Brabham. Williams
worshipped the ground Piers walked on and Courage, in turn, was
spurred on by a tremendous determination to show the motor racing
establishment that a private team could take on the works entries.

Driving for Frank, Piers Courage developed a polished edge to his
driving that had been sadly lacking during the rough and tumble of his
spell with the BRM team, a period characterized by worrying over-
exuberance on his part. Second chances come infrequently in Formula 1,
so now he was determined to make the most of it with Williams.

Second places in both the Monaco and United States Grands Prix
were the high spots of that 1969 season, leading to a link with the Italian
firm de Tomaso for the construction of a brand new car for the 1970
season. Frank, with typical enthusiasm, embraced the new project
wholeheartedly, although it was to prove enormously expensive. And
tragic, as things turned out.

Frank's world was torn apart on lap 22 of the Dutch Grand Prix at
Zandvoort when Piers crashed heavily. The de Tomaso burst into flames
and the debonair English driver perished in the inferno. Frank was
crushed, anguished, and desolate. Witnesses recall how helpless and alone
this wiry figure looked in the Zandvoort paddock. It was a turning point
for him, helping him develop a resilience and singlemindedness that
would see him surmount even more daunting problems in the future.

Alessandro de Tomaso effectively lost interest in the programme after
Piers's death and the team just bumped along to the end of the season
with young Australian Tim Schenken driving. For Frank to keep going
into 1971 he needed a driver who could bring sponsorship. Frenchman
Henri Pescarolo fitted the bill and the team purchased a new March 711.
For the next few years this was the way Frank went racing, squeezing by
on minimal budgets, paying last year's bills with next year's money.
Several times the 'phone was cut off due to non-payment of bills, but

Frank continued his business out of the 'phone kiosk a short walk from his Reading factory ...

Energy and enthusiasm notwithstanding, Frank wasn't much of a businessman. Bumping along at the back of the grid wasn't much of a way to go motor racing, so when Austro-Canadian oil man Walter Wolf appeared on the scene in 1975, and offered to buy a majority shareholding in the company, Frank decided to sell. The cars may have Walter Wolf Racing on their cockpits now, but everybody who matters in this business will still know it's my team, Frank reasoned. Trouble was, it still looked like Frank's team. The 1976 season proved even more chaotic than before, so Wolf took Frank out of the management front line and replaced him with ex-Lotus team manager Peter Warr.

For 1977, Frank made the split with Wolf and set up again on his own. Starting from square one with an off-the-peg March 761, driven by Belgian Patrick Neve, Williams began to claw his way up the ladder. With talented young engineer Patrick Head in charge of the technical side, Williams began making real progress in 1978 when the rugged Australian driver Alan Jones joined the team. The team's efforts financed now by a string of Saudi Arabian companies, they were on the verge of the big time.

Finally, in 1979, Clay Regazzoni won the British Grand Prix at Silverstone in the ground-effect Williams FW09, a machine that established Patrick Head's status in the absolute front rank of Grand Prix car designers. Once on the high wire, the victories came cascading in. In 1980, Jones won the World Championship, Williams the Constructors' crown. The team retained its title in 1981, although Jones lost his to Nelson Piquet, while Keke Rosberg won the Drivers' Championship again in 1982 following Jones's retirement, the Constructors' title falling to Ferrari. With Honda turbo power Williams won the Constructors' title again in 1986 and 1987, with their man Nelson Piquet also taking the Drivers' crown in 1987.

With Nigel Mansell at the wheel of the brand new Renault-engined FW14, Williams Grand Prix Engineering challenged the dominant McLaren-Honda team hard for the World Championship in 1991. Mansell took the Drivers' Championship battle all the way to the penultimate round of the title chase before losing to Senna, while the struggle for Williams to win the Constructors' crown was only lost to McLaren in the final race of the year.

On a personal level, Frank never relaxed once he'd hit the big time. Years of struggling against the odds had taught him how difficult success was to achieve. Once his team was tasting it, he would fight to sustain a position in the sun. Williams was every bit a racer as ever, sleek and lean, with a fitness bred from years of consistent and determined running to keep himself in trim.

Yet his biggest challenge would not be his partnership with Keke

Rosberg, Honda, Nigel Mansell, or Nelson Piquet. Frank's biggest battle would be waged on a personal level.

In March 1986, returning to Nice airport from a test session at the Circuit Paul Ricard, Frank was seriously injured when his rental car crashed on a rural byway. His spine severed, he almost died in the crucial weeks that followed. Now his years of training, running, and maintaining a super-fit physical frame paid dividends, enabling him to turn the corner and return to some semblance of normality.

Today, Frank Williams still fulfils the role of Managing Director of the company he founded. But he is an almost complete invalid, totally dependent on others. The accident has imposed upon him the frustrations of restricted mobility, forcing management delegation he might otherwise have been reluctant to concede.

Yet, remarkably, Frank Williams continues to present a cheerful front to the passing world. He admits he has been mercifully free of the depression that haunts many who have known his physical anguish. The way he puts at ease all those around him, talking about his handicaps with the dispassionate objectivity previously reserved for recalcitrant racing cars, testifies to an inner tranquility.

49

Walter Wolf

WALTER WOLF SPENT something over a million dollars between 1975 and 1977 establishing himself as the last of Grand Prix racing's private owners, bankrolling a serious World Championship challenge that saw Jody Scheckter come extremely close to taking the title in 1977 by winning the Argentine, Monaco and Canadian Grand Prix. Only a slow puncture prevented him adding a fourth victory at Long Beach, with Scheckter dominating the Californian street race from the word go almost until the finish.

Wolf remains cheerful, extrovert, and full of gusto over a decade after his Formula 1 team effectively closed its doors by amalgamating with Fittipaldi Automotive. He thoroughly enjoyed his time in Formula 1, reckons it was money well spent, and has absolutely no regrets. He remains on the fringe of the Formula 1 business, periodically turning up at races as far apart as Hockenheim and Mexico City. And he always seems to have the inside track on what's going on.

That's not surprising in the slightest. He bounced onto the Grand Prix scene in 1975 as a sponsor of Frank Williams's then crumbling Formula 1 empire, eventually buying out control of the team for 1976 while leaving Frank in charge. But anybody who thought Wolf was a rich dilettante was seriously misjudging his personality.

Walter had been born in the Austrian provincial city of Graz just before the outbreak of the Second World War and went to the United States at the age of 19 to seek his fortune. As early as 1966 he was buying shares in an oil drilling company and subsequently became involved in drilling throughout the world. By the mid-1970s he rose to control a multi-national group of companies that dealt with all facets of the oil drilling business.

However, his enthusiasm for motor racing had been fired by a visit to the Italian Grand Prix at Monza when he was a schoolboy, not by high-faluting connections within the international oil business. He wanted to have a go himself, but he was well into his mid-thirties by the time he had accumulated the necessary finance.

In 1974 he acquired a 2-litre March-BMW sports car, but his aspirations for personal fame behind the wheel were somewhat cooled when he flipped it spectacularly over a guard rail whilst testing at Varano in Italy. At around the same time he had become extremely close to

Lamborghini and even talked to designer Gianpaolo Dallara about the possibility that a Countach might be prepared for Le Mans. In the event, Dallara, who was an old pal of Frank Williams, suggested that he might take an interest in Formula 1. Frank was duly tipped off, invited Walter to the 1975 International Trophy meeting, and, before long, they had done a deal.

Later, Walter would look back with affectionate amusement on his first sponsorship involvement with the struggling Williams equipe. 'Frank was always quite a salesman,' he acknowledged. 'First I helped him out by buying the team an engine—one engine—but by the end of the year I ended up owning eight of them.' At the time, the popular view in the Formula 1 paddocks was that Frank could make the grade as Formula 1 team owner if only he had the necessary financial backing. Walter listened, was impressed—and invested.

Walter decided he would buy a controlling stake in Frank's team for 1976, but he concedes that it wasn't a particularly happy or fruitful association. 'I wasn't quite convinced that money doesn't buy success in itself,' he admitted. 'I could accept that talent gets the money—but knew full well that not everybody had that talent to get it in the first place. I became extremely worried ...'

With good reason, one might add. At the start of 1976, Walter Wolf Racing acquired the underdeveloped rubber-sprung Hesketh 308Cs from his lordship's now-defunct Grand Prix team. They had been designed by Harvey Postlethwaite and, not putting too fine a point on it, they turned out to be duds. With Jacky Ickx driving, the team didn't qualify for Monaco, nor for the British Grand Prix at Brands Hatch. Wolf was on the verge of pulling out. It was a disaster.

Nevertheless, Walter liked Harvey's straight, uncomplicated thinking about Grand Prix racing. Taking a considered view as to how he might dig the team out of the mire, Walter decided to start with a clean slate for 1977. Frank was to be taken out of front-line management and replaced by former Lotus team manager Peter Warr. The intention was that Williams would now fulfil a roving role as Walter's right-hand man, but that turned out to involve missing some races. Frank couldn't take it, left on amicable terms, and started up again on his own.

For 1977, Postlethwaite designed a straightforward and uncompli-cated flat-bottomed contender, the Wolf WR1, at the start of a season that would see Colin Chapman produce his first ground-effect machine, the Lotus 78. The first pure Wolf Formula 1 car was just like the man whose name it carried—rugged, uncomplicated, and reliable. Scheckter, after three increasingly unproductive seasons with Tyrrell, liked the idea of a one-car team exclusively tailored round his efforts.

Winning on its début outing at Buenos Aires was a dream come true, but it didn't lull Wolf Racing into a mood of over-optimism. The short-chassis, Cosworth-engined machine was a natural over-steerer and splendidly complemented Scheckter's exuberant driving style. More-over, Jody himself was maturing into a skilled and accomplished performer, the impetuosity that had marked his early career now well and truly put behind him.

The team won at Monaco, commandingly, then fortuitously in front of Walter's adoptive home crowd at Mosport Park. Mario Andretti's Lotus 78, which had dominated the Canadian race, retired in the closing stages with engine failure and Jody slipped through to win. It was another glorious day for Walter's personal ambitions.

At the start of 1978 it quickly became clear that any team was going to need a ground-effect chassis to have a chance of competing with the sensational new Lotus 79s. Harvey rushed through the new Wolf WR5, a snub-nosed, angular, and highly promising contender, in time for the start of the European season. It was promising, but didn't yield Jody even a single Grand Prix win. At the end of the season he jumped ship and signed with Ferrari for 1979.

By now you could sense that Walter Wolf was cooling in his interest towards Formula 1 racing, almost as if he knew it had been fun while it lasted and the good times were coming to an end. James Hunt briefly drove a second generation ground-effect Wolf Formula 1 car for the first few races of 1979 before deciding, too, that he'd had enough, quitting the scene for good. Keke Rosberg filled his vacant seat, the talented Finn being part of the assets transferred to Fittipaldi when the two teams merged at the end of the season.

That was the end of Walter Wolf's direct involvement in Formula 1. He had got out before becoming disenchanted with the business, spent a great deal of his own money, and concluded that it had been a worthwhile project. But now the moment had passed.

Remaining on the touchlines, he was happy to watch as Frank Williams, the man who'd attracted him into the business in the first place, finally achieved Formula 1 success at the turn of the 1980s. Walter could be said to have accurately predicted Frank's arrival in the big time.

In 1977, he told me 'Frank is still one of my best friends, even though we have parted company. I hope I'm around to see him win a World Championship within the next five years.'

It was certainly a prescient observation.

50

John Wyer

JOHN WYER'S TEAM management abilities paid dividends for Aston Martin, Ford, and Porsche over a quarter century of intense commitment to top line international sports car racing. A steely disciplinarian whose stern-faced visage earned him the soubriquet 'Death Ray' from a generation of otherwise respectful drivers, he exemplified the philosophy that flawless planning and meticulous attention to detail were as much a part of the winning formula as actually having the right technical package at one's disposal.

Born in Kidderminster, Warwickshire, in 1909, Wyer took up a five-year apprenticeship with the Sunbeam company on leaving school, after which he moved to the Solex carburettor company in 1934. After the war he briefly became an unofficial Bugatti agent, did some hillclimbs in a 3.3-litre Molsheim machine, and then swapped it for an HRG.

In 1947 he changed jobs again, taking a position with respected racing car preparation specialist Monaco Engineering, one of whose directors, Dudley Folland, was racing his own 2-litre Aston Martin in selected European events, and Wyer was frequently taken along as an unofficial team manager.

It was in 1949 that industrialist David Brown offered Wyer the post of racing manager for his Aston Martin Lagonda group, and what was initially intended as a temporary position in fact lasted for thirteen years. Their association was crowned in 1959 when Roy Salvadori and Carroll Shelby won Le Mans and Aston Martin beat arch-rivals Ferrari to win the World Sports Car Championship.

Up to John Wyer's arrival at Aston Martin, the business of team management had all been rather casual and haphazard. Nobody, it seemed, had taken a leaf out of Alfred Neubauer's book and copied the example set by him at Mercedes-Benz in the immediate pre-war years. Now Wyer applied a logical, diligent, and highly disciplined mind to the business of operating a racing team—and David Brown quickly came to appreciate just what an asset he had in this rather serious young man.

Shortly after Wyer joined up, he found himself facing a potentially very embarrassing situation when David Brown himself indicated that he wanted to drive one of his own cars at Le Mans in 1950. Wyer was privately aghast, feeling that he had come to try and organize a professional racing team, not an amateur set-up catering for the whims of its owner. In his own mind he decided that, if this was how things were to be, he would have no real choice but to resign.

As things turned out, he was spared any such awkwardness. Thankfully, the RAC Competitions Department declined to issue the requisite visa to approve David Brown's participation. Wyer informed the Aston Martin boss of this decision and, happily, he shrugged it aside in good part. No further mention was ever again made about the possibility of the proprietor racing his own cars!

There should be no mistake, however; the drivers deferred to Wyer, handling him in very circumspect fashion. From an early stage in his Aston Martin career he made it very plain that he intended to do his job properly. He was not a man to be trifled with and his drivers quickly came to grips with that reality.

During the emergent years of Aston Martin many of the drivers were accomplished amateurs who were glad of the chance to drive for a factory team. But this, and the fact that they were paid purely nominal fees, was no reason for a casual approach.

Study the photographs of Eric Thompson telephoning to the pits, having climbed from his badly dented Lagonda V12 after shunting it at the Esses during the early stages of the 1954 Le Mans 24-hour race. Quite clearly, the prospect of explaining the matter to John Wyer is not something that rests easily on his mind.

At the end of 1956 David Brown offered Wyer the post of General Manager of Aston Martin Lagonda and Reg Parnell, who had made a timely retirement from active driving, took over team management duties. But John was still there playing an even more crucial role in both road car and racing plans right through to the end of 1962, when Aston Martin finally wrapped up their racing involvement for good.

In 1963, with long distance sports car racing enjoying the prestige and popularity that is accorded to F1 in the 1980s, it was no surprise that Wyer became a key member of Ford's multi-million dollar assault on Le Mans. He worked closely with Eric Broadley's Lola company on the development of the central-engined Lola GT, which ran at Le Mans in 1963 as the precursor to the Ford GT40's arrival the following year.

Wyer again had to demonstrate his quietly diplomatic manner, mediating in contractual hiccups between Broadley and the Ford management, and eventually he set up Ford Advanced Vehicles to oversee the GT40's racing development from the European end. In 1967, after Ford finally pulled out of a works involvement, this metamorphosised into JW Automotive, which, with sponsorship from Gulf Oil, would win Le Mans with its own GT40s in 1968 and '69.

Later Wyer took over what was effectively the works Porsche team and won another World Sports Car championship in 1971 under the JW/ Gulf banner, using the sensational 5-litre Porsche 917s with Pedro Rodriguez and Jo Siffert spearheading the driving force. By this time he was rather fading into the background from an organizational point of view, his able lieutenants John Horsman and David Yorke increasingly taking responsibility for day-to-day operations.

At the end of the 1971 season Wyer effectively retired, dismayed at the instigation of a 3-litre engine capacity ceiling and deeply saddened by the deaths of both his top drivers. Rodriguez was killed at the wheel of a private Ferrari 512M at the Norisring, while Siffert died in his blazing BRM P160 at the end-of-season Brands Hatch non-championship F1 event.

Wyer remained a non-executive director of Gulf Research Racing, which was subsequently formed to build its own Cosworth V8-engined 3-litre cars, dubbed Mirages, coming out of retirement to watch Derek Bell and Jacky Ickx win at Le Mans in 1975. By now living in France, he and his wife Tottie later moved to Scottsdale, Arizona, on the suggestion of his former right-hand man John Horsman, who was working on Harley Cluxton's 1977/78 Le Mans assault using Renault turbo-engined Mirages.

Thereafter he would stay on in the Arizona sunshine where the lack of humidity helped ease progressively worsening bronchial problems from which he eventually died in 1989, just short of his 80th birthday.

John Wyer was a man of considerable presence who not only raised the standards of professional racing team management but treated the pit lane as his own personal domain where he tolerated no argument or dissent from the many great names who drove for him over the years.

'He was a real disciplinarian,' recalls Derek Bell, 'although not so much from what he said to you, more from his overall attitude. You did what he asked and respected him a great deal. It was very much like being at school, with John acting out the role of headmaster.'

Index